THE OAKWOOD PRESS

Weymouth to the Channel Islands

A Great Western Railway Shipping History

by

B.L. Jackson

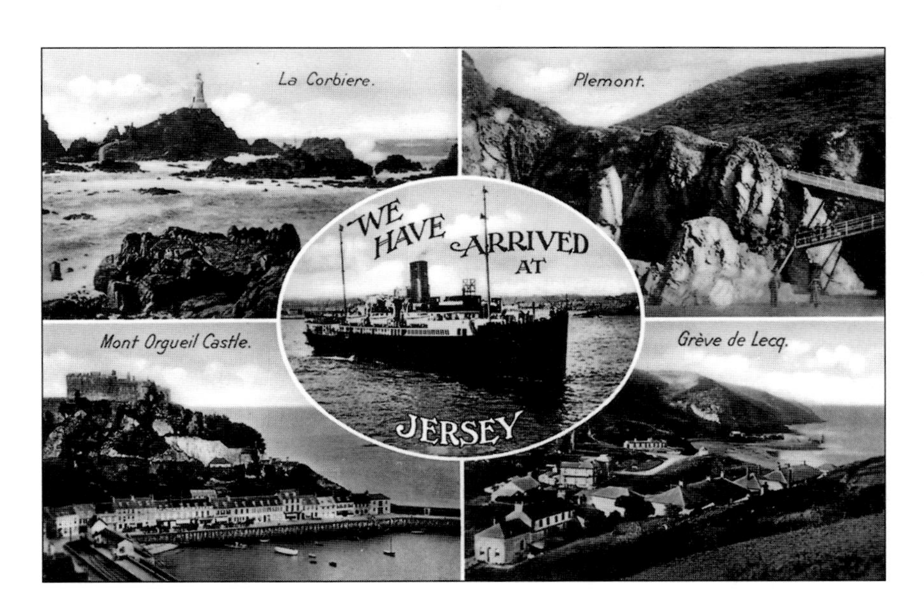

THE OAKWOOD PRESS

British Library Cataloguing in Publication Data
A Record for this book is available from the British Library
ISBN 0 85361 596 9

Typeset by Oakwood Graphics.
Repro by Ford Graphics, Ringwood, Hants.
Printed by Cambrian Printers Ltd, Aberystwyth, Ceredigion.

Above: This comic postcard posted in Weymouth on 27th August, 1914 has a certain ring of irony, war had been declared on 4th August and the Channel Islands services were to be much reduced for the duration. *Author's Collection*

Title page: A typical pre-war postcard depicting four views of Jersey with either *St Helier* or *St Julien* forming a centre-piece. *Author's Collection*

Front cover: *St Julien* entering Weymouth Harbour prior to the 1937 alterations clearly showing the livery of the GWR steamers of the inter-war period.
Kestin/Caddy collection. Computer colouring by KN Print, Berkeley, Glos.

Rear cover, top: The *Sambur (left)* and *Roebuck* moored alongside the cargo section of the pier on 22nd December, 1963, by then nearing the end of their lives. They were without doubt the two most successful cargo vessels ever employed on the service, and the only two especially built as cargo ships for the GWR. The high piles on the wall astern of *Sambur* were to enable the vessels to lay their sterns on when swinging around within the harbour. *C.L. Caddy*

Rear cover, bottom: The last revenue-earning sailing of a former GWR ship from Weymouth took place on 24th August, 1968 when *St Patrick* sailed to the Channel Islands to replace the *Caesarea* which was undergoing repair following collision damage. The GWR crest had been removed from the bows and she was painted in Sealink livery and rust streaked, one quayside observer was heard to say, 'well at least she has a red funnel'! This last departure of *St Patrick* brought down the final curtain on GWR marine operations from Weymouth. Today the GWR crest from her bows resides in the National Railway Museum at York. *R.C. Clammer*

Published by The Oakwood Press (Usk), P.O. Box 13, Usk, Mon., NP15 1YS.
E-mail: oakwood-press@dial.pipex.com
Website: www.oakwood-press.dial.pipex.com

Contents

Sites of GWR Shipwrecks off Guernsey

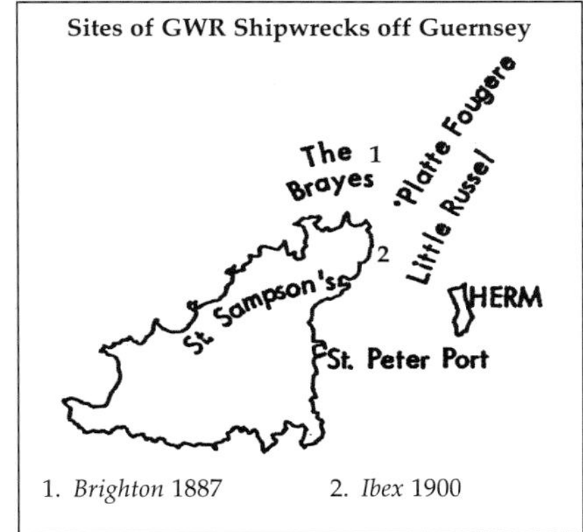

1. *Brighton* 1887
2. *Ibex* 1900

Sites of GWR Shipwrecks off Jersey

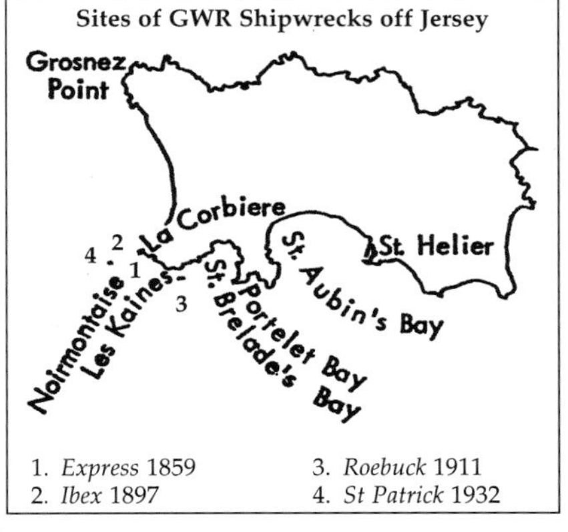

1. *Express* 1859
2. *Ibex* 1897
3. *Roebuck* 1911
4. *St Patrick* 1932

Glossary

For those not familiar with nautical terms the following notes are of assistance.

Knot. A nautical mile = 6,080 ft =1.12 land miles.
Fathom. A unit for measuring the depth of water, 6 ft = 1 Fathom.
1 League. Equal to 3 miles.
Port. Left-hand side of the vessel, when looking forward aboard the vessel (shows a red light).
Starboard. Right-hand side of the vessel, when looking forward aboard the vessel (shows a green light).
Rules of navigation. When ships pass each other in restricted space they pass 'Port' to 'Port', (in motoring language, they drive on the right). When crossing each other's path ships give way 'Starboard to Port', either by the ship giving way going slowly, stopping, or steaming around the stern of the other vessel (in motoring language, they give way to vessels approaching from the right).
Forecastle. The raised deck in the bows (the front).
Poop Deck. The raised deck at the stern (the back).
Beam. The width of the ship (minus paddle boxes if fitted).
Draught or *Depth.* The measurement of the part of the hull underwater.
Top Hamper. High superstructure, etc.
Boat Deck. The deck on which the lifeboats are placed.
Gross Tonnage (gt). The total cubic capacity of all enclosed spaces at 100 cubic feet to the ton. The Net Tonnage being measured by the same process, deducting the space for engines, boiler rooms, crew accommodation, stores, and all spaces necessary for the working of the ship, leaving the cubic capacity of all earning space. It is on this calculation that harbour dues are usually paid.
NHP. Nominal horse power.
Oscillating engine. Used by the earliest vessels in the Weymouth fleet. The cylinders were placed in the bottom of the ship with the piston rod directly connected to the crankshaft above thus saving space. To enable this arrangement to work the cylinders were mounted on hollow bearings (through which the steam passed) and swung back and forth with the revolutions of the crankshaft.
Triple expansion engine. The steam is exhausted from the high-pressure cylinder into the intermediate pressure then the low-pressure cylinders, each being of a larger diameter as the expended steam requires a larger surface to work on.
Turbines. High-pressure steam is forced through nozzles between fixed blades and moving blades on a shaft, the expansion causing the shaft to revolve at approx 4,000 rpm. Before this power can be transmitted to the propeller shaft it has to be reduced in speed through a gearbox. Turbines also worked on the expansion system, passing used steam to a second turbine of larger proportions.

Conversion Table

During the period covered by this work Britain used the Imperial system for measurement and currency. These units are used throughout the book, no conversions being provided within the text to avoid interrupting the flow of the narrative.

The following table sets out the metric units against the traditional measurements.

Length
1 inch = 2.54 cm
1 foot = 12 inches= 30.5 cm
1 yard = 3 feet = 91.4 cm
1 mile = 8 furlong = 1.6 k

Currency
1*d.* (penny) = 0.4p
6*d.* (sixpence) = 2½p
1*s.* (shilling) =12*d.* = 5p
£1 (pound) = 20*s.* = 240*d.* = 100p

Weight
1 qtr (quarter) = 127 kg
1 cwt (hundredweight) = 4 qtrs = 50.8 kg
1 imperial ton =20 cwt = 1.02 metric tonnes

Introduction

The history of cross-channel shipping services between Weymouth, the Channel Islands and France is long and interesting. This work deals principally with the vessels of the Great Western Railway (GWR) and its predecessors the Weymouth & Channel Islands Steam Packet Company who operated the service on their behalf until 1889.

Weymouth was unusual by virtue of it being one of the few railway ports not owned (or even partly owned) by a railway company. Weymouth harbour had always has been municipally owned, although the pier and cargo stage area had many GWR features and was very much under the influence of that company. There was also the unique Weymouth Harbour Tramway, running from the town station through the streets to the pier, carrying both goods and passengers to the quayside. It was the only place in Great Britain where a main line passenger train travelled along the public highway for a mile!

Locally the affairs of the cross-channel boats were of great interest, as directly and indirectly they created employment and their harbour dues and other incomes contributed towards the local economy. Ships are the largest moving objects devised by man, and they have a mystique and romance about them as they glide through the water. Using a comparatively small harbour where all movements were within public view the ships could be viewed at close quarters, both when alongside and when entering or leaving harbour and vessels moored at certain berths could literarily be 'touched' by passers-by. The arrivals and departures of the boats and other quayside activities, especially the operation of the Harbour Tramway, were a constant source of interest to both residents and visitors alike.

In the past various books have been written covering the Channel Islands services, the most important being *The Great Western at Weymouth* by the late J.H. Lucking, who was also author of *The Weymouth Harbour Tramway*. It was John Lucking's abiding interest in these two important facets of local railway history that made these books the standard works on the subject. It is now over 30 years since the publication of *The Great Western at Weymouth* and much new material has come to light during that time. Therefore other associated services and harbour arrangements are only dealt with in outline in this publication which is primarily a history of the ships that operated the service.

It is hoped that the detail within will go some way in describing the vast improvements in both naval architecture and marine engineering that took place within a hundred years. Between 1850 and 1910 the evolution of marine steam machinery moved ahead so rapidly that many revolutionary ideas were superseded within a few years. Had the turbine been developed 10 years earlier what a difference that would have made to the Weymouth fleet! Unlike the LSWR which had acquired new ships, even with their vast resources the GWR could not just purchase new vessels at a whim as they had already invested heavily, and Weymouth had to wait until 1925 to reap the benefit of turbine technology.

Whilst researching this work the author thought at one stage that the title *Wreck & Rescue on the Channel Islands Route* might be more appropriate, but as with any other form of public transport the service featured in the press only when there were problems. The thousands of mundane journeys were never recorded or remembered. The exceptional tides and rock-infested coastline of the Channel Islands (in the days before modern navigational aids) were a recipe for disaster, but thanks to good seamanship accidents were comparatively few given the circumstances.

This book is dedicated to the officers and crews of the cross-channel boats who over the years served with distinction both in peace and war, upholding the finest traditions of the Merchant Navy, and to the late John H. Lucking who carried out so much of the original research on the history of the Weymouth steamer services.

St Julien heads across the English Channel towards the end of her career in 1960.
Dorset Evening Echo

Chapter One

The Port of Weymouth

Weymouth lies at the mouth of the River Wey, which rises four miles inland at the base of the Ridgeway in the village of Upwey. Flowing south through Broadwey it broadens out at Radipole into a flood plain now known as Radipole Lake, becoming the upper part of Weymouth Harbour before turning left through a right angle to pass under the Town Bridge, then turning left again for its final length before entering the south end of Weymouth Bay.

The Weymouth area has been inhabited since prehistoric times and finds from the Bronze Age suggest the earliest use of the River Wey. The Romans are believed to have used Radipole Lake as a harbour, sailing their galleys up the Wey and beaching them at Radipole where goods could be unloaded and transported overland to the new Roman town of Dorchester (Durnovaria). Two towns grew up on either side of the river, small communities which cannot be definitely identified in the great Norman survey of 1086, the Domesday Book, although their shipping trade would have been developing by this date.

Weymouth grew up on the south side of the harbour and Melcombe on the north, two separate and rival towns, maintaining their own civic authorities and regularly disputing each other's rights to the harbour dues. These arguments, frequently violent, would continue for 300 years. Some sharing of the trade in mediaeval times when Weymouth was created a staple port for the export of wool and Melcombe a staple port for the import of wine did little to ease the situation, but it does indicate the growing importance of the coastal towns and in 1347 they were called upon to supply ships for the Siege of Calais. Vulnerable to attacks from the sea, one account stated that whilst the townsfolk were at church:

> The Normans, Genoese, Bretons, Picardes, and Spaniards entered into the town and robbed and pillaged the town, and slew divers, and defouled maidens, and enforced wives, and charged their vessels with that pillage, and so entered again into their ships, and when the tide came, they disanchored and sailed to Normandy, and came to Dieppe, and there departed and divided their booty and pillages.

Another unwelcome visitor in 1348 was the Black Death, believed to have entered England via a vessel from the Continent which had tied up at Melcombe quayside. Melcombe's suffix 'Regis' dates from the mediaeval period and indicates that its lands were in royal ownership.

Elizabeth I granted the two towns a charter of union in 1571, although resentment continued and it was not until the construction of the first bridge across the harbour linking them in 1597 that the rivalry began to subside. In a new charter granted in 1606 the term 'Weymouth' became accepted as meaning the town as a whole and not just the ancient borough south of the river. The towns at that period were still comparatively small, Weymouth consisting of the area along the south side of the harbour and extending a little way up into Chapelhay, whilst Melcombe Regis occupied the sand spit on the north side, the present town centre area. The full title 'Borough of Weymouth and Melcombe Regis' was

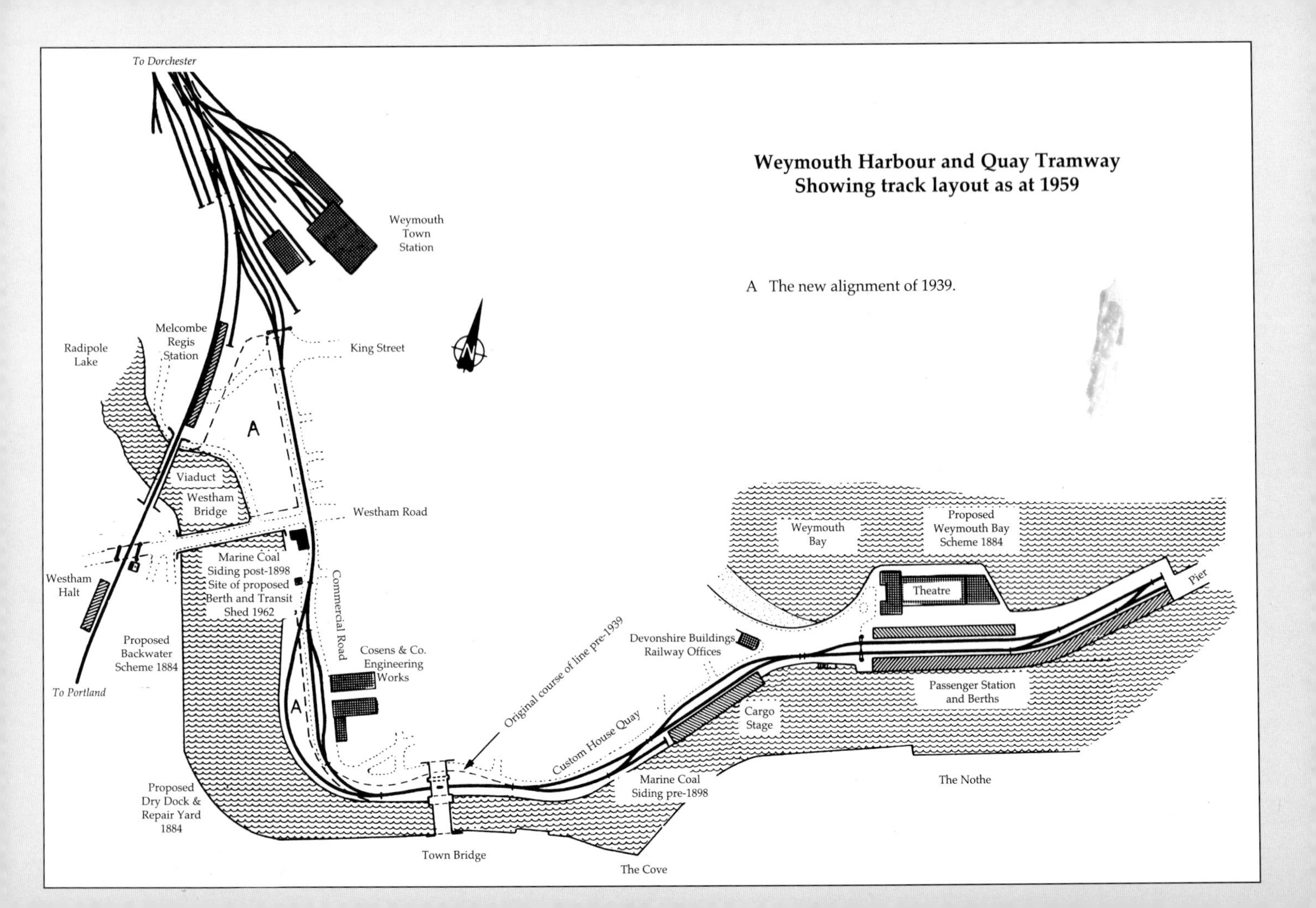

Weymouth Harbour and Quay Tramway
Showing track layout as at 1959
A The new alignment of 1939.
To Dorchester
Weymouth Town Station
King Street
Westham Road
Commercial Road
Cosens & Co. Engineering Works
Melcombe Regis Station
Radipole Lake
Viaduct
Westham Bridge
Marine Coal Siding post-1898 Site of proposed Berth and Transit Shed 1962
Westham Halt
Proposed Backwater Scheme 1884
To Portland
Proposed Dry Dock & Repair Yard 1884
Town Bridge
The Cove
Original course of line pre-1939
Custom House Quay
Marine Coal Siding pre-1898
Devonshire Buildings Railway Offices
Cargo Stage
Weymouth Bay
Proposed Weymouth Bay Scheme 1884
Theatre
Passenger Station and Berths
The Nothe
Pier
A
A
A

displayed on municipal documents until the 1970s, but today Melcombe Regis is just an electoral seat on the combined Weymouth and Portland Council.

In 1588 ships were supplied to fight the Spanish Armada. In the early days much of the sea-borne trade was coastal, but later ships sailed to the Continent, Mediterranean, the West Indies and America, trade increasing until the Civil War after which there was a decline.

The visits to the Borough of King George III between 1789 and 1805 gave the Royal seal of approval, and from then onwards the town became a holiday resort, firstly for the upper classes and later the masses, this being assisted by the opening of the railway in 1857.

Trade was regained in the early 19th century and brought about various harbour improvements including the reconstruction of the harbour walls, the reconstruction of the Pile Pier in 1859, the construction of the Nothe Fort at the harbour entrance, and the extension of the Stone Pier in 1878. The modernisation of several slipways to take small steamers and the construction of the Weymouth Harbour Tramway, which opened in October 1865 on the east side (after which some quayside warehouses had a proper quay wall in front of them), all added to the facilities and usage of the port. On the south side of the harbour adjacent to Cove Row, a section of quay wall and several buildings were removed in the 1880s to permit the swinging in harbour of larger steamers. Other improvements were carried out over the years following the arrival of the cross-channel steamers.

The original wooden bridge after many repairs and alterations had been replaced in 1713, and again in 1770, to be replaced by a stone structure in 1824. Modified in 1880 it survived unti1 1928 when it was demolished to make way for the present structure, a twin span lifting bridge opened in 1930. With an open span of 80 feet it freed the inner harbour of the restrictions that previously had allowed only the smaller vessels up to it.

Other works such as the construction of the original Westham Bridge in 1859 and the bridge carrying the Portland Railway across the Backwater had concluded any idea of navigation north of that point, although by that time silting up had taken place. The construction of the new Westham Bridge in 1921, a solid dam with sluice gates which enclosed the Backwater turning it into 'Radipole Lake'. The subsequent construction of Westwey Road in 1932 reduced the west side of the harbour area and the building of a new harbour wall in 1938 on the east side, allowing a large radius curve for the Weymouth Harbour Tramway, reduced the water area still further.

The Channel Islands trade apart, by the late 1880s a good trade in timber and block ice from the Baltic ports, cement from the Thames, grain for the local mills, coal and other commodities made for a busy harbour. Apart from the ice and grain trade, the others survived until the war. Beyond the Town Bridge small coastal petrol tankers would berth at the Shell and Esso storage facilities well up harbour and a small tanker collected tar from the gasworks alongside Westwey Road.

The outbreak of World War II was to drastically cut all trade, although the harbour remained busy. Vessels of the Contraband Patrol operated from the harbour, and Messrs Cosens had many vessels alongside for repairs. The Royal Navy requisitioned the cargo stage and pier area in 1942 as *HMS Bee,* a training base for the working up of coastal forces. This was relocated in October 1943

Weymouth Harbour photographed from the air between 1925 and 1927, *St Helier* or *St Julien* lies at the passenger stage. *Reindeer* is laid up in the Cove, with one of the two cargo boats *Roebuck* or *Sambur* moored outside, whilst the other sister is at the cargo stage. In the foreground is the old Town Bridge demolished in 1928. Weymouth town centre is to the left and the Nothe and Old Stone Pier to the top right. *Author's Collection*

when *HMS Grasshopper* was established for preparations towards D-Day. On 1st May, 1944 it became *USS Grasshopper* as the US navy built up for the D-Day assault. Weymouth and Portland harbours were the main departure points for US Force 'O' which headed for Omaha Beach. The first U Boat to surrender following the German surrender, U249, was escorted into Weymouth on 10th June, 1945, quickly followed by two others.

Trade never fully recovered following the war, timber being the only one to expand. During 1959 fifteen timber ships were unloaded, the remainder being mainly opportunist cargoes that needed loading or unloading. In the early 1960s sand was brought in to Trinity Road and transported to several ready-mix cement plants. The main trade was firmly in the hands of the Channel Islands boats. Messrs Cosens whose paddle steamers had been part of the local scene since 1848, also handled vessels for refit alongside the quay walls and their two slipways were employed in the repair of smaller craft - a trade that was to be reduced from the late 1950s. Eventually the company vacated their quayside premises, moving to Portland in 1987 to specialise in metal prefabrication work.

Although the trade had already declined, it is questionable whether in today's Health and Safety conscious society, timber and other cargoes could be unloaded on what is a public road, watched by the general public who took a great interest in those activities. Today the major part of the harbour above the Town Bridge forms a marina with space for approximately a thousand boats, whilst large sections of the lower harbour are also given over to yachts and fishing boats. Likewise the quayside businesses have turned from trade and industry to the yacht and tourism market. Commercial trade is restricted to the ferry terminal and the occasional cargo vessel utilising a berth to the east of that point. Ironically the recent creation of Portland Port in the former dockyard has created what the Great Western Railway failed to achieve over one hundred years ago.

Chapter Two

Post Office Packets

Weymouth, the closest point on the English coast to Cherbourg (62 miles), Guernsey (70 miles) and Jersey (80 miles) has always held an attraction as a cross-channel port, and in years past the less time spent at sea on the spartan vessels of the period the better!

The earliest recorded involvement of Weymouth trading with the Channel Islands and Cherbourg dates back to 1582 with references to the cargo of the *Margaret*. The first attempt to operate a regular service to the Islands took place in 1794 when the Post Office organised sailing packets. The first crossing took place on 13th February, 1794 using the former Dover Packet *Royal Charlotte*, the *Rover* being the other vessel employed on the weekly service.

These small sailing vessels were between 50 and 60 feet long and cutter rigged. Although usually designated 'HM' Mail Packets they were actually hired from private owners, and only the mails and passengers were carried. Except for the passengers' luggage no cargo was allowed so as not to compete with commercial vessels. Although indemnified against the capture of his vessels in time of war (England was often at war with France during that period) the owner had to cover all other losses and expenses himself, and with the limitations set on his cargo the passenger receipts were greatly relied upon; one of the oldest professions - smuggling - was engaged in by both crew and captains to boost funds!

Naturally any successful business will attract competition, and within a short while 'The Bye Boat' had appeared. The term was often used to describe a Post Office standby vessel, although in this case the *Alert* was operated by a Guernsey merchant Nicholas Robilliard. Unofficially he carried letters, which were addressed, 'Care of Mr Nicholas Robilliard, Weymouth' to circumvent the regulations! By 1806 the Packet Boats were losing so much trade to the *Alert* that extra vessels and an improved service were put into operation within three years, resulting in the *Alert* going out of business.

Despite all the difficulties of the time, the *Chesterfield* packet, having been captured by a Cherbourg privateer, and the intervention of several other commercial services the Packet Boats maintained the service. The turning point came in 1823 when, during the night of 9th-10th June, the steam vessel *Medina* crossed from Southampton to Guernsey, and then ran an excursion to Jersey. The interest this event caused resulted in the Lieutenant-Governor of Jersey writing to the Postmaster General to urge the use of steam vessels for the Channel Islands mails with a contract-operated service from either Portsmouth or Southampton. The Post Office however, stated that if steamers were to be employed they would run from Weymouth - the shortest route - where smaller, more economic vessels could be employed, and that the service would be operated by the Post Office.

In December 1824 Treasury approval was given for a scheme for the Post Office to operate its own vessels. In March 1825 a new steamer was ordered and it was planned to transfer the *Ivanhoe* and *Meteor* from Milford. Although the new steamer, the *Watersprite,* was launched on 9th May, 1826 and made a trial crossing to Guernsey on 26th June and (with the *Ivanhoe)* put in occasional appearances at Weymouth, the service to all intents and purposes was still in the hands of the sailing packets, which were in difficulties. The *Hinchinbrook* was wrecked off Alderney on 2nd February, 1826 and on 26th September the *Francis Freeling* disappeared with all hands between Weymouth and the Channel Islands, it being thought she had been run down by a brig off Portland Bill.

Officially the Post Office took over the Weymouth-Channels Islands station on 5th July, 1827 with the *Watersprite* and *Ivanhoe,* and on the night of Saturday 7th July the first mail was officially carried by a steam vessel when *Watersprite* crossed from Weymouth. The old sailing cutters were withdrawn, resulting in a speedier and more reliable service. The *Dorset County Chronicle* for 19th July, 1827, reported:

> His Majesty's Steam Packets are now regularly fixed for this station to convey the Mails and Passengers to Guernsey and Jersey; and such is the rapid expedition of these vessels, that on Wednesday last, two gentlemen having taken their breakfast in London, departed by the Magnet coach and arrived at the Golden Lion, Weymouth, the same evening, in good time for the packet, so that on the following morning they were seated at their breakfast at Payns Hotel, Guernsey, all accomplished within 24 hours. They are dispatched on Wednesdays and Saturdays at nine o clock in the evening and return to Weymouth every Sunday and Wednesday morning.

The same regulations applied to the steam vessels as to the former sailing cutters in that no cargo could be carried. The Weymouth operation was reported as working satisfactorily, and in March 1828 it was decided to add an additional sailing as an experiment for the summer season, the outward sailings from Weymouth becoming Tuesday, Thursday, and Saturday evenings, returning from the islands on Monday, Thursday and Saturday. The *Meteor* was transferred to Weymouth making her first sailing on 13th April, 1828. The additional sailing was not a financial success and was discontinued the following year, but the third vessel was retained in reserve.

Meteor became the victim of fog on 23rd February, 1830, when on an inward sailing she ran ashore on the east side of Portland at Church Ope. Fortunately there was no loss of life and the mails were brought ashore, although there were reports that as the tide receded Portlanders looted the passengers' luggage. After the salvage of her machinery and other gear the wooden hull was sold locally. A replacement steamer *Flamer* arrived at Weymouth in July 1831. Although considered superior to others on the station she was not the best sea-boat, and in December 1833 on passage to the islands she received such a battering during a gale that she was forced to turn back off Alderney and run for Weymouth. Her captain and five men were seriously injured, one fatally.

The weather apart, other problems beset the packets. The first responsibility of the Post Office was the delivery of the mail; the requirements of the passengers, their only other source of revenue, took second place resulting in many passengers using the other ships available, usually from Southampton. In true Civil Service fashion a report on the Packets' failings was made in 1830, with another in 1832 and a third in 1836 - the latter on five services which all ran at a loss. It did, however, state that Weymouth's loss was modest, and that incompetence and fraud - which was rife elsewhere - was entirely absent at Weymouth!

This report also highlighted the fact that the Post Office was not a suitable authority to manage a large fleet of steam vessels, this resulting in the entire Packet service being taken over by the Admiralty from 16th January, 1837, the Post Office only having jurisdiction over the routes and sailing times. Having acquired a fleet of dubious quality, the Admiralty immediately set about improving the general standard. *Ivanhoe* was sent to Woolwich Dockyard for repairs, but owing to her age and condition did not return, she was renamed *Boxer* and lasted several years on other duties. The *Flamer* was renamed *Fearless* and *Watersprite* became *Wildfire,* this being followed by changes of vessel. *Pluto* took up the station whilst *Fearless* underwent refit. In April 1838 *Dasher,* a replacement for *Ivanhoe,* arrived. She had been launched that January and was a vast improvement on previous vessels. *Wildfire* underwent refit and re-boilering. In August 1839 *Cuckoo* replaced *Fearless.* Although dating back to 1824 she was well regarded as a good sea-boat and her accommodation was of a high standard.

Despite all the improvements to vessels and captains wearing cocked hats and swords in the Admiralty fashion, the service was no match for the commercial operations being established with the improvements in steam power. The Commercial Steam Packet Company, operating a coastal service from London as far west as Weymouth, extended its sailings across the channel to Cherbourg in April 1839, and in September added Alderney and Guernsey to its ports of call. The Channel Islands calls ceased after 1st November the same year although Cherbourg continued until the following year. Albeit short-lived, it was Weymouth's first steam-operated commercial cross-channel service.

Other considerations were now coming to the fore as the railway age arrived and the old mail coach and stagecoach routes were shortly to make way for the iron road. The opening on 11th May, 1840 of the London & Southampton Railway was the beginning of a great change in the transport system in the South and West. The London & Southampton Railway became the London & South Western Railway (LSWR) which looked upon the steamers of the various companies as a useful extension to its line, and the financial difficulties encountered by the Commercial Steam Packet Company late in 1841 allowed the LSWR to become involved. The LSWR Act of Parliament prevented it from operating or owning steamships, but the establishment of a separate company, 'The South Western Steam Packet Company', was a means of circumventing the Act. The fact that the new company contained virtually the same shareholders as the LSWR was immaterial! Thus the new company took over the bankrupt Commercial Steam Packet Company on 1st May, 1842. By that time the Post Office had approved, subject to certain conditions, that the mail could be carried on the commercial steamers.

Despite the competition and Southampton's swift connection with London, in 1841 the Admiralty still considered Weymouth had certain advantages because of the shortest sea crossing, and being nearer to Falmouth and its connection with the Ocean Mails. However, the transfer of many mail services from Falmouth to Southampton in September 1843, compounded by the efforts being made in the development of Southampton, reduced Weymouth's claim still further at a time when - despite many keenly debated schemes - there was no definite plan for a railway to the town. With the loss of passenger revenue to commercial undertakings and the other limitations enforced upon it, there must have been mutterings in the corridors of the Admiralty asking why they were involved in the packet trade at all!

In 1844 it was announced by the Post Office that a contract had been agreed to transfer the mail to the Southampton steamers. Despite protests the Weymouth Packet service ceased the following year. *Dasher* departed on 5th April leaving the *Wildfire* and *Cuckoo* to complete the service. *Wildfire* made her last crossing on 19th April, having been at Weymouth since the beginning of steam operation. *Cuckoo* made the final crossing on 5th May, 1845; built in 1824, she had introduced steam to the Milford-Ireland service under her original name of *Cinderella*.

An engraving depicting the rescue of passengers and crew by ropes from the Royal Mail Steam Packet *Meteor* from rocks at Church Ope, Portland on 23rd February, 1830. The mail reached Weymouth at 2 am the following day, it being reported that the following night more than 100 Portlanders swarmed aboard and pilfered a large proportion of the baggage. *Maureen Attwooll Collection*

Chapter Three

Railway Intervention and the Weymouth & Channel Islands Steam Packet Company

With the departure of the Post Office packets Weymouth's prospects as a cross-channel port looked bleak. Southampton had both the shipping service and the railway connection. At the time Dorset was without a railway, although two Acts of Parliament received the Royal Assent that year (1845). The Wilts, Somerset & Weymouth Railway, was authorised to construct a line from near Chippenham to Weymouth; and the Southampton & Dorchester Railway from a junction with the London & Southampton line at Southampton to Dorset's County town. The latter was swiftly completed and opened to Dorchester on 1st June, 1847, whilst the Wilts, Somerset & Weymouth Railway ran unto financial difficulties and proceeded very slowly.

The opening of the Southampton & Dorchester, with its branch from Hamworthy Junction to Hamworthy (on the south side of Poole Harbour), encouraged a shipping service from Hamworthy to the Channel Islands. During that time the South Western Steam Packet Company had been in competition with The South of England Steam Navigation Company, but they joined forces on 1st October, 1846, to form the New South Western Steam Navigation Company.

On 2nd May, 1848 the new paddle steamer *Dispatch* sailed on her maiden voyage from Poole to the Channel Islands and France. *Dispatch* only made two sailings from Poole, being replaced by the *South Western*. On 14th August, 1848 the LSWR obtained powers to operate its own shipping services, thus bringing to an end the fiction of an independent company for the purpose. The New South Western Navigation Company was formally absorbed by the LSWR in February 1849. Before that date the status of Poole as a cross-channel port suffered a blow on 30th September, 1848 when the *South Western* ran aground in Poole Harbour, where she remained firmly stuck fast until the next spring tide. The LSWR withdrew the service immediately - somewhat surprising as the Steam Ship Act included provisions for the purchase of land and the erection of buildings and wharves at Hamworthy. It was to be another 120 years before Poole again became a serious contender for the cross-channel trade.

Despite the fact that the railway had not yet reached Weymouth the LSWR commenced to operate a service between that port and St Malo via Guernsey, Jersey and Granville on 14th August, 1850, using the *South Western*. The service was however short lived. As the railway terminated at Dorchester and passengers had to continue to Weymouth by horse bus it failed to attract sufficient patronage and was withdrawn that December, the LSWR then concentrating its efforts on Southampton.

March 1850 saw the Wilts, Somerset & Weymouth Company taken over by the Great Western and soon progress was made on the construction of the line. Completed to Yeovil in 1856 it opened through to Weymouth on 20th January, 1857. On the same date a spur connecting the LSWR line at Dorchester came

WEYMOUTH & CHANNEL ISLANDS STEAM-PACKET COMPANY.
LIMITED LIABILITY.
CAPITAL, £40,000,
In Shares of £10 each, and £1 per Share to be paid in 1857, and the remainder by instalments in 1858.

THE GREAT-WESTERN RAILWAY will indmnify this COMPANY against loss. Two Thousand Shares have been allotted to Jersey, and taken up by 250 merchants, tradesmen, and others of that island. Thus the goods traffic from London, Birmingham, Manchester, and West of England has been secured to this Company. The passenger traffic will follow the fancies of travellers, some preferring the long and others the shorter sea voyage, with the longer or shorter land journey. All travellers, however, to the West of England, Bristol, Bath, the manufacturing towns, Wales, and South of Ireland will naturally take the Weymouth route as the shortest and most economical. One thousand Shares have been allotted to Weymouth and one thousand to Guernsey, six hundred and twenty-five of which latter have already been taken up by ninety gentlemen, merchants, and others interested in the trade and prosperity of the island. The greater part of the goods traffic, as in Jersey, has been thereby secured to this Company, insuring its ultimate prosperity. As the Guernsey Directors have only a limited period for passing off the Shares allotted to this island, and as its prosperity depends on its being closely united with England by the shortest sea route, they appeal to the patriotic feelings of their countrymen, and request all interested in the welfare and prosperity of Guernsey to subscribe their names without delay, in order to secure a Direction to protect the interests of the island. The Share List may be seen at Mr. Greenslade's, Mr. Redstone's, and at Mr. John Jones's Office, No. 4, High street, where Shares taken will be registered.

HENRY TUPPER, THOMAS PRIAULX, } Provisional Directors.

Guernsey, March 26, 1857.

STEAM COMMUNICATION BETWEEN WEYMOUTH, GUERNSEY, AND JERSEY ON AND AFTER SATURDAY, 11TH APRIL, 1857.—(CIRCUMSTANCES PERMITTING.)

THE WEYMOUTH AND CHANNEL ISLANDS STEAM PACKET COMPANY.—(LIMITED.)

THE COMPANY'S fast Iron Steam Boats AQUILA and CYGNUS, fitted up in the most splendid style, with every requisite accommodation, and making *daylight* passages both ways, will ply between WEYMOUTH, GUERNSEY, and JERSEY as follows :—

From Jersey to Weymouth, calling at Guernsey.		*From Weymouth to Jersey, calling at Guernsey.*	
On Mondays, Wednesdays, Fridays, Saturdays,	at 8 a.m.	On Mondays, Tuesdays, Thursdays, Saturdays,	at 8 a.m.

N.B. Further particulars as to fares, rates of goods, &c., and through booking to the different towns on the Great Western Railway, and to places on lines in connection with the Great Western will appear in a future advertisement. JOHN JONES, Agent.

Guernsey, April 4th.

WEYMOUTH AND CHANNEL ISLANDS STEAM-PACKET COMPANY.

AS the Jersey Directors have bespoken whatever number of Shares unallotted after Thursday, the 10th of April, the day appointed for closing the Guernsey Share List, all who are desirous of giving their support to the Company are requested to subscribe their names prior to that date. The deposit of £1 British per Share is now in course of payment at the Old Bank.

HENRY TUPPER, THOMAS PRIAULX, } Provisional Directors.

WEYMOUTH AND CHANNEL ISLANDS
STEAM PACKET COMPANY, LIMITED.

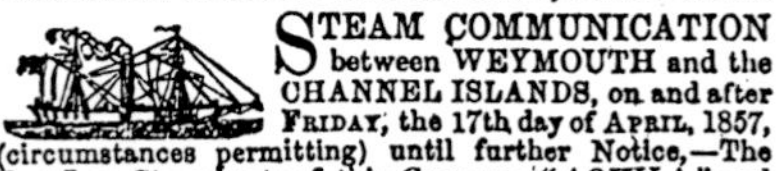

STEAM COMMUNICATION between WEYMOUTH and the CHANNEL ISLANDS, on and after FRIDAY, the 17th day of APRIL, 1857, (circumstances permitting) until further Notice,—The Fast Iron Steamboats of this Company "AQUILA" and "CYGNUS," fitted up in the most splendid style, with every requisite accommodation, and making Daylight Passages both ways, will ply between WEYMOUTH and CHANNEL ISLANDS as follows :—

FROM WEYMOUTH TO JERSEY,
Calling at Guernsey on Tuesday, Thursday, Friday, and Saturday in every Week, at ½ past Eight A.M.

FROM JERSEY TO WEYMOUTH,
Calling at Guernsey on Monday, Wednesday, Friday and Saturday in every week, at ½ past Seven, A.M.

The "Aquila" will leave Jersey, and the "Cygnus" will leave Weymouth, circumstances permitting, for their first Trips, on Friday, the 17th day of April instant.

☞ For further particulars of Fares, Rates for Goods, and through Booking to the different Towns on the line of the Great Western Railway, and other lines in connection therewith, apply to the Company's Agents, Capt. W. ROBERTS, Weymouth; Mr. RENOUF, Jersey; and Mr. JONES, Guernsey.

Weymouth, April 13, 1857.

WEYMOUTH, AND GUERNSEY AND JERSEY.
On and after MONDAY, 13th APRIL, 1857.

THE SOUTH WESTERN RAILWAY COMPANY'S Fast Iron STEAM PACKETS, fitted up in splendid style for Passengers, will (commencing on MONDAY, 13th APRIL,) sail *from Weymouth* every Monday, Wednesday, and Friday, at 8 o'clock, a.m.; and from Jersey (calling at Guernsey about 1½ hours afterwards) every Tuesday, Thursday, and Saturday, at 6 o'clock a.m., arriving at Weymouth, under ordinary circumstances, in time for the afternoon Trains from Weymouth to London, Bristol, Bath, and the West of England.

FARES :—London to Guernsey and Jersey, 31s., first class, or 21s. second class.

FARES :—Weymouth to Guernsey and Jersey, 18s. first class, or 12s. second class.

Tickets, between London and Guernsey and Jersey, viâ Weymouth, are available for THREE days from the date of issue, and passengers may stop at Southampton, Dorchester, or Weymouth.

The Royal Mail Packets will sail viâ Southampton, every MONDAY, WEDNESDAY, and FRIDAY, as usual, after the arrival of the 8.30 P.M. train from London.

For further particulars, see Handbills.

BY ORDER.

Waterloo Bridge Station,
London, April, 1857.

Left: Adverts appearing in the *Southern Times* during March and April 1857 announcing the formation of the Weymouth & Channel Islands Steam Packet Company, the first sailings commencing on 11th April; in the event these did not commence until the 17th of the month.

Above: Two adverts that appeared in the *Southern Times* on 18th April, 1857 advertising the commencement of both the Weymouth & Channel Islands Steam Packet Company service, and that of the South Western Railway Company.

into use, thus bringing Weymouth in direct contact with both Paddington and Waterloo. The time was ripe for the commencement of a steamer service to the Channel Islands now that the shortest sea route was accessible by railway.

Towards the end of 1856 minds were turning to the matter, the LSWR, which had the ships and the necessary Parliamentary powers, sending two of its captains to Weymouth to plan a return to the port. The Great Western on the other hand had no powers to operate steam ships, and having just completed the railway to the town at considerable expense gave little thought to a cross-channel service. However, in the Islands there was dissatisfaction with the monopoly enjoyed by Southampton and now Weymouth was on the railway map there was a call to reopen the route.

Captain Stevens, a former Mail Packet master who had retired to Jersey, commenced canvassing for a Weymouth service in November 1856, gaining the support of Weymouth Alderman William Eliot. The Great Western became quite willing to be of assistance, two of its Directors going to Weymouth and the Channel Islands to address public meetings for the establishment of a proposed company. A Prospectus was issued for the Weymouth & Channel Islands Steam Packet Company Limited. By forming an independent company matters could move quickly without the delay an Act of Parliament would entail if the Great Western wished to operate its own service.

The company seal of the Weymouth & Channel Islands Steam Packet Company Limited.
Public Record Office

Express opened the Weymouth-Channel Islands service for the LSWR on 13th April, 1857. Constructed in 1847, she was the first new vessel built for the New South Western Steam Navigation Company. A vessel with a good turn of speed, she was wrecked off Corbière in September 1859. *J. Attwood Collection*

A pre-1866 view of either *Aquila* or *Cygnus* moored at Weymouth. The appearance of the vessel and the flags flying suggests it could well be at the inauguration of the service in 1857. *R.C. Clammer Collection*

Enthusiasm was high in the Islands, particularly in Jersey, whilst Weymouth was cautious, no doubt owing to past events. The promoters pressed ahead, although the company had not yet been legally formed, with plans to commence sailings on 11th April, and looked around for suitable vessels as they could not wait for new construction. Two second-hand vessels, *Aquila* and *Cygnus* were chosen and a race against time began to have them overhauled and ready for service. On 27th March the LSWR informed the GWR that its service would commence on 13th April. The paddle steamer *Express* arrived from Southampton on the 8th and was open for inspection by the public. The first sailing on Monday 13th April took place in unfavourable weather, only seven passengers braving the crossing which took 10 hours!

There was already disagreement between the LSWR and GWR; there had been proposed inter-availability of tickets, but the LSWR then announced that its fares between London and Guernsey and Jersey via Weymouth would be 35*s*. first class and 25*s*. second class. As the fares from Southampton were only 31*s*. and 21*s*. the GWR protested but the LSWR refused to raise the Southampton fares. However, when it was announced that the Packet Company was going to charge 31*s*. and 21*s*. the LSWR was forced to fall into line, but the inter-availability scheme was abandoned.

The Packet Company promoters were in the meantime frantically setting their company on a legal footing, the Weymouth & Channel Islands Steam Packet Company Limited being formally incorporated on 14th April, 1857. The authorised capital was £40,000 in £10 shares with a provision to increase the capital to £100,000 by a special resolution. Two thousand shares were allocated to Jersey, 1,000 to Guernsey, 500 to Weymouth and 500 to the Great Western Railway. Two of its shareholders were Brunel and Gooch! All the shares were quickly taken up except at Weymouth, where only 241 were sold.

TO JERSEY & GUERNSEY, FROM WEYMOUTH,
BY THE SOUTH-WESTERN COMPANY'S

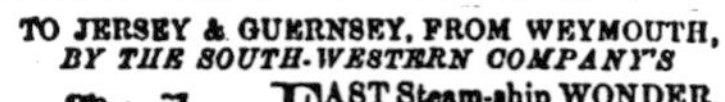

FAST Steam-ship WONDER, leaving Weymouth MONDAYS, WEDNESDAYS, and FRIDAYS, at Eight o'clock A.M.; returning from Jersey (Calling at Guernsey) TUESDAYS, THURSDAYS, and SATURDAYS, at Half-past Six o'clock A.M.; and arriving at Weymouth, under ordinary circumstances, in time for the Afternoon Trains to London, Bristol, Bath, Exeter, Plymouth, and the West of England.

FARES:—
Weymouth to Jersey or Guernsey, 18s. First Class; or 12s. Second Class.

Fast Steam-ships sail between SOUTHAMPTON and JERSEY and GUERNSEY, MONDAYS, WEDNESDAYS, and FRIDAYS, at Quarter to Twelve, Midnight; returning from Jersey, *via* Guernsey, MONDAYS, WEDNESDAYS and FRIDAYS, at seven, A.M., arriving at Southampton, under ordinary circumstances, in time for the Afternoon Trains to London, Bristol, Bath, Exeter Plymouth, and the West of England.

By order,
ARCHD. SCOTT.
Waterloo Bridge Station, London, July, 1857.

WEYMOUTH AND CHANNEL ISLANDS STEAM PACKET COMPANY LIMITED.
AQUATIC EXCURSION.

EVERY MONDAY in JULY, 1857, (weather and circumstances permitting),—One of this Company's Fast and Splendid STEAMERS, "AQUILA," or "CYGNUS," will make a Trip round the Bay; the Bill of Portland; and the Victoria Harbour of Refuge, leaving Weymouth Harbour after the Arrival of the Great Western Railway Excursion Trains.

Provisions may be obtained on Board upon moderate Terms.

FARES 1s. each.—Tickets to be had on Board.
J. MAUNDERS, Manager.

WEYMOUTH and CHANNEL ISLANDS STEAM PACKET COMPANY, LIMITED.
NOTICE, ALTERATION OF TIME.

Steam communication between Weymouth, Guernsey, and Jersey. On and after the 1st JULY, 1857, the AQUILA and CYGNUS will leave WEYMOUTH HARBOUR with GOODS and PASSENGERS for GUERNSEY and JERSEY, as under, viz.:—

On Tuesdays at 8 A.M.	On Fridays at 3 A.M.
On Wednesdays at 3 A.M.	On Saturdays at 8 A.M.

Fares from London, 1st Class 31s., 2nd Class 21s.
" from Weymouth, do. 18s., do. 12s.
Steward's Fees, 1st Class, 2s., 2nd Class, 1s., Children half-price.

Further particulars may be known on application at any of the Stations of the Great Western Railway Company; of Mr. THOMAS RENOUF, Jersey; Mr. JOHN JONES, Guernsey; Mr. ROBERT BESANT, Weymouth; or of
JOSEPH MAUNDERS,
Manager and Secretary.

Adverts from the *Southern Times* of 11th July, 1857: the South Western Railway advertising both its Weymouth and Southampton services; the Weymouth & Channel Islands Steam Packet Company advertising weekly 'Aquatic Excursions' and alterations to the timings of its Channel Islands service.

WEYMOUTH AND CHANNEL ISLANDS

STEAM PACKET

COMPANY LIMITED.

STEAM COMMUNICATION BETWEEN

WEYMOUTH

AND THE

CHANNEL ISLANDS

ON AND AFTER

FRIDAY, THE 17th DAY OF APRIL, 1857,

(CIRCUMSTANCES PERMITTING) UNTIL FURTHER NOTICE

THE IRON

FAST STEAMBOATS OF THIS COMPANY,

AQUILA & CYGNUS,

Fitted up in the most splendid style, with every requisite accommodation, and making DAYLIGHT PASSAGES both ways, will ply between Weymouth and the Channel Islands as follows:

FROM WEYMOUTH TO JERSEY,

Calling at GUERNSEY on Tuesday, Thursday, Friday, and Saturday in every week, at half-past Eight A. M.

From JERSEY TO WEYMOUTH,

Calling at GUERNSEY on Monday, Wednesday, Friday, and Saturday in every week, at half-past Seven A. M.

The "AQUILA" will leave Jersey, and the "CYGNUS" will leave Weymouth, circumstances permitting, for their first Trips, on Friday the 17th day of April inst.

For further particulars of FARES, RATES FOR GOODS, and through Booking to the several different Towns on the Line of the GREAT WESTERN RAILWAY, and other Lines in connection therewith, apply to the Company's Agents, Capt. W. ROBERTS, Weymouth; Mr. RENOUF, Jersey; and Mr. JONES, Guernsey.

JEFFERY, Printer, St. Mary Street, WEYMOUTH.

Poster announcing the commencement of the Weymouth & Channel Islands Steam Packet Company service to the Channel Islands in April 1857.

Twelve provisional Directors were nominated, Elias Neel, a banker and States Deputy of Jersey was nominated Chairman, Jersey and Weymouth were both represented by four Directors, Guernsey and the Great Western Railway by two each. Mr Joseph Maunders was appointed Secretary and Manager, setting up office at South Parade, Weymouth. Mr W. Roberts was appointed Weymouth agent, with Mr Renouf for Jersey and Mr Jones for Guernsey.

The original planned opening of the service for mid-May was hurriedly brought forward to the 17th April, with the *Cygnus* sailing from Jersey and *Aquila* from Weymouth. The initial service consisted of four return crossings each week departing Weymouth at 7 am on Tuesday, Thursday, Friday and Saturday, returning from Jersey at 6.30 am on Monday, Wednesday, Friday, and Saturday.

In the early days the steamer anchored outside St Peter Port, Guernsey, passengers and cargo being transferred by boat and barge - a most unsatisfactory procedure. Indeed much concerning the early days of the operation was unsatisfactory. The service having been commenced in such haste there were difficulties in obtaining crews, including officers, and the charter of the vessels was on the personal guarantee of one shareholder. No letters of allotment concerning the shares had been issued, and no documents concerning the charter of the vessels or agreements with the GWR had been signed. It was not until 14th May that both charter agreements and agreements with the GWR were eventually signed, everything until then having relied on a gentleman's agreement!

The terms of the original agreement between the Packet Company and the Great Western Railway - which was for 18 months - included the provisions that the Packet Company would run a minimum of two return crossings each week to connect with train services provided by the GWR; that through rates and apportionment of receipts would apply as might be agreed; and at the end of 12 months any loss on the steamer service be made good by the GWR from its share of receipts from through traffic, after deducting cartage and terminal charges.

The local press reported favourably, stating that receipts for the first five weeks were about £300 for cargo and £678 for the 847 passengers carried during that period. However, this was only about one-third of the number sailing via Southampton, where the trains ran virtually to the quay. This was not the case at Weymouth, a good half-mile separating the railway station from the quay. Furthermore, the early morning sailing required passengers (other than those from Weymouth) to arrive overnight and either stay at one of the hotels or sleep aboard the vessel.

If the facilities for passengers were sadly lacking there were even less for the vessels themselves! At the April Council meeting the LSWR requested that two piles be driven in at the edge of the quay opposite the Custom House to prevent the paddle boxes of the steamers riding over the top of the harbour wall, trapping the vessel as the tide fell and damaging the paddle wheels. Likewise two piles were required at the end of the coal stage projecting into the harbour on the other side. It was agreed that this work would be carried out, as the Packet Company would doubtless make a similar request, 'but that it be explained to the LSWR that the Council are not authorised to assign any particular berth to a steamer'.

The *Southern Times* followed the new service with interest, reporting on Saturday 23rd May:

> The traffic with Guernsey and Jersey continues to progress most satisfactorily, both as regards goods and passengers. The boats of either company seldom arrive without bringing twenty or thirty passengers and as the season advances a considerable addition to this number may be expected. A great deal of attention was excited on Saturday last by a trial of speed between the *Express* and the *Aquila*. Both steamers started at the same time, and kept well together during the whole passage over. On their arrival at Weymouth the *Aquila* was obliged to slacken speed for the purpose of taking the pilot on board, and the *Express* - having previously taken in her pilot - obtained the lead, and reached her destination two minutes and a half ahead of her competitor, but for the unavoidable delay on the part of the *Aquila* it would most probably have been a neck and neck race. The occurrence attracted a considerable number of persons on the quay, and the contest was watched with keen interest.

The Packet Company held its first general meeting on 1st July, 1857 when, with the exception of one Guernseyman, the provisional Directors were all confirmed, as was the Chairman Elias Neel. Those assembled, being satisfied with the two chartered vessels, decided to take up the option of purchase - although at a reduced price owing to the amount of work required on them. This offer was refused by the owners. Seven days later the boilers on *Cygnus* failed and the Packet Company had perforce to rely on *Aquila* which, despite suffering from faults, maintained a reduced service of three return crossings weekly until the return of *Cygnus* at the end of August.

During that period the company further discussed the purchase of the steamers, including the option of having a high-class steamer constructed by the following March. As finances were stretched, this was no doubt an artful attempt to obtain the chartered vessels at a reduced price. Whilst these discussions and repairs to *Cygnus* were taking place the LSWR steamer *Express* was withdrawn for refit, the *Wonder* being sent as a replacement. As this vessel had a good turn of speed it can be assumed that the LSWR had chosen her to outstrip the mediocre *Aquila*!

In August the Council received the first complaint from yacht and other boat owners concerning the wash from the Packet Company and LSWR steamers entering and leaving harbour - a matter that still causes friction nearly a century and a half later!

Eventually the matter of purchasing the charter vessels was settled by independent valuation and they became the property of the Packet Company on 21st November, 1857. On the same day it was reported that *Express,* just returned from re-fit, made the passage from Jersey in the shortest time then on record, having departed at 7 am to arrive in Weymouth harbour at 1.55 pm, just 6 hours 55 minutes.

During the first year of operation the Packet Company carried nearly 9,000 passengers, which gave receipts of £11,811 when cargo traffic was added. Unfortunately expenses totalled £19,575, the deficit of £7,764 being far in excess of the Great Western's mileage proportion, so the first year had proved to be unprofitable for both companies!

Despite the financial situation the Packet Company decided to commence a service between Weymouth and Cherbourg in co-operation with the Great Western Railway and the Western Railway of France. The completion of the massive harbour works at Cherbourg and the opening of the railway between Caen and Cherbourg completed the line to Paris, this making Weymouth ideal as the point of departure on a through route from the West of England to Paris and beyond. *Cygnus* had run two excursions to the French port that July, no doubt as a trial run for the future service. An additional steamer, *Brighton,* was purchased in the same month. *Brighton* made her maiden voyage to Cherbourg on 7th August when she undertook an excursion for the grand opening ceremony of the harbour works. The regular service commenced on 2nd September, 1858, sailing from Weymouth on Monday, Thursday and Saturday, returning Tuesday, Thursday and Monday, the outward sailing on Saturday and inward sailing on Tuesday calling at Alderney.

From October the Cherbourg mails were carried and Alderney mail was conveyed from the following March. Unfortunately expenses again exceeded income, the company being obliged to accept loans from Directors secured by mortgages against the three steamers. By the end of June 1859 the loss on the service was well in excess of £6,000, and both the GWR and the Western Railway of France had lost interest, so after 111 return voyages the service ceased.

The lack of capital and some unwise decisions, together with competition from the LSWR had reduced the Packet Company almost to bankruptcy. Neel resigned, and at the July meeting a Guernsey linen-draper, Abraham Bishop, was elected Chairman. The future of the company looked bleak indeed. Although the Cherbourg service had suffered substantial losses, it was stated that the Channel Islands traffic had shown an increase in the gross receipts of 20 per cent over the previous year, and was fully up to expectations considering the formidable competition of the LSWR. Trade further increased in September. With Brunel's steamship *Great Eastern* lying in Portland Harbour and open to visitors, the opportunity was taken to run excursions out to the great vessel.

The LSWR also met with difficulties when the *South Western,* running an excursion to view the *Great Eastern,* struck a hulk laying alongside which destroyed a paddle box and resulted in her undergoing substantial repairs at Weymouth. However, this paled into insignificance on 20th September, 1859 when the *Express* on departure from Jersey struck rocks at Corbière. Although run ashore in an attempt to save her, she broke up and became a total loss. The service continued using the *Wonder* and the *South Western* until suspended on 12th December, 1859 when *Wonder* made the final voyage. Both vessels then returned to Southampton, and the service was never revived.

This left the Packet Company as sole providers of a service from Weymouth. In December 1859 agreement was reached with the Post Office for the exclusive conveyance of all supplementary mails to and from the Channel Islands by the company steamers, it being estimated that between 60,000 and 70,000 letters a month were conveyed at a charge of £80, thus opening up another source of revenue. In order to comply with the Post Office and the wish of the shareholders the sailing days from Weymouth were changed to Monday, Wednesday and Friday.

WEYMOUTH & CHANNEL ISLANDS STEAM PACKET COMPANY (LIMITED.)

DAY PASSAGES, SHORTEST SEA ROUTE.

RETURN TICKETS to JERSEY and GUERNSEY, by the Fast Paddle-wheel STEAMERS, *Aquila* and *Cygnus*, every TUESDAY, THURSDAY, and SATURDAY, at 8.0 A.M., on and after the 1st JUNE, AVAILABLE FOR ONE MONTH.

Fares:—Between Weymouth and the Islands and Back, 30s. First Class, 20s. Second Class, allowing passengers to Break the Journey at Guernsey, *en route* to or from Jersey.

JOSEPH MAUNDERS,
Manager and Secretary.

SUMMER SERVICE.

COMMENCING 1st MAY, 1858.

TO GUERNSEY and JERSEY from WEYMOUTH, by the SOUTH WESTERN COMPANY'S Fast STEAM SHIPS, *Express* or *Wonder*, leaving WEYMOUTH on WEDNESDAY and FRIDAY mornings, at EIGHT, and on SATURDAY evenings at half-past ELEVEN.

From JERSEY (viâ Guernsey) on TUESDAY, THURSDAY and SATURDAY mornings at half-past SIX.

FARES:—

Weymouth to Guernsey or Jersey, 12s. Second Class; 18s. First Class.

DOUBLE JOURNEY TICKETS, available for One Month:—20s. Second Class; 30s. First Class.

In addition to the above the Company's Packets Sail from Southampton to Guernsey and Jersey, on MONDAYS, WEDNESDAYS, and FRIDAYS, at a quarter to Twelve Midnight, returning to Southampton on the same Days.

BY ORDER.

SUMMER SERVICE.

COMMENCING 1st MAY, 1858.

TO GUERNSEY and JERSEY from WEYMOUTH, by the SOUTH WESTERN COMPANY'S Fast STEAM SHIPS, *Express* or *Wonder*, leaving WEYMOUTH on WEDNESDAY and FRIDAY mornings, at EIGHT, and on SATURDAY evenings at half-past ELEVEN.

From JERSEY (viâ Guernsey) on TUESDAY, THURSDAY and SATURDAY mornings at half-past SIX.

FARES:—

Weymouth to Guernsey or Jersey, 12s. Second Class; 18s. First Class.

DOUBLE JOURNEY TICKETS, available for One Month:—20s. Second Class; 30s. First Class.

In addition to the above the Company's Packets Sail from Southampton to Guernsey and Jersey, on MONDAYS, WEDNESDAYS, and FRIDAYS, at a quarter to Twelve Midnight, returning to Southampton on the same Days.

BY ORDER.

Left and above: The adverts that appeared in the *Southern Times* during the summer of 1858, advertising both the services of the Weymouth & Channel Islands Steam Packet Company, and that of the South Western Company.

WEYMOUTH & CHANNEL ISLANDS STEAM PACKET COMPANY (LIMITED.)

DAY PASSAGES, SHORTEST SEA ROUTE.

RETURN TICKETS to JERSEY and GUERNSEY, by the Fast Paddle-wheel STEAMERS, *Aquila* and *Cygnus*, every TUESDAY, THURSDAY, and SATURDAY, at 8.0 A.M., on and after the 1st JUNE, AVAILABLE FOR ONE MONTH.

Fares:—Between Weymouth and the Islands and Back, 30s. First Class, 20s. Second Class, allowing passengers to Break the Journey at Guernsey, *en route* to or from Jersey.

JOSEPH MAUNDERS,
Manager and Secretary.

WEYMOUTH and CHANNEL ISLANDS STEAM PACKET COMPANY (LIMITED.)

VISIT of QUEEN VICTORIA, PRINCE ALBERT, The EMPEROR of the FRENCH, &c., &c., to CHERBOURG.

SHORTEST SEA PASSAGE from ENGLAND!

One of this Company's Powerful STEAMERS, *Aquila* or *Cygnus*, will make an EXCURSION from WEYMOUTH to CHERBOURG, on the above occasion.

A limited number of Tickets only will be issued.

FARES:

From Weymouth to Cherbourg and back, ... 20s.
Ditto, with liberty to sleep on board, with such accommodation as may be provided on Deck, 30s.
Ditto, with liberty to sleep on board, in the Saloon or Fore Cabin, ... 40s.

A Plan of the Berths, regularly numbered, will be prepared, corresponding with the numbers on the Tickets issued.

To Prevent Confusion, no Person will be admitted on board without a Ticket, previously obtained.

Further particulars of Mr. THOMAS RENOUF, Jersey; Mr. JOHN JONES, Guernsey; or Mr. ROBERT BESANT, Weymouth.

JOSEPH MAUNDERS, Manager and Secretary.
Weymouth, 13th July, 1858.

Above: A special excursion to coincide with the Royal visit to the new breakwater works at Cherbourg was operated by the Packet Company. Alongside were the regular adverts for both the Packet Company and the South Western Co.'s regular services.

WEYMOUTH AND CHANNEL ISLANDS STEAM PACKET COMPANY LIMITED.

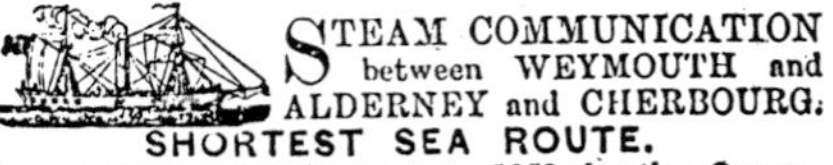

STEAM COMMUNICATION between WEYMOUTH and ALDERNEY and CHERBOURG.

SHORTEST SEA ROUTE.

On and after the 2nd SEPTEMBER, 1858, by the *Cygnus*, *Aquila*, or *Brighton*, Fast, Powerful, and Paddle-wheel STEAMERS.

FROM WEYMOUTH,

Every Monday, at 11.30 P.M... ... To Cherbourg direct.
Every Thursday, at 9.30 A.M... ... To Cherbourg direct.
Every Saturday, at 9.30 A.M...To Alderney and Cherbourg.

FROM CHERBOURG,

Every Tuesday, at 9.30 A.M...To Alderney & Weymouth.
Every Thursday, at 11.30 P.M... ... To Weymouth direct.
Every Monday, at 0.30 morn ... To Weymouth direct.

FARES.	Single Journey. 1st Class. s.	d.	2nd Class. s.	d.	Return within 1 month. 1st Class. s.	d.	2nd Class. s.	d.
Weymouth to Alderney or Cherbourg and vice versa	18	0	12	0	30	0	20	0
Steward's Fee, each way	2	0	1	0	2	0	1	0
Alderney to Cherbourg, and vice versa	7	0	5	0	11	6	8	0

Provisions may be obtained on Board at moderate rates.

Through Booking from the principal Stations on the Great Western Railway, England, to and from the principal Stations on the Western Railway of France.

Further particulars at the offices of the Great Western Railway, England, and at the Western Railway of France; of Mr. ROBERT BESANT, Weymouth; Mr. GAUVAIN, Alderney; Mr. KIRKHAM, Cherbourg; Mr. RENOUF, Jersey; or Mr. JONES, Guernsey.

JOSEPH MAUNDERS, Manager and Secretary.
Weymouth, August, 1858.

Above: The opening of the short-lived Cherbourg service by the Weymouth & Channel Islands Steam Packet Company on 2nd September, 1858 was announced with this detailed poster in the *Southern Times*.

PS Brighton moored in the Cove at Weymouth. This early photograph was taken pre-1877 when during a major refit a turtle-back was fitted to the bows of the vessel. Note also the buildings behind and to the left of the ship's bow. The latter were later demolished for enlargement of the cove to allow larger vessels to swing in the harbour. *J. Attwood Collection*

WEYMOUTH & CHANNEL ISLANDS STEAM PACKET COMPANY (LIMITED).

NOTICE TO THE PUBLIC.

SUSPENSION OF THE CHERBOURG AND ALDERNEY ROUTE.

The DIRECTORS of this COMPANY hereby give Notice, that on and after the 30th of JUNE inst., the SAILINGS from WEYMOUTH to CHERBOURG and ALDERNEY, and *vice versa*, will be SUSPENDED until further NOTICE.

N.B.—The Steamers to the Channel Islands will continue to run as heretofore, viz., on TUESDAYS, THURSDAYS, and SATURDAYS, at 8.0 A.M.

JOSEPH MAUNDERS, Secretary.

Weymouth, June 23, 1859.

WEYMOUTH AND CHANNEL ISLANDS STEAM PACKET COMPANY LIMITED.

EXCURSIONS TO ALDERNEY AND CHERBOURG.

THE AQUILA, CYGNUS, or BRIGHTON Steam Ships, will make TWO EXCURSIONS to ALDERNEY and CHERBOURG on THURSDAY, the 14th, and SATURDAY, the 16th JULY, leaving Weymouth Harbour at 7.0 A.M., returning from Cherbourg on Friday, 15th, and Monday, July 18th, at 7.0 A.M., and from Alderney at about 9.0 A.M.

Fares for the Double Journey to Alderney or Cherbourg and back, 12s. and 8s., and one Steward's Fee for the Double journey.

JOSEPH MAUNDERS, Manager and Secretary.

Weymouth, 1st July, 1859.

SUMMER SERVICE.

COMMENCING 1st JUNE, 1859.

TO GUERNSEY and JERSEY from WEYMOUTH, by the SOUTH WESTERN COMPANY'S Fast STEAM SHIPS, *Express* or *Wonder*, leaving WEYMOUTH on WEDNESDAYS, and FRIDAYS, at Eight morning, and on SATURDAYS, at Half-past Eleven night, and returning from JERSEY (via Guernsey) on TUESDAYS, THURSDAYS, and SATURDAYS at Half-past Six morning.—FARES:—

Weymouth to Guernsey or Jersey, 12s. Second Class; 18s. First Class.

DOUBLE JOURNEY TICKETS, available for One Month:—20s. Second Class; 30s. First Class.

In addition to the above the Company's Packets Sail from Southampton to Guernsey and Jersey, on MONDAYS, WEDNESDAYS, and FRIDAYS, at a quarter to Twelve Midnight, returning to Southampton on the same Days.

BY ORDER.

Adverts from the *Southern Times* of 2nd July, 1859 inform of the suspension of the Packet Company service to Cherbourg, with an advert immediately below giving details of excursions to both Alderney and Cherbourg, clearly demonstrating that where a regular service cannot succeed the odd excursion can make money, and can be cancelled if insufficient patronage is forthcoming. The South Western Company also ran an advert for its service to the Channel Islands from both Weymouth and Southampton.

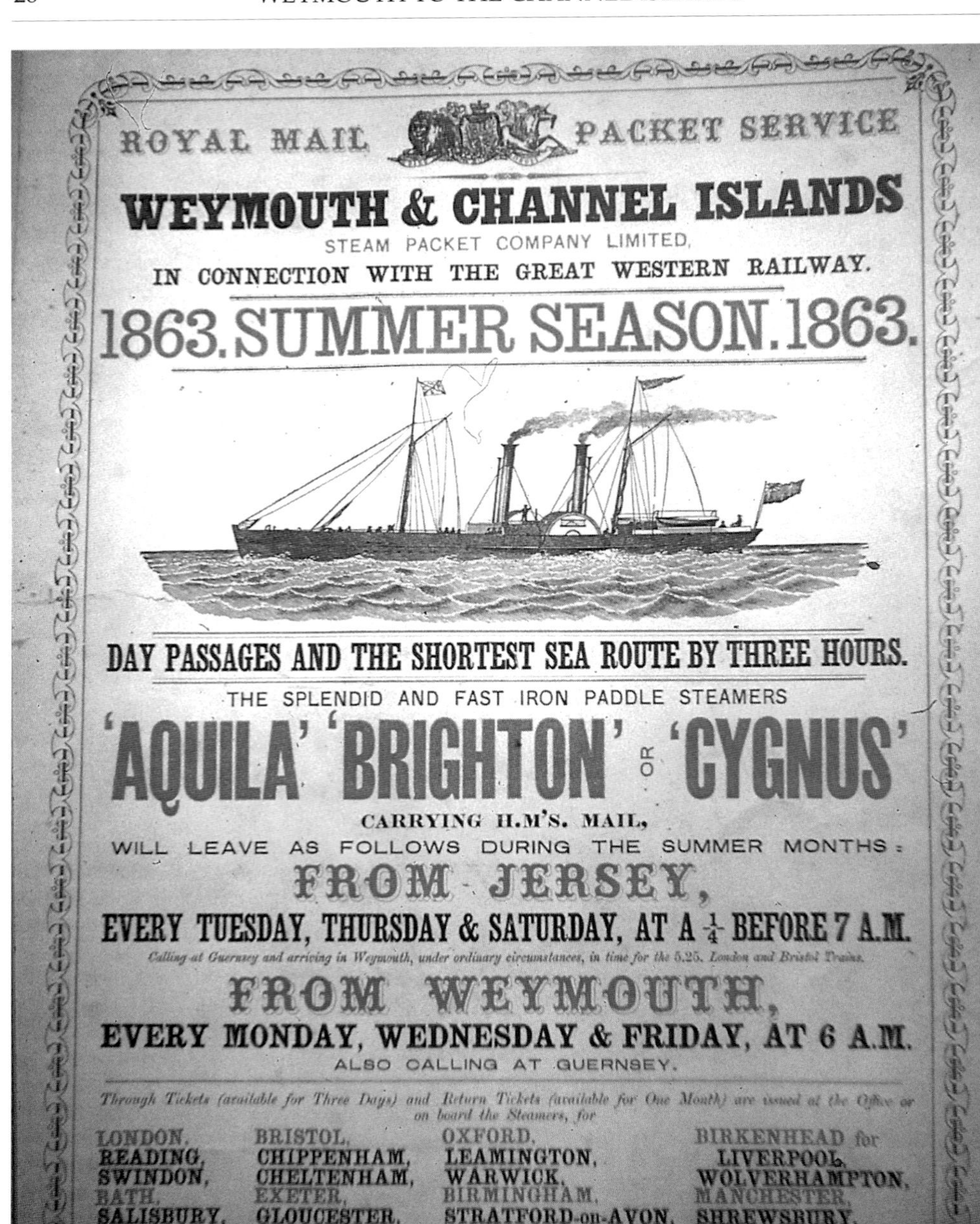

Poster advertising the sailings of the Weymouth & Channel Islands Steam Packet Company vessels for the 1863 summer season. The vessel illustrated is the *Brighton* in her original form.

Although still working under a great financial handicap, the GWR offered an annual subsidy of £2,000 on top of its existing commitment. Of course, every deal has its price, and the railway company stipulated more control. Although an agreement to the new terms was signed in August 1860 Bishop, the Packet Company Chairman, was dissatisfied with it and pressed for better terms. Indeed, he wanted the GWR to take the service over completely, but they agreed only to invest more money into the company.

Lack of capital was one of the main causes of the Packet Company's financial difficulties. Receipts for the first year were £11,811 16*s*. 7*d*., the second year £13,579 6*s*. 5*d*., the third £15,589 13*s*. 9*d*., and the fourth, £16,753 11*s*. Although this showed a steady increase, a meeting in Jersey on 5th June, 1861 was held for the purpose of increasing the capital of the company by the creation of an additional 12,016 £10 shares. It was stated that from the commencement of operations the annual receipts had increased uniformly at the rate of £2,000 per annum, but they had only just arrived at the position where receipts about covered their normal expenditure. It was therefore clear that capital was required to improve the service and the Board of Trade were stipulating further requirements at annual surveys. The above facts were also reiterated at the annual general meeting held in Weymouth on the 17th July.

There was a fear in Weymouth that the Packet Company could collapse and a meeting was held in the Guildhall on 25th July in an effort to sell the preference shares. This had been difficult when the company had been formed originally, but Mr J.A. Devenish, a Weymouth Director, thought £3,000 worth of shares could now easily be raised among the hotelkeepers, publicans and other tradesmen of the town as they gained most from the steamers.

Affairs had improved by the 1862 ordinary general meeting, when an excess of £2,356 18*s*. over expenses was announced. Of this £1,500 would go towards reducing mortgage debt whilst £856 18*s*. would be written off against depreciation of the company's vessels. One of the Directors, a Mr Wimble, had accepted the post of superintendent and agent at Jersey and was therefore not eligible for re-election to the Board.

The upturn in the potato trade during the early 1860s brought an added bonus to the struggling company, and the opening of the Weymouth Harbour Tramway in October 1865 connecting the Quay with the Town station, albeit for goods traffic only (and horse drawn), enhanced the facilities at Weymouth by allowing wagons to load and unload directly on the quayside, although the space was very limited.

From the earliest days the running of excursions and other special trips was practised to utilise a spare vessel and raise additional revenue, some of the earliest being trips around the course taken by competing yachts at Weymouth Regatta during the summer of 1857. In June 1860 both *Cygnus* and *Brighton* were advertised as giving cheap day trips to the Islands, although these were not 'day trips' in the accepted sense, as passengers could stay over a period of a few days and during their stay undertake an excursion to one of the other islands at the price of a single fare. Today's bargain packages are nothing new!

Local excursions were also operated. On 1st July, 1867 *Aquila* took many excursionists who had arrived in Weymouth by train for a trip to see the fleet and the breakwater under construction, thence towards Portland Bill adding a little competition for the local paddle steamers. The Isle of Wight had been the destination for an excursion the previous year, landing at Cowes, whilst on 29th June, 1867 a visit was made to Ryde. The Grand Fleet Review at Spithead that July involved both the *Brighton* and *Aquila* making excursions to Portsmouth on the 13th and 16th respectively, and then running cruises around the assembled fleet from Portsmouth Piers.

Poole and Cherbourg had again come to the fore during the summers of 1865-1866, the PS *Albion* being chartered by the Somerset & Dorset Railway to run the service which was part of a bold plan to link South Wales with Paris. This journey involved ship Cardiff to Burnham-On-Sea, train over the Somerset & Dorset to Wimborne, and the LSWR thence to Hamworthy, ship again to Cherbourg and finally train to Paris, tickets also being available with connections from various Midland Railway stations. It was unsuccessful, the service ceasing at the end of the 1866 season. The Poole & Cherbourg Steam Packet Company was formed to run the following season with the PS *Spicy*; but this was also short-lived. It was to be 120 years before a successful cross-channel service began operating from Poole.

Weymouth was not however the only port with which the GWR were experiencing difficulties, a similar situation existing at Milford from where a service operated to Ireland. Like Weymouth, it was worked by agreement with a separate company, Messrs Ford & Jackson. The GWR was dissatisfied with the arrangements and, as the Irish trade was important, decided to seek powers to operate its own service, resulting in the Great Western Railway (Steam Vessels) Act of 13th July, 1871. The Act authorised the company to own and work steamers between Weymouth and/or Portland and the Channel Islands, Cherbourg and St Malo, and between Milford Haven and Cork and Waterford. The Milford service was taken over quickly, the vessels being transferred to the GWR early in 1872.

There appeared to be no hurry to take over the Weymouth services although the agreement with the Packet Company expired in 1871. There were several good reasons for this delay, as even at that time Weymouth was not the most suitable harbour for the railway's requirements, The original Portland breakwater works were almost complete and were considered to offer a suitable site from where to operate a service, especially as a branch line had opened to the island in October 1865. During 1871 the GWR and LSWR had discussed the possibility of a joint scheme, but the latter company declined the offer. The GWR, having lost 'the battle of the gauges' had the millstone of the broad gauge to deal with. Its conversion was to cost a great deal of money and took the focus off other schemes.

The Great Western Railway, interested in obtaining the French trade, began negotiations with the Western Railway of France during 1875 to operate a joint service between Weymouth and Cherbourg again. The matter was discussed at great length as there were many problems to be resolved. The French had a zoning agreement with the London, Brighton & South Coast Railway (LBSCR) concerning Dieppe-Newhaven traffic, additional harbour works were required at Cherbourg, and although the Great Western had obtained powers to operate its own shipping services it was looking for an arrangement involving the

A view *c.*1880 showing *Aquila* moored alongside the original cargo stage of 1877, upon which can be seen the steam crane, with the Marine Hotel in the background. Astern lays the GWR vessel *South of Ireland*, which operated the Cherbourg service until wrecked on Christmas Day 1883. *R.C. Clammer Collection*

Western Railway of France and the Packet Company. The Great Western would transfer two vessels - *Great Western* and *South of Ireland* - to the ownership of the Packet Company in return for shares in that concern equal to the value of the vessels. The Packet Company would run the daily Cherbourg service and improve its Channel Islands service, but having failed at Cherbourg previously the offer was declined. The French Railway favoured a third party independent of the railways running the steamer service. This arrangement could have been considered, as owing to French Government restrictions the French Railway was unable to become involved directly in the running of the steamer service.

More improvements were required at Weymouth, although Weymouth Corporation had agreed to provide a wooden landing stage for the use of the steamers. It was ready for use on 12th June, 1877. Only 200 feet long and 22 feet wide and partly built out into the harbour, its inner edge was of a suitable height for railway wagons, and it provided valuable working space. The GWR provided a steam crane. Within a short time this new facility was proving valuable as the time required to unload cargo was greatly reduced, and there were reports of greater tonnages being shipped through the port during the season. The *Southern Times* for 30th June reported that two days previously five steamers including the *Aquila* had arrived with potatoes and business was brisk. There were, however, complaints before long, the *Southern Times* reporting,

> The residents of Pulteney and Devonshire Buildings have complained to the Corporation of the nuisance they are subject to on account of the increased trade brought into the harbour since the erection of the platform by the Great Western Railway Company.

This was indeed a constant cause of complaint until the final departure of the cross-channel steamers. Perhaps because of this complaint a scheme for the mass import of cattle from the Channel Islands and France and the construction of a lairage to handle the traffic was never proceeded with, although it was noted that 649 head of cattle had passed through the port in the first nine months of 1877.

Apart from the Weymouth landing stage, a necessary requirement with or without the Cherbourg traffic, little else had happened, but it was hoped to commence the service in May 1878 at the start of the Great Paris Exhibition. A visit to Cherbourg by Great Western officials found no progress there either, the company refusing to commence the service until the required improvements had been made. On 15th July *South of Ireland* took an official party to Cherbourg where a very short (18 ft long) temporary landing stage had been constructed, and somewhat reluctantly arrangements were made for the service to start on 1st August, 1878.

Following the commencement of the Cherbourg service an interesting aside was revealed during the latter part of August. Mr Davis, who ran the Marine Hotel (later known as the Cherbourg Hotel, and then The Edward Hotel) applied to the Magistrates for a licence, for which both the Great Western Railway and the management of the Packet Company were pressing. Indeed a personal letter to the Justices from Sir Daniel Gooch supported the application! It was stated the premises had been closed until that May, but if the licence was granted Davis planned to raise the building with an additional storey to contain 15 more bedrooms. Davis' application was opposed on the grounds that there were already 105 public houses in the Borough to serve 13,259 inhabitants. But the real reason was that the proximity of his premises to the landing stage compared to other hostelries would give him a near monopoly. Passengers from the boats, which often arrived in the night, who would go straight to it.

Davis stated that the terms of his lease obliged him to have servants up and waiting for the arrival of the steamers, and that he was also restricted to supplying passengers with refreshments at a fixed tariff which worked out at the same prices they paid aboard the steamers. During the hearing it transpired that Wimble, the Packet Company Manager, and James Nobbs, the Weymouth agent, held the lease on the premises, in which Wimble had a private room and office.

Despite high expectations the Cherbourg service was in difficulties from the outset. The poor facilities at Cherbourg lost much potential cargo, and passenger figures were much lower than expected. It seemed that all concerned had wildly over-estimated Weymouth and Cherbourg as the gateways to the continent. One of the problems was the poor train service to and from Weymouth which affected both Cherbourg and Channel Islands traffic, it being rumoured that some Island traders who were also Packet Company shareholders sent goods to England via Southampton to ensure speedy delivery.

There was also the requirement for a spare vessel to cover the Cherbourg service, this matter being resolved by a loose agreement with the Packet Company whereby their vessels could run to Cherbourg and the Great Western vessels to the Channel Islands if required. A fresh agreement between the Packet Company and the Great Western was negotiated during 1879, the 'loose charter' arrangements being formalised and the financial arrangements altered. The Great Western waived all further mortgage interest, the debt having been reduced from £15,000 to under £9,000. The £2,000 subsidy was discontinued and replaced by an annual payment of £700 for depreciation in addition to the £900 dividend payment.

Weymouth Corporation completed an extension to the east end of the cargo stage in June 1880. Additional steam cranes were installed and a total length of 380 feet of working space was then available. The Tramway alongside was altered to form a run-round loop, and from 7th June, 1880 a steam locomotive replaced the horse for much tramway work. Towards the end of the year additional dredging work that was required in the harbour was carried out.

For several years the service enjoyed financial stability mainly owing to the potato traffic. The GWR made a gross working profit on the Channel Islands traffic until 1882 when extensive repairs to the vessels proved costly. It was then decided that only work required by the Board of Trade would be carried out, and the future of the service was even in doubt, but the question of facilities at Weymouth and Portland forestalled a decision.

Despite the improvements carried out at Weymouth there were still many difficulties of which the GWR marine superintendent Captain Lecky was acutely aware, and in January 1883 he looked towards Portland as the answer to the problem. He drew up a scheme consisting of an 'L'-shaped pier projecting out into the harbour from the Admiralty coal depot. As a railway already connected this to the Portland branch there would be little difficulty in upgrading the line to carry passenger traffic. Captain Lecky estimated the entire cost of the project would be £30,000 to £35,000, but the scheme was only suitable for the volume of traffic passing at that time. To cater for expansion plans were drawn up for an alternative scheme to construct docks on an area known as 'The Mere' in the south-west corner of Portland Harbour, a site that could be developed as required to deal with increasing trade and which was also only a short distance from the existing Portland railway station. Captain Lecky estimated that for £50,000 two piers complete with cranes and buildings, a slipway and workshops could be constructed. This plan was given serious consideration for provisional approval to be obtained from the Board of Customs. Trial bores for foundations were undertaken, after which revised estimates costed the scheme at £108,000 and doubtless caused the idea to be dropped.

Early the following year it was proposed that the Harbour Tramway be doubled and the cargo stage extended with associated harbour works. Two more radical plans were produced to improve facilities at Weymouth; one was for a dock and dock basin to the north of the Pile Pier (on a site now occupied by the Pavilion Theatre). The second was for the construction of a 10 acre dock on the west side of the inner harbour (later reclaimed as Westwey Road and part of the gasworks site) complete with workshops and a dry dock. It would have covered the whole area, including the present Asda site. A second viaduct would have achieved a rail connection across the Backwater alongside the Portland branch from Weymouth station, but as with the Portland schemes no progress was made.

However by that time any improvements were academic as the Cherbourg service was in trouble. Firstly the *South of Ireland* was wrecked on Christmas Day 1883, leaving only the *Great Western* to maintain the service until the purchase of the *Gael*, the official relief steamer *Vulture* being incapable of performing the work. *Gael* later suffered boiler problems, which called for the chartering of a screw steamer, the *St Andrew*, in March 1885 to keep the service running.

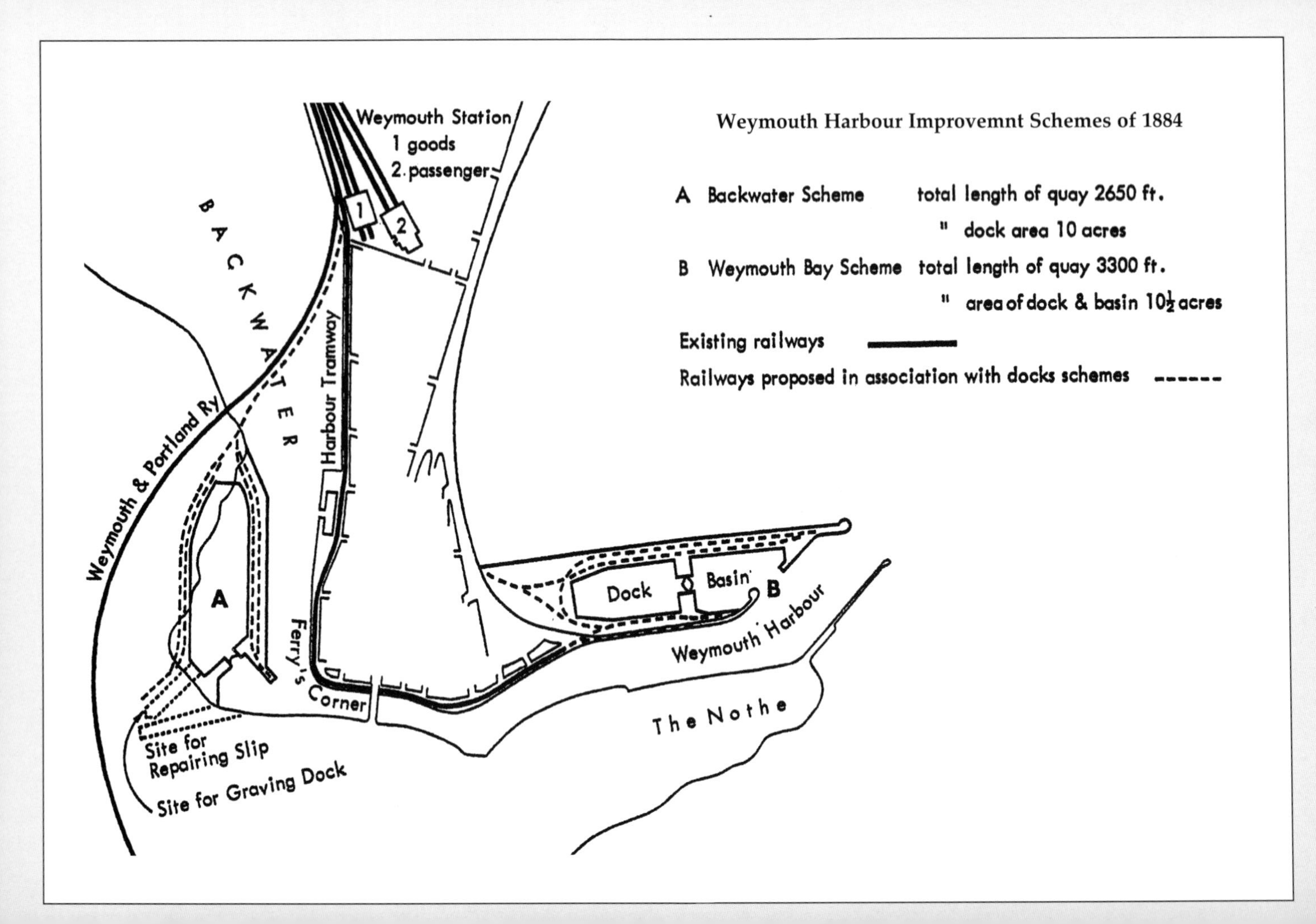
Weymouth Harbour Improvemnt Schemes of 1884
A Backwater Scheme total length of quay 2650 ft.
" dock area 10 acres
B Weymouth Bay Scheme total length of quay 3300 ft.
" area of dock & basin 10½ acres
Existing railways
Railways proposed in association with docks schemes
Weymouth Station
1 goods
2. passenger
BACKWATER
Harbour Tramway
Weymouth & Portland Ry
A
Ferry's Corner
Dock
Basin
B
Weymouth Harbour
The Nothe
Site for Repairing Slip
Site for Graving Dock

After seven years Cherbourg still failed to come up to expectations. Much of the traffic was of a seasonal nature, and the French wished to terminate the service at the end of the 1885 season because of the unsatisfactory results. The Great Western, being unwilling to continue alone, agreed to the closure. It has to be said that insufficient effort by both companies had been put into marketing the service, which goes down in history as the route by which thousands of tons of pipes made by a British firm for the drainage of Paris were exported. *Great Western* and *St Andrew* maintained the service until it ceased after 30th June, 1885. *Gael* did not return from boiler repairs and *Vulture* went to the breakers. Despite plans for new vessels none had been forthcoming, the slow outdated paddle steamers employed doing little to enhance the situation.

During that time the Packet Company had continued with the Channel Islands service using their three antiquated vessels, but matters were made worse on 29th January, 1887 when *Brighton*, the least decrepit of the three, struck rocks approaching Guernsey and was lost, the Packet Company having to charter the *Great Western* from the railway company during the following summers.

At a Board meeting of the Great Western Railway in 1888 it was decided to operate the service to the Channel Islands with its own vessels, an order being placed with Messrs Laird's of Birkenhead for three twin-screw steamers. It was clear that the GWR could no longer support the local company, which had enjoyed its limited financial support over the years. Although it could not be claimed that the LSWR had the latest and finest vessels afloat, they were well ahead of the Weymouth fleet of ageing paddle steamers. Southampton also had the advantage of direct rail access for passengers, whereas at Weymouth passengers had to make their own way to the quay from the Town station. The result was that Weymouth received only about one-third of the potential trade!

The final chapter in the history of The Weymouth & Channel Islands Steam Packet Company commenced in the last week of June 1889, when on Thursday 27th *Cygnus* arrived on her last journey from the Islands, departing the next day to Southampton to await her fate. On Saturday 29th *Aquila* sailed to the Islands and returned to Weymouth at 5 pm, this being the last Weymouth & Channel Islands Steam Packet Company vessel to use the port. On Sunday 30th the *Great Western* on charter to the Packet Company, arrived in the Islands with the final sailing from Weymouth.

Following the final settlement of accounts with the Great Western Railway the surplus assets were valued at £25,193 (less liquidation expenses). In July the final ordinary general meeting of the company took place, disagreement amongst the shareholders as to how the assets be distributed causing the matter to be settled in Chancery. The holders of the original 2,917 paid up shares received £7 a share, 10 years earlier these same shares had been worth less than £1! On 15th August an extraordinary general meeting of the company took place in the Lyric Hall, St Helier, to appoint John Wimble as liquidator for the purpose of winding up the company. On 19th February, 1891, after all expenses had been paid, the final dividend of 19*s*. a share on all shares was declared and the books were closed. This brought to an end the life of the Weymouth & Channel Islands Steam Packet Company which had provided the GWR with a means of competing for the Channel Islands traffic without itself becoming directly involved, although its timely intervention had on several occasions saved the Packet Company from sinking. It had been a difficult 32 years for all concerned.

The passenger facilities at Weymouth during the 1890s. One of the 'Lynx' class boats is alongside the baggage shed and in the platform one of the former B&E tanks waits with the boat train. To the left of the pier tollhouse the original Pavilion Theatre has yet to be built.

R.C. Clammer Collection

A turn of the century view of the passenger landing stage and baggage shed showing the 1897 extension to the stage at the left-hand end. Although over the years this area has changed out of all recognition, the buildings in the background forming Weymouth Esplanade have changed little in the intervening hundred years. *Author's Collection*

Chapter Four

The Great Western Railway Steamer Service 1889-1948

The taking over of the service by the GWR was a far more involved affair than just replacing the Steam Packet Company vessels. In co-operation with Weymouth Corporation improvements were made to the very inadequate harbour facilities. To operate an efficient service, deep water and direct passenger transfer between ship and train were requisites - as was accommodation for passengers, Customs, and other associated business. The main harbour improvements were incorporated in the Weymouth & Melcombe Regis Corporation Act of 1887. Basically, the Corporation was to provide a landing stage, passenger accommodation and direct rail access, demolishing a small amount of property on the south side of the harbour (a section of the east side of the Cove) to allow larger vessels to swing around, and dredging the harbour to allow the larger vessels access at all states of the tide.

The GWR for its part was to provide the necessary vessels to maintain the service and to improve the Tramway allowing passenger trains access to the pier. There was the usual let-out clause to cover the Corporation should the railway cease to use the port, and all the above were to be ready for 1st July, 1889. In the event the harbour works (in particular the dredging) was incomplete, as were the tramway alterations, and the new vessels were delayed. The Great Western informed the Corporation that owing to the dredging being incomplete it would use smaller vessels for the first month, these being *Great Western* and *Gael*. It was a case of the old being replaced by the not quite so old! With these vessels sailing to the new timetable it became a pure work of fiction as far as arrival times were concerned.

The *Great Western* made the first sailing from the Islands on Monday 1st July, but this state of affairs remained until the arrival of *Lynx*, the first of the new ships, on 21st July, followed by *Antelope* in time to allow a start to the intended service on 4th August. A third vessel, *Gazelle*, joined her sisters in September.

The new service was an instant success. With the combination of the boat train a London passenger could cut three hours off the Southampton times! This caused a decline in Southampton patronage, and an end to the LSWR near-monopoly of the Channel Islands traffic. By the end of the 1889 season figures for passengers travelling on both routes were virtually equal. Although the LSWR ships had been far superior to the old Packet Company vessels, the new GWR trio were even better than the LSWR fleet (such were the rapid advances being made in ship building technology). In retaliation the LSWR ordered three new ships from Clydebank builders, the Great Western ordering an extra vessel for the Weymouth service to act as a relief, and also - during the season - to operate a thrice-weekly daylight service. Thus the arrival of the *Ibex* in September 1891 added to the competition, each company improving its train service or clipping a few minutes off the voyage.

Despite official denials there certainly was racing. It was the age of the 'Railway Race', and railway ships were part of the family. Risks were without a

GREAT WESTERN RAILWAY

NEW AND IMPROVED SERVICE

TO AND FROM THE

CHANNEL ISLANDS

VIA WEYMOUTH,

BY

THE EXPRESS STEAMERS,

"ANTELOPE," "GAZELLE," AND "LYNX,"

AND

THROUGH TRAINS IN CONNECTION.

DAILY (SUNDAYS EXCEPTED).

SHORTEST SEA PASSAGE.

QUICKEST AND BEST ROUTE.

WEYMOUTH TO GUERNSEY IN ABOUT 4¼ HOURS.	GUERNSEY TO JERSEY IN ABOUT 1¼ HOURS.

THE SERVICE BETWEEN

WEYMOUTH AND THE ISLANDS OF GUERNSEY & JERSEY

IS NOW CONDUCTED BY MEANS OF THE COMPANY'S OWN STEAMERS.

These Steamers have been specially built for this service upon the most approved principle, possess all the requisite qualifications of first-class ships, and are fitted with the Electric light and all the latest improvements and conveniences.

NEW EXPRESS TRAINS

ARE RUNNING BETWEEN

LONDON AND WEYMOUTH,

in connection with the Steamers, and direct connections have been established to and from all parts of the Great Western Line.

These Trains work to and from the Landing Stage at Weymouth and enable Passengers to pass direct from the Train to the Steamer, and vice versa.

Poster announcing the commencement of the new GWR steamer services to the Channel Islands in 1889.

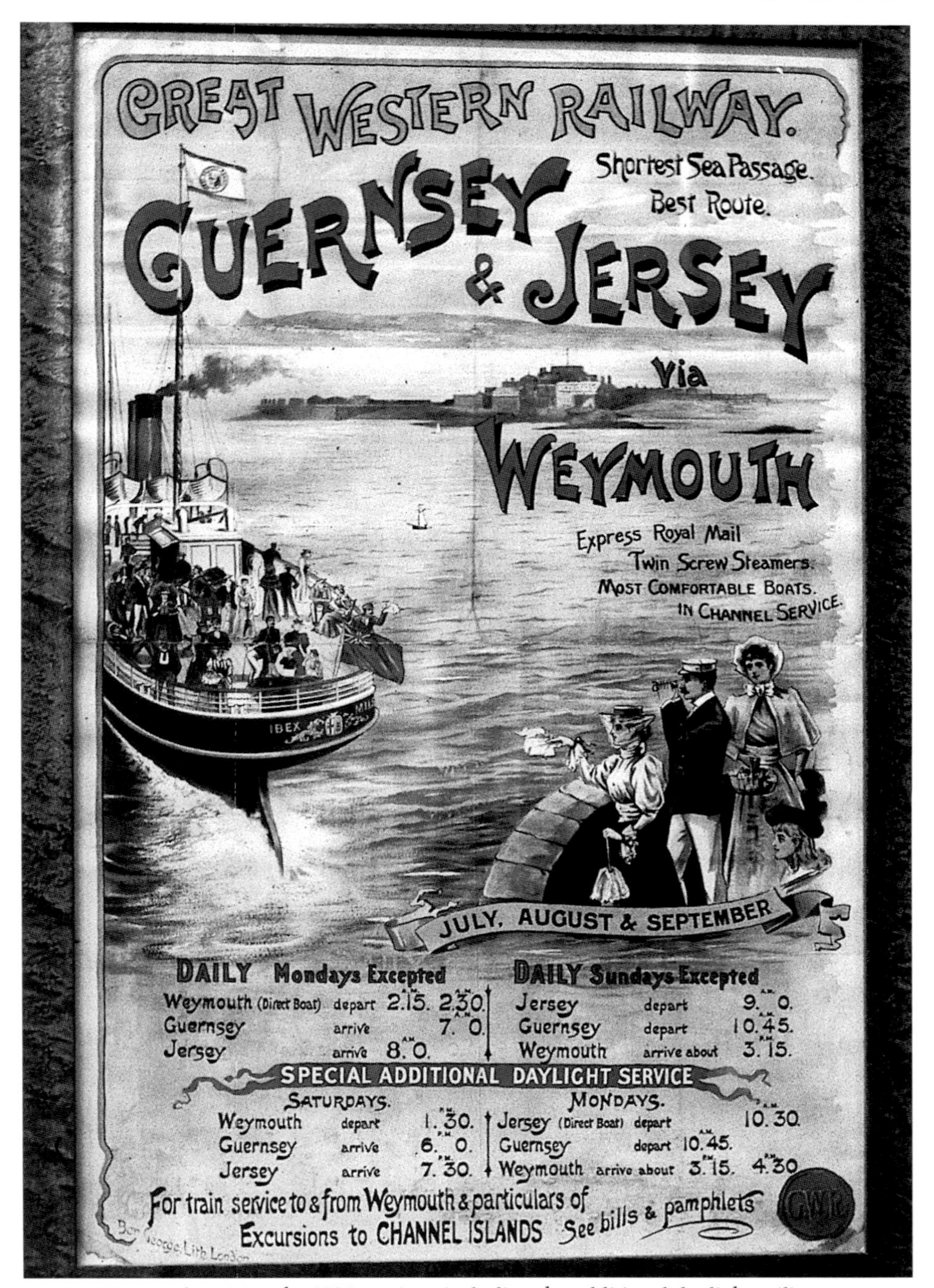

Poster advertising the 1891 services, including the additional daylight sailings.

Antelope entering Weymouth Harbour during 1895, her low, narrow, and sleek lines giving the impression of speed. Indeed, for their day they were fast ships. The open bridge gave no protection whatsoever to the crew in the boisterous conditions the English Channel could often present. *SE&CR Society*

The *Lynx* and *Reindeer* laid up in the Cove, Weymouth Harbour. This view, taken during the early 1900s, clearly shows the difference in size between the *Lynx* of 1889 and the *Reindeer* of 1897. The *Lynx* (on the outside) was 235 ft long, the *Reindeer* (on the inside) 280 ft, the gross tonnages being 596 and 1,281 respectively. To the left is Cosens' paddle tug *Albert Victor*, above which - to the right of her funnel - can be seen the crane and workshops of the GWR Marine Department situated on Nothe Parade. *Mrs N. Fuller Collection*

doubt taken, and there were reports of passengers lining the ships' rails cheering or jeering as the opposition closed in. Certainly the engine room staff wanted to prove their ship had that little bit extra and it became something of a sport in the Islands, great interest being taken in who arrived first. The restricted facilities and tidal problems also created a 'first come first served' situation at the quays.

The *Ibex/Frederica* episode of Good Friday 1897 (*see Chapter Nine*) was indeed the gypsies' warning, and both companies then talked about a co-ordinated service - although little was done in that direction. The addition of the *Roebuck* and *Reindeer* to the Weymouth fleet and the operation of a full daylight service with an improved train service from Paddington in the Summer of 1897 only added to the cut and thrust of the situation.

The new train departed from Paddington at 8.50 am arriving at Weymouth Quay at 1.10 pm, with the ship sailing just 20 minutes later, and departing Guernsey at 5.15 pm for Jersey with a 7 pm arrival there. These new timings gave the Great Western an advantage over their rivals and passenger numbers increased. Further dredging was required, both in the Islands and Weymouth Harbour, for the two new steamers that commenced the new daylight service on 1st July, 1897. The west end of the passenger landing stage was also lengthened by 40 feet to accommodate the new vessels.

Unfortunately, although exploratory meetings had taken place, there was still no agreement over an amalgamated steamer service, and disaster struck again. On Maundy Thursday 30th March, 1899, the LSWR vessel *Stella* - racing on at 19 knots through patchy fog - struck the Auguiere rock on the Casquets. Within eight minutes she had gone, taking 105 of her 217 passengers and crew with her.

The race was over. From 1st October, 1899 it was to be a joint service; during the winter months each company would run only on three nights a week from the mainland and alternate days from the Islands. During the summer each company would run six times a week: from Southampton by night and by day from Weymouth with both companies sailing to the mainland by day. Tickets would be interchangeable, and the gross receipts (less deductions) would be placed in a common fund and divided.

The workings of the Weymouth vessels at the turn of the century are noteworthy. In July 1899 the daylight service was worked by *Roebuck* and *Reindeer* alternately, the night service by *Antelope* and *Ibex* with *Gazelle* moored in the Cove as a stand-by boat. The *Lynx* was working the Milford-Waterford fast service with the Milford-based *Pembroke. Lynx* was laid up for overhaul on 2nd October, *Antelope* taking over the Waterford service. Both *Roebuck* and *Reindeer* proceeded to Milford at the same date to lay up in Barn Lake Pill where special moorings had been laid for them. At Weymouth *Ibex* took up the winter sailings with *Gazelle* as spare boat.

Following the early example set by the packet company the GWR was keen to promote special charters and excursions - principally to utilize a ship during the quiet periods. The conveyance of servicemen to and from the Channel Islands garrisons provided one such opportunity. During 1899 *Reindeer* conveyed the 1st Worcestershire Regiment from Weymouth to Guernsey, and on 23rd October, 1899 *Lynx* carried 120 troops from Weymouth. Unfortunately

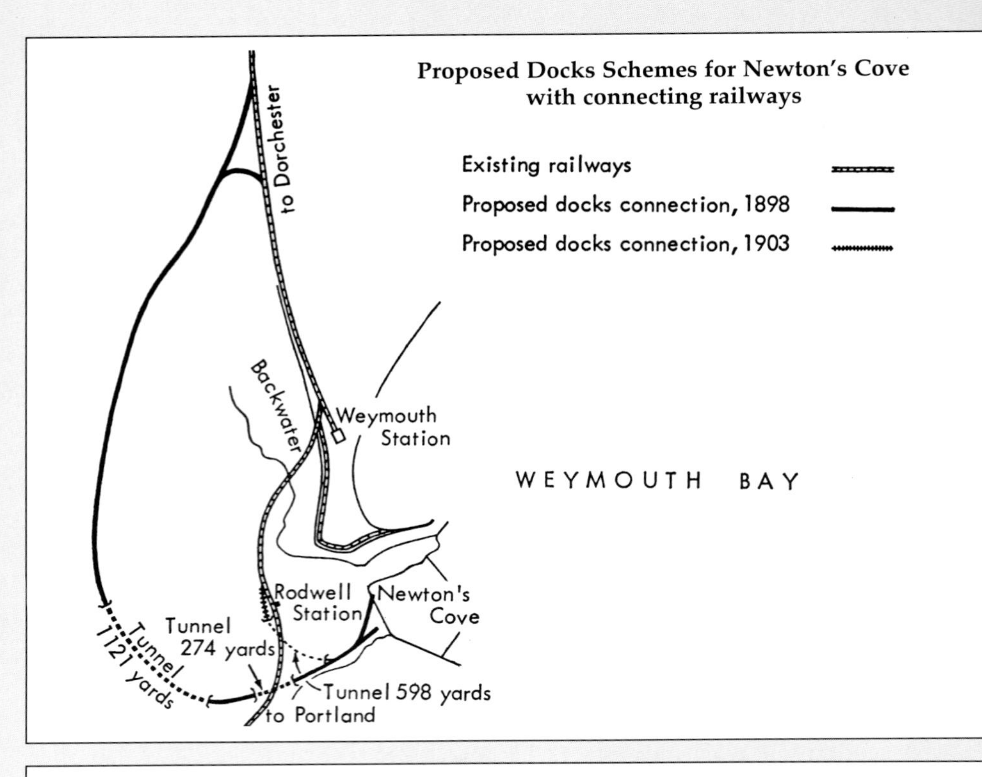
Proposed Docks Schemes for Newton's Cove
with connecting railways
Existing railways
Proposed docks connection, 1898
Proposed docks connection, 1903
to Dorchester
Backwater
Weymouth
Station
WEYMOUTH BAY
Rodwell
Station
Newton's
Cove
Tunnel
274 yards
Tunnel
1121 yards
Tunnel 598 yards
to Portland

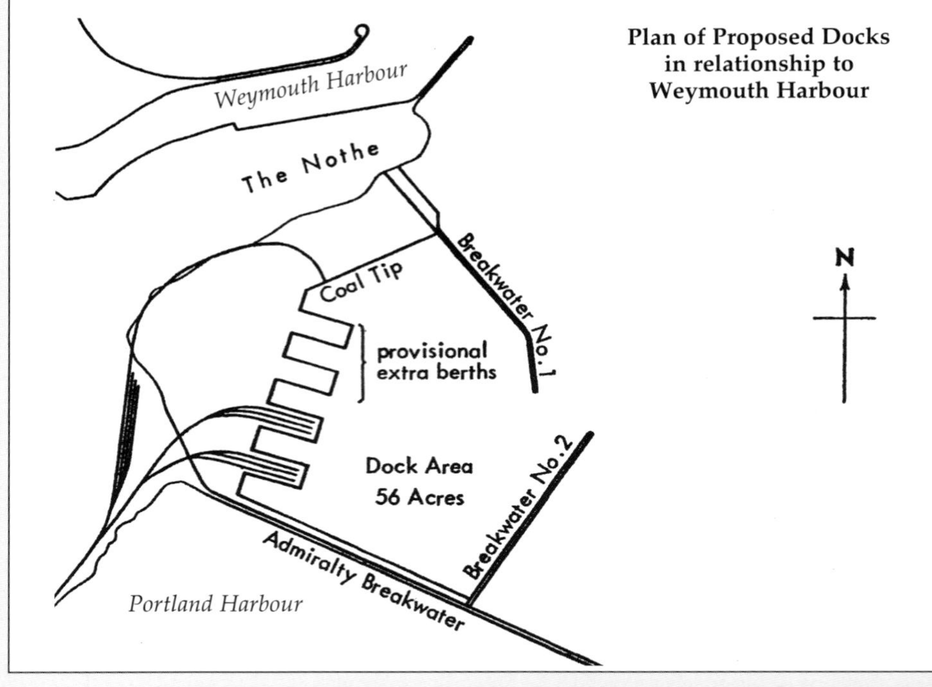
Plan of Proposed Docks
in relationship to
Weymouth Harbour
Weymouth Harbour
The Nothe
Coal Tip
Breakwater No.1
provisional
extra berths
N
Dock Area
56 Acres
Breakwater No.2
Admiralty Breakwater
Portland Harbour

some were the worse for drink, and one was lost over the side! *Ibex* took the 3rd Battalion of the Devonshire Regiment from Plymouth to Jersey around the same time.

The inadequacies of Weymouth Harbour again came to the fore, and Captain Lecky saw Portland Harbour as the answer to the problem. With the threat of the newly invented torpedo the Admiralty was engaged in the construction of two extra breakwaters to enclose Portland Harbour. The northern one would project out from the cliff under Bincleaves at Weymouth, Lecky proposing a dock inside this breakwater under the cliffs, but the Admiralty objected to this. The Great Western then proposed to construct a harbour outside the breakwater in Newton's Cove to which the Admiralty did not object, and a Bill went before Parliament and received the Royal Assent on 12th August, 1898. The scheme was for a 56 acre dock shielded by two breakwaters and a 4½ mile railway leaving the main line at Upwey and swinging around the west of Weymouth, and would have cost £375,000. Work on the Admiralty breakwater was proceeding and the Great Western assumed responsibility for some of the work at the Bincleaves end. A little construction work had been carried out by 1902, mainly to satisfy the Admiralty. The planned railway was reduced to a short and steeply graded spur branching off the Portland branch near Rodwell. The Fishguard project was costing far more than originally intended, resulting in the Weymouth scheme being dropped and the work carried out - which had already cost £70,000 - was handed over to the Admiralty. Thus for years a railway-type footbridge over Newtons Road, and a public house nearby named 'The Railway Dock Hotel' were memorials to yet another scheme that failed to materialize, and it proved to be the last. Despite all its failings, Weymouth was the shortest sea journey to the Channel Islands, and that alone justified its continued existence.

From 1900 it had become a regular feature to send the older vessels to Plymouth to assist with tendering duties and later to operate sailings to Brest. Following the passing of a further Bill through Parliament in August 1909 to increase the company's shipping powers, a service between Weymouth and Nantes was commenced on 9th September, a passenger and cargo service sailing from Weymouth on Saturday and returning on Tuesday. It was slow to develop, the sailing days being changed to Wednesday and Saturday the following January. For the summer months the service was transferred from Weymouth to Plymouth, ostensibly to make space at Weymouth. Operating agreements with other railway companies and the lack of trade caused the last Nantes sailing to depart from Weymouth on 6th June and from Plymouth on 30th September, 1911. The Plymouth-Brest service had ceased in July 1910, and with little other work for the older Weymouth steamers, two were converted to cargo vessels and the other disposed of, the French connection again having been unsuccessful.

The visit of the French fleet to Spithead in the summer of 1905 was an opportunity not to be missed for special excursions, *Ibex* sailing from Weymouth and *Antelope* from Plymouth and Torquay.

The Outbreak of World War I in August 1914 was drastically to reduce the service. During the early weeks the three passenger vessels were engaged in

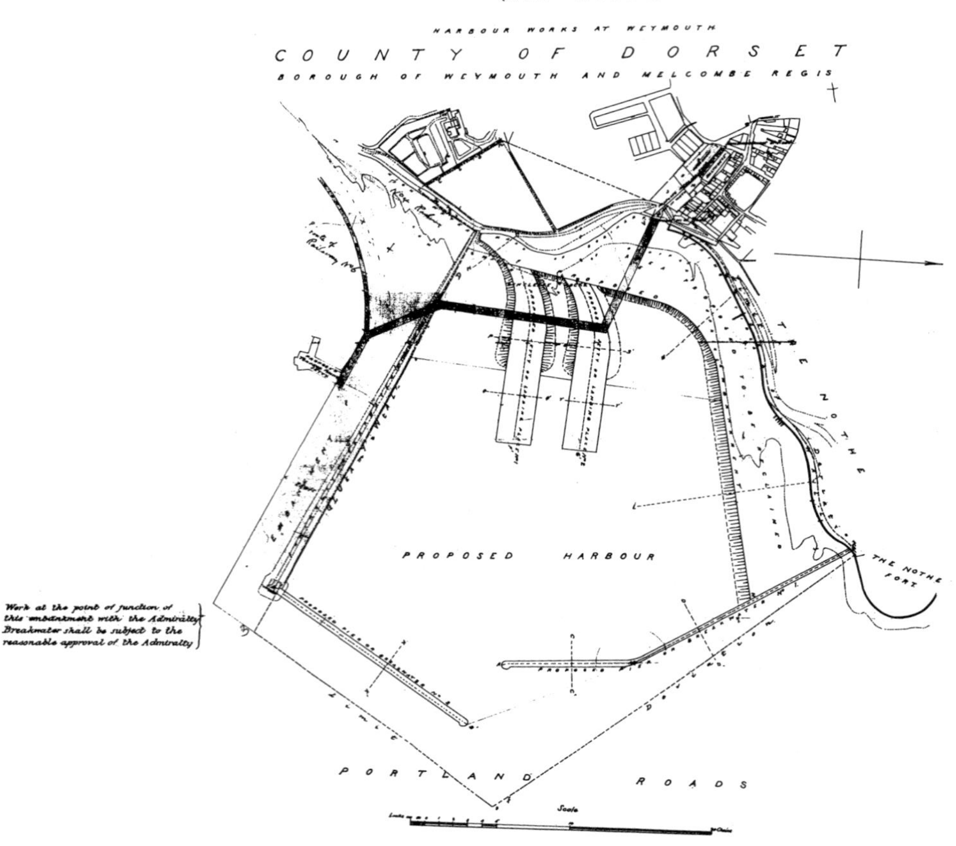

GWR proposals of 1902 for new works.

GREAT WESTERN RAILWAY.

NEW STEAMSHIP SERVICE

BETWEEN

ENGLAND and FRANCE

Via Weymouth and Nantes.

By the S.S. "MELMORE"

IMPORTANT NOTICE.

The Sailings between WEYMOUTH and NANTES will be amended from December 18th as follows:—

Leave WEYMOUTH (Landing Stage) for NANTES.		Leave NANTES for WEYMOUTH.	
1909. Saturday, December 18th; Tuesday " 28th; 1910. Wednesday, January 5th; And every following Wednesday until further notice	At 2.30 p.m.	1909. Monday, December 20th; Friday " 31st; 1910. Saturday, January 8th; And every following Saturday Afternoon until further notice.	Afternoon.*

* Passengers are requested to enquire of the Captain as to actual time of departure.

Steamer Fares between Weymouth and Nantes—

Single Ticket - - 15s.

Return Ticket - - 25s.

Through Fares with Nantes—

NANTES AND	FARES— 3rd Single.	3rd Return.
LONDON	27/-	40/-
BATH	21/-	36/-
BRISTOL...	21/6	37/-
CARDIFF	25/-	43/-
SWANSEA	28/9	49/-
BIRMINGHAM	29/-	50/-
WOLVERHAMPTON	29/9	51/-
OXFORD	25/6	44/-

Accommodation is provided on the Steamer for 12 passengers only, and passengers desirous of travelling by it in either direction must therefore give not less than 24 hours' notice at any Station or Office of the Company, so that it may be ascertained if a Berth is available.

Passengers desirous of taking return tickets, must at the time of application state date on which they wish to return.

Children under Three years of Age are conveyed Free; Three and under 12, Half-Price. The Free Conveyance of 100lbs. of Luggage is allowed.

Every endeavour will be made to adhere to the times of sailing as shewn above, but the Company hereby give notice that they will not be responsible for any delay, expense, or inconvenience caused to passengers owing to any alteration that may be found to be necessary.

For any further information respecting the sailings application should be made to Capt. Hemmings, Marine Department, G.W.R., Weymouth, and for particulars as to Fares, Tourist Arrangements, and Parcel Rates, application should be made to Mr. J. MORRIS, Superintendent of the Line, Paddington Station, W.

PADDINGTON STATION, LONDON, W.
December, 1909.

JAMES C. INGLIS,
GENERAL MANAGER.

35,500 WYMAN & SONS, Ltd., Printers, Fetter Lane, London, E.C., and Reading.—10410a.

Circular announcing changes to the Weymouth-Nantes service commencing on 18th December, 1909.

The scene at Weymouth Quay pre-1908. *Roebuck* or *Reindeer* has just arrived from the Islands, and luggage porters and other interested parties await the passengers. At the platform one of the two former Bristol & Exeter Railway tank locomotives Nos. 1376/7 stands with the boat train. *Author's Collection*

A delightful period postcard showing either *Roebuck* or *Reindeer* alongside the landing stage. The stock of the boat train stands in the platform and horse-drawn carriages and porters with trucks await the passengers. In the foreground is the track of the Weymouth Harbour tramway and a gentleman contemplating the scene at the ferry steps. In the background is the Pavilion Theatre a quintessential Edwardian structure that set the seaside scene, but was unfortunately destroyed by fire in 1954. *Author's Collection*

A busy Edwardian scene at Weymouth as passengers unload direct from the boat train onto the cargo stage and board the *Roebuck*. In the background is the Marine Hotel and the back of Pulteney and Devonshire Buildings whose residents constantly complained about the activities at the cargo stage. The youth in the foreground on the right has stuck his tongue out at the photographer, proving bad manners are nothing new! *R.C. Clammer Collection*

A stern view of the *Gazelle* alongside the cargo stage around 1910, shortly after she was converted into a cargo vessel. Note the fruit baskets loaded in every available space.
Author's Collection

Busy times in Weymouth Harbour. This view taken *circa* 1910 shows on the left - one of the 'Lynx' class as a cargo vessel alongside the cargo stage, with Cosens' paddle steamer *Premier* moored outside. Ahead is the paddle steamer *Albert Victor*, with *Roebuck* or *Reindeer* moored inside. On the passenger landing stage is a 'Lynx' class vessel in passenger service, and to the far right the paddle steamers *Majestic, Emperor of India*, and *Victoria*. *Author's Collection*

Either *Roebuck* or *Reindeer* is moored outside *Ibex* at the passenger stage, Cosens' paddle steamer *Queen* is moored at the steamer jetty whilst *Helper* (the former GWR tender *Sir Francis Drake*) goes astern out of harbour, both the latter vessels acting as liberty boats to the Fleet in Portland harbour. To the left *Melmore* is alongside the cargo stage whilst in the foreground several steam yachts lay at their moorings. *Author's Collection*

various trooping sailings between Weymouth, the Channel Islands and France. With all other vessels requisitioned by late October only the *Ibex* remained to maintain a service three times a week, this at times being impossible with maintenance, the requirements of Government service at short notice, and other problems. She was assisted by various chartered vessels until *Pembroke* was brought to Weymouth. There were also difficulties in obtaining labour to unload the vessels, troops being employed at one stage. Following the armistice returning troops were landed at Weymouth, in particular Australian forces, the first vessel to arrive being the Isle of Man steamer *Mona's Queen* on 15th January, 1919. This was the last time a large cross-channel paddle steamer visited the port. Also to arrive were the LBSCR steamer, *Dieppe* and *Ibex*.

A thrice-weekly service during the summer of 1919 become possible once more, the duty again falling on the *Ibex*, but it was not until the summer of 1920 with the return of *Reindeer* and the cargo vessels that a full summer service could resume. The loss of *Roebuck* had reduced the fleet, although the summer use of the Fishguard vessels *Great Western* or *Great Southern* helped, but in general the steamers had become outdated and the port facilities inadequate

The harbour facilities had changed little since the 1889 construction, and the arrival of the new steamers in 1925 strained them to the limit. The only work carried out was the cutting back of the harbour wall by a few feet under the Nothe to allow the new steamers to swing within the harbour. A steam crane had been erected at the west end of the baggage shed but again it was inadequate for the work required. Prior to this all vessels, after unloading at the passenger berth, proceeded to the cargo stage to discharge and load cargo. Laid-up ships went into the Cove. At busy times ships were 'double parked', as the GWR were not the only users of the harbour. There were numerous coastal vessels and the local paddle steamers. The *Southern Times* for 15th May, 1920 reported 'On some days this week as many as six GWR boats have been in the harbour at the same time'.

In July 1923 a party of Directors and principal officers of the Great Western reviewed the situation, and the following year four new steamers were ordered - two turbine passenger vessels *St Julien* and *St Helier* and two cargo ships, *Roebuck* and *Sambur*. The two passenger vessels were named after the Patron Saints of Guernsey and Jersey respectively. The four new vessels of 1925 quickly settled into a routine and gave an enhanced service, and during the General Strike the following year the fact that they were oil fired made them indispensable. For several weeks during the subsequent coal strike only the Weymouth route to the Channel Islands was open and one of the steamers was transferred to the Fishguard service.

Talks with Weymouth Corporation concerning improvements began in the early 1920s, and by 1925 a draft plan had been prepared, with agreement finally being reached on 31st December, 1930. The Corporation financed the work, with the GWR supplying the cranes and other equipment and giving a 20 year guarantee on the loan charges. Work commenced in February 1931. The original pier was completely rebuilt, but the baggage shed, although extended with a refreshment room added, was incorporated into the new work, which included a pleasure pier on the east side with two berths for the pleasure steamers at the end.

During World War I certain ships were painted in what was described as 'Dazzle Paint', a scheme devised to confuse the range-finding equipment of the enemy. How effective this was at sea is open to question but in harbour it helped the ship to blend in with quayside buildings as shown in these views. *Above,* is *Ibex* laid up in the Cove, and *below,* the *Pembroke* alongside Custom House Quay. *(Both) J. Attwood Collection*

Disembarking troops at Weymouth in 1919 is the *Mona's Queen* of the Isle of Man Steam Packet Company. Painted in camouflage to distract enemy gun sights she had served as a troopship since 1915 her notable achievement being the sinking of an enemy submarine. A massive steamer built in 1885 she remained in service until 1929. She was 320 ft long, 1,559 tons gross and was powered by a four-cylinder compound oscillating engine, and undoubtedly was the largest paddle steamer ever to visit Weymouth. *Author's Collection*

The London Brighton & South Coast Railway steamer *Dieppe* unloading 'Anzac' troops at Weymouth in January 1919. Many of these troops went to dispersal camps in the Weymouth area before later returning to Australia and New Zealand. *Author's Collection*

Above: The need for improvements is clearly shown in these views taken in 1926/7 as *Roebuck* (1925) lays at the cargo stage with *Great Western* ahead. Double-banked at the passenger stage are *St Helier* and *St Julien,* whilst to the right *Reindeer* lays in the Cove. *Below: Great Western* at the cargo stage with *St Helier* on the passenger landing stage, whilst *Roebuck* (1925) and *Reindeer* are laid up in the Cove. *(Both) R.C. Clammer Collection*

The commencement of the accelerated summer service on 29th June, 1925; *St Helier* awaits departure from Weymouth. All the smoke was coming from the forward funnel, the aft one being a dummy. Note the officer standing on the aft docking bridge. On the quay the new boat train consisted of the first set of GWR articulated stock to enter service.
Author's Collection

The working part of the pier could accommodate one passenger boat and three cargo steamers simultaneously. Constructed in reinforced concrete, the entire structure was nearly ¼ mile long. Six electric cranes with lifting capacities ranging from 30 cwt to 5 tons were provided, and two railway platforms, each capable of holding a full-length passenger train or about 50 wagons, were also provided. Like all reconstruction work of that nature in those days life had to go on around it, and enough progress had been made to allow *Roebuck* to unload tomatoes on the partly-completed pier on 18th May, 1933, the completed work being officially opened by the Prince of Wales on Thursday 13th July, 1933. The first official vessel to use the new pier was *St Helier*, which ran a special excursion from the Islands for the Ceremonies. Before long the face of the landing stage in front of the baggage shed was reconstructed to complete the works. The previous year new buildings had been provided at both Jersey and Guernsey, and as an economy measure the Island's GWR and SR staff were amalgamated.

Reindeer, being the spare and weekend steamer, was ideal for running excursions during the week as a means of covering the cost of her crew and harbour dues. On Tuesday 26th August, 1926 she ran a day excursion to Guernsey. A total of 670 excursionists left Weymouth at 7.30 am, arriving at 12.30 pm and returning at 6.30 pm to arrive back in Weymouth at 1 am, at a fare of 10*s*. 6*d*. The excursion trade was soon expanded with trips to Cherbourg and Guernsey being run from Weymouth, Torquay, Dartmouth and Plymouth. The positioning sailings to and from Weymouth were advertised as a combined sea and rail circular tour, or return two days later with the ship. Even in those days of a good railway system travel between Weymouth and the West Country was still something of an ordeal, and these trips did not prove popular, the rail element soon being abandoned. An innovation in August 1934 was the introduction of a six hour grand channel cruise from Weymouth at 6*s*. with the idea of emulating a liner with music, dancing and deck games, but the latter fell on stony ground. However, the idea was basically sound and in succeeding years up to the war afternoon and evening cruises were popular at 4*s*. and 2*s*. Indeed they proved very popular, and must have undermined the traditional paddle steamer trade. After all, for the average working man a cruise on a cross-channel steamer towards Bournemouth or into Lyme Bay was as near as he would ever get to boarding a liner!

Another way of raising revenue was to provide a cruise when returning the summer vessel to Fishguard. In September 1933 *St Patrick* made a first class all-in weekend cruise leaving Weymouth at 5 pm on Friday 22nd September. Limited to 120 passengers who could start at either Weymouth, Plymouth, Bristol or Cardiff, the inclusive fare of £5 5*s*. covered first class rail travel to Weymouth or Plymouth for passengers from Bristol and Cardiff, and return rail travel from Fishguard. Departing Weymouth at 5 pm on Friday 22nd September the first port of call was Plymouth where a 14 hour stop was made before leaving at 1 pm on Saturday. She then steamed to the Scilly Isles where Sunday was spent before sailing for Fishguard, which was reached at 6 am on Monday.

Improvements were made to the train service in 1934, when the boat train ceased to run via Swindon and was rerouted over the Berks & Hants line, the journey time being reduced by 55 minutes, with further improvements in September 1936. The excursion programme was progressing, although (disappointingly) only 143 passengers sailed aboard *St Helier* on a special trip to witness the maiden voyage of the *Queen Mary* on 27th May, 1936. But 562 undertook an excursion to Cherbourg on 5th July, whilst 910 passengers sailed to within half a mile of Bournemouth pier on an afternoon cruise on 16th July. Proving the short cruise was popular the same destination drew 720 passengers on 7th July, 1938, and 996 partook of an evening cruise to St Albans Head on 4th August, whilst cruises from Torquay were also popular.

The improvements carried out to the accommodation aboard *St Helier* and *St Julien* during 1937 added to the progress made with the service. The 1938 season again broke records, when over 133,000 passengers used the service and 22,370 took advantage of the excursion programme, 4,624,612 chips of tomatoes and 307,604 boxes of flowers also being carried. Unfortunately war clouds were again gathering, and the booked summer service ended abruptly at the end of August 1939, the last daylight sailing being on Friday 1st September. A night-only service commenced the following day.

War was declared on Sunday 3rd September, 1939, and immediately the Admiralty set up a contraband base at Weymouth. On 7th September instructions were received from the Immigration Office to suspend the service from Weymouth, the last passenger sailing being at 2.30 am on Saturday 9th September. The cargo service remained although the quayside had to be shared with vessels unloading contraband cargo, this continuing into the summer of 1940. The Weymouth traffic agent, Mr D.G. Hoppins, was appointed chairman of the Port Emergency Committee on 9th April. On 18th May the first refugees were landed; it was the beginning of a busy and harrowing time as following the fall of France and the Low Countries, refugees and troops came in from the Channel Islands and the Continent in their thousands. There was also an outward traffic in French troops who had escaped Dunkirk and wished to be repatriated.

The situation was to test the facilities at Weymouth to the full, with the Southern Railway steamers *Canterbury* and *Maid of Orleans* arriving with refugees from Cherbourg on 20th May. This was only a prelude to the mass arrival of other refugees and troops in the port during the following month. Amongst the vessels recorded were the LNER steamers *Amsterdam Archangel* and *Vienna* on 31st May with British troops from Cherbourg, *Vienna* returning with repatriated French troops. On the same day the LMS steamer *Duke of Argyll* arrived with troops from North West France, returning the following day with 957 repatriated French troops, the *Vienna* returning 937 the same day. The 2nd June saw the Southern Railway steamers *St Briac* and *Brittany* arrive, the latter returning to Brest with 776 French troops, and *Archangel* with 1,000 French troops. The *Antwerp* was the first of three ships to arrive on 4th June with British troops from Cherbourg, returning with repatriated French troops, and on the same day the Dutch steamer *Batavier IV* made the first of two crossings bringing back British troops and returning French troops to Cherbourg, whilst on the 5th *St Briac* returned more French troops to Cherbourg. On 6th June the Southern Railway mail steamer *Isle of Sark* unloaded at Weymouth owing to magnetic mines further up channel.

The evacuation of those wishing to leave the Channel Islands commenced with the arrival of the Southern Railway's *Haslemere* from Guernsey on 20th June, followed by the LNER steamer *Malines* with troops from Jersey and the LMS steamer *Duke of York* made the first of two crossings bringing evacuees from Guernsey, including 2,000 mothers and 700 children, one sick child dying on voyage whilst another was born. *Duke of Argyll* then brought more refugees and *Batavier IV* brought Guernsey school children. On the 21st the Southern Railway vessels, *Fratton, Minster,* and *Ringwood* arrived from the Islands, whilst on the following day *Biarritz, Deal, Maidstone,* and *Whitstable* arrived, together with the Belgian steamer *Prinses Astred.* On 23rd the Southern Railway cargo vessel *Tonbridge,* which 36 hours earlier had departed from Guernsey with 250 women and children, managed to berth at Weymouth.

Added to this there were several other unspecified vessels and some 70 loaded Belgian trawlers. Of these unfortunate people over 3,000 were moved from the quay by special trains, others departing from the town station.

Amongst the chaos a limited amount of cargo working continued until the fall of the Islands, the quay having to be shared with the Contraband Patrol vessels. It had required the co-operation of all concerned, including many outside organisations, to organise the dispersal of so many displaced persons.

With the invasion scare the tramp steamer *Kenfig Pool* was tied up at the general berth to be swung across the harbour as a block ship if required, replacing the paddle steamer *Monarch* that had previously stood by. On 25th July, 890 survivors of the French liner *Meknes* were landed at Weymouth and dispatched by special trains from the quay. From that point Weymouth ceased to be a channel port. The refreshment rooms closed on 10th August and were requisitioned by the Admiralty on 1st October, and on the 7th the marine stores were transferred to Fishguard and Swindon. In October the workshop and yard at Nothe Parade was inspected by the Admiralty and later taken over by them, the Weymouth marine department having closed.

The harbour then came under the control of the military authorities; during this time the sole representative of the railways was the Southern Railway Isle of Wight paddle steamer *Freshwater* engaged on the contraband patrol service. Following use as an MTB base under the name *HMS Bee*, Weymouth Harbour prepared for D-Day. Included in this planning was the construction of a temporary train ferry ramp up-harbour from the cargo stage, at which either of the Southern Railway train ferries, *Hampton Ferry* and *Shepperton Ferry* could lie to take stock via the ramp which was connected to the Weymouth Harbour Tramway. There are no records of the ramp ever being tested with a ship, and in the event it was never used. Very soon after the war this wooden pile structure was removed without trace, and the old wooden cargo stage which had suffered from wartime over-use never went back into service and was later rebuilt.

A limited cargo service was restarted by the *Sambur* on 18th September, 1945. However the two passenger steamers had to be released from Government service and refitted, and the terminal facilities also had to be restored before the restoration of the passenger service in June 1946.

The restrictions on foreign travel and the public's desire to have a holiday after years of war strained the service to capacity in 1947 - the final year of GWR operation. A total of 145,287 passengers were carried on the steamers: 64,234 outwards, 57,653 inwards, and 23,400 between the islands. Outward cargo was 31,820 tons, including 1,940 motorcars and 2,000 containers of general merchandise. Inward tonnage was 36,445. On 31st December, 1947 the Great Western (along with the other three main railway companies) ceased to exist, and all railway ships came into the ownership of British Railways. The Great Western era had come to an end.

St Julien returns to Weymouth on 29th November, 1946 following her post-war refit. Much of the pre-war brown paintwork had been replaced by white, and apart from a change of funnel colour two years later, the sisters remained in this condition to give a further 14 years' service. *The late E. Latcham Collection*

Chapter Five

The British Railways Steamer Service

Passenger numbers were rapidly increasing as trade returned to normal, and the arrival of the *St Patrick* allowed the resumption of the excursion programme. The first post-war day excursion from Torquay to Guernsey took place on 18th August, 1948, *St Helier* undertaking the £1 5*s*. voyage. The short coastal cruises were also resumed but only ran for two seasons, the last on 8th September, 1949 by the *St Helier*. In 1948 the railway steamers saw competition on the Channel Islands service when the Radcliffe Channel Islands Steam Ship Company commenced a service between Weymouth, Guernsey, and Alderney. Weymouth Council were unable to offer full berthing facilities owing to other shipping commitments and the condition of parts of the harbour wall, also HM Customs were concerned over the lack of covered facilities for their inspection of goods and the search of inward passengers. This resulted in the SS *Radford* (1935), which during the war had served as an armed minesweeper-trawler HMS *Basset*, making her maiden voyage on 1st August taking passengers on the outward sailing only. However this difficulty shortly became academic, for having acquired a second vessel - SS *Radbourne* - the following year, financial difficulties resulted in bills for work carried out by Messrs Cosens being unpaid. A writ was issued, and by December 1949 the company was in receivership.

On the shore side the reconstruction of the cargo stage between September 1948 and July 1951 allowed extra space during the season, and as it was outside the quay station proper the outer edge could be used either as a platform for loading railway trucks or, just as easily, motor vehicles, a useful feature in later years.

On 1st November, 1948 the Weymouth vessels were transferred to the Southern Region under the control of the Docks & Marine Manager at Southampton. The red funnels of the Great Western had already been replaced by buff, the standard colour of all British Railways ships. The final act to end the Great Western Marine Department took place at 10 am on 4th April, 1949, when the house flag of the Great Western Railway was hauled down for the last time, to be replaced by the new British Railways flag - a 'half starved' lion astride a railway wheel on a blue background.

Trade continued to increase, and although the ships were still reliable they were fast becoming dated. The announcement in the *Dorset Daily Echo* on 9th November, 1955 that the *St Julien* and *St Helier* were to be replaced by new and larger ships was the turning point in the previous traditional cross-channel service, although it was to be almost five years before any serious changes took place, the order for the vessels not being placed until the end of 1957. Of a more political nature the boat train which, despite Southern Region control, had continued to run from Paddington, ceased after the 26th September, 1959, the service being transferred to Waterloo.

With the exception of the cargo stage the facilities at Weymouth had not improved since 1933 but with even larger vessels on order it was desirable that something be done. As usual, a compromise situation was agreed. The passenger berth would be extended at the west end joining to the rebuilt cargo stage, still allowing for the harbour ferry and local motor boat owners to operate from a new set of steps incorporated into the structure, and there was a definite need to completely revamp the terminal arrangements. As in 1933, this was not completely a railway matter. In February 1960 agreement was reached with Weymouth Corporation for the complete reconstruction of the buildings on the pier, these being replaced by two storey structures to save space and allow an open area for cargo handling. A third line and platform were to be added, and extra loop sidings laid inside the curve in Commercial Road to allow the storage of wagons.

There were also plans for a cargo berth and transfer shed in the inner harbour on the site of the former coal siding, but this part of the scheme was never proceeded with, thus depriving everybody of the sight of *Roebuck, Sambur* and other vessels passing through the Town Bridge. It would have required a vast amount of dredging and associated harbour works, and been difficult to navigate with large vessels.

The two new passenger ships on order, *Caesarea* and *Sarnia* were to set new standards, being one class vessels suitable for both day and night sailing with sheltered seating for 1,400 passengers, a selection of single and double cabins, and two small sleeping lounges. The sisters were the last conventional ferries built for the Channel Islands service. *Caesarea* made her maiden voyage on 2nd December, 1960, and *Sarnia* on 17th June, 1961. With the closure of the Southampton-Channel Islands passenger service from 13th May, 1961 the former Southern Railway steamer *Isle of Guernsey* (1929) moved to Weymouth as a relief boat to assist the *Caesarea* until the arrival of *Sarnia* and the return of *St Patrick* from refit. Making her last sailing from Jersey to Weymouth on 10th June *Isle of Guernsey* sailed for lay up and the breaker's yard, ending yet another chapter in cross-channel history.

The 1961 season saw the entire passenger service operated through Weymouth and, although there were some problems, the fact remained that the three ships had carried 11 per cent more passengers than six ships had from two ports the previous year. Slight timetable adjustments to both rail and ship times during 1962 alleviated most difficulties, but there was still a deficit. The only part of the programme to be truly successful were excursions, which showed increased bookings. Ironically, these were to be more than halved in 1963 when *St Patrick* was diverted to operate the Jersey-St Malo service, returning to Weymouth only at weekends to assist with the extra sailings. It was to be a short-lived arrangement. Although a limited St Malo service was sandwiched in with the excursions passenger figures were declining, resulting in *St Patrick* being transferred to Dover at the end of 1964. Following the departure of the *Sambur* earlier in the year, the departure of *Roebuck* in July 1965 brought the regular use of former Great Western ships to an end.

Although the additional platform was built and extra tracks laid there was a delay in the construction of the new terminal buildings, the new steamers appearing out of place against the 1889 structure. It was not until June 1967 that the new passenger facilities were finally completed. Following a brief visit by *St*

Patrick in August 1968 the final GWR steamer departed forever, and there ends our story. However, for the sake of historical continuity a brief account of the final years is not out of place.

In November 1969 it was announced that British Rail shipping services were to be re-branded as 'Sealink' and shortly the livery was changed to a blue hull, white upper works (after a disastrous experiment with grey) and red funnels.

The Guernsey tomato traffic had been concentrated on Weymouth since 1960. With the chips replaced by pallet-loaded boxes and increased mechanical handling, plus extra sailings, an average of 41,000 tons a year was passing through the port. Unfortunately when the grower's contract came up for renewal in 1964 British Rail increased the rate by up to 40 per cent resulting in an immediate loss of trade to the Commodore Shipping Company of Guernsey sailing into Shoreham, and by 1969 of the annual 9½ million boxes only 4 million were handled by British Rail. The Jersey flower trade was also being lost as more was being sent to the mainland by air. Attempts to extend the use of containers at Weymouth were hindered by the lack of space and the perennial battle between the holiday and the commercial trades and, as with the railways in general, their shipping services were only picking up the freight traffic nobody else wanted. A steady decline resulted in cargo services being withdrawn from Weymouth in February 1972 the last sailing being undertaken by *Elk*.

Left with only passenger traffic it was just a matter of time before a 'Roll on-roll off' (Ro-Ro) car ferry appeared. There were various schemes, including a terminal on the Nothe side of the harbour, and in November 1972 work commenced on the construction of a ramp at the east end of the passenger berth. The service commenced on 1st June, 1973, operated by *Falaise* (1947) which had been converted into a car ferry for the service. This was the beginning of the end for the conventional ferry, and in 1976 *Caeserea* departed eastwards to be followed by *Sarnia* in 1978. By that time Weymouth was already being served by a succession of good, bad, and indifferent vessels which had usually already seen service on other Sealink routes, and their history is generally outside the remit of this publication.

After 89 years the Weymouth-Cherbourg service re-opened on 6th April, 1974 as a summer-only operation, the Dover Ro-Ro ferry *Maid of Kent* being transferred for its operation. History was made in February 1976 when *Earl Godwin* took over the Channel Islands service from *Caesarea*, which departed for Dover. *Earl Godwin* a Ro-Ro ferry built in 1966 as *Svea Drott* was purchased during 1974, and was Weymouth's first regular diesel-propelled passenger vessel. In June 1977 *Sarnia* represented *Sealink* at the Spithead Silver Jubilee Review. Making her last crossing to Guernsey on 10th September she was laid up before disposal thus ending the use of conventional ferries on services out of Weymouth.

A disturbing event took place on 8th November, 1977 when Sealink opened a Ro-Ro ferry service between Portsmouth and the Channel Islands. It was the first signs of Weymouth's decline as a channel port. The popular *Maid of Kent* made her final sailing to Cherbourg on 2nd October, 1981, but owing to *Earl William* striking a rock she was diverted to the Channel Islands service until

With a sea running, *St Julien* steams past Corbière Lighthouse homeward bound for Weymouth. *J.D. Ward Collection*

St Helier departs from Weymouth Harbour for the last time on 17th December, 1960, in tow of the Dutch tug *Schouwenbank*. *Dorset Evening Echo*

30th October when she crossed from Guernsey to Weymouth, the last Sealink sailing by steam vessel. She then went to Newhaven for disposal on 24th November, and the last steam-propelled cross-channel vessel had left the port 124 years after the Packet Company bravely set out with the *Aquila* and *Cygnus*.

Sealink was privatised in July 1984 being sold to Sea Containers Ltd, and a rival service between Portsmouth and the Channel Islands commenced on 3rd April, 1985. This competition caused a reduction of staff at Weymouth at the end of the season. The following year the operation was marketed as Sealink British Ferries. Disputes between the rival companies the following year and industrial unrest by Sealink staff culminating in a strike and 'sit-in' at Weymouth caused the service to be curtailed in the September.

During the 1987 and 1988 seasons Sealink operated only a Cherbourg service with the *Earl Harold* whilst Channel Island Ferries ran a service to the Channel Islands with the chartered vessel *Portelet* (1967) (formerly the *Lion*). *Earl Godwin* returned to operate the Cherbourg service during 1989, but owing to engine failure the Isle of Man Steam Packet Company vessel *Mona's Queen* was chartered between 14th and 24th September. Being a side loader she had difficulties in loading and unloading, but added to the variety of vessels employed over the years. *Earl Godwin* completed the season before sailing for Portsmouth. She returned to Weymouth on 24th December for lay up, being sold to Navarma Lines of Italy. Renamed *Moby Baby*, she sailed from Weymouth on 30th March, 1990, the last railway-connected ship to leave the port. The final link was broken, and today the only island connections are the Condor sea cats, a far cry from those pioneering steam vessels of the 1850s.

Painted in the new British Railways livery, *St Helier* at the passenger berth in Weymouth Harbour during the autumn of 1949. In the foreground is the relief lifeboat *John & Mary Meiklam of Gladwood* (1923), which was sold for £950 in 1952 to British Railways and renamed *'Pen Cw'*. She served as a work boat at Fishguard until the early 1980s before being sold to the RNLI for £5 in 1985. Today restored, she is on display at Gorleston on Sea lifeboat house, her station between 1924 and 1939. *Kestin/Caddy Collection*

Chapter Six

Management and Operation

Joseph Maunders was both Secretary and Manager of the Weymouth & Channel Islands Steam Packet Company from its inception until 1868, but from that date until 1878 he held only the office of Secretary as John Wimble had been appointed Manager. A native of Sussex, Wimble went to reside in Jersey in 1851 where he represented a London firm. From his early days there he was involved in obtaining trade for the Island, and in 1853 he embarked upon a scheme to export the island's produce, quickly becoming involved with the Packet Company and succeeded Mr E. Neel as Jersey agent until he was appointed General Manager. With the commencement of the GWR Cherbourg service he also acted as their superintendent, then residing mainly at Weymouth. After the closure of the Cherbourg service Wimble became the district superintendent for the GWR's Channel Islands traffic, as well as Manager of the Packet Company and its liquidator upon closure. His other interests over the years had included starting the first daily paper, the *Jersey Independent* in September 1858, and he was Secretary and Manager of the Jersey Eastern Railway during its construction and early years, a Director of Jersey Waterworks, and also established the Jersey Mutual Plate Glass Insurance Company.

The affairs of the Great Western Marine Department come under the marine superintendent who was originally based at New Milford but from 1878 John Wimble managed Great Western marine matters at Weymouth for the company. With the take-over of the Channel Islands service Captain Henry William Hemmings was appointed assistant marine superintendent. Formerly commodore captain of the LBSCR Newhaven-Dieppe steamers, he was the son of a Dover mail steamer captain. Apprenticed in a sailing ship, at the age of 13 he joined the LBSCR in 1865. Whilst at Weymouth he oversaw the salvaging of the *Ibex* on two occasions and the *Roebuck*, retiring in December 1915 aged 71 years.

His successor was Percy Boyle who had commenced his career at New Milford in 1883, where his first job was the taking of wagon numbers in the yard, moving to Weymouth with the GWR take-over in 1889 to become chief clerk to Captain Hemmings. When Boyle replaced Hemmings, as he was classed as a non-technical officer his new appointment was designated as traffic and marine agent - a post he held until his own retirement in December 1935. He was also a Lloyds Agent and Vice Consul for Belgium. Awarded the MBE for services to the Country, and a leading member of the Weymouth Chamber of Commerce, he became a town councillor in 1924 and was elected Mayor both in 1928 and 1929.

Boyle was succeeded by Douglas Giles Hoppins who had commenced his career in the Docks Department at Plymouth in 1902, rising to the position of chief clerk before becoming assistant dock manager at Newport in 1932. His stay at Weymouth was short as the position was withdrawn following the fall of the Channel Islands in 1940. William George Salmon from Cardiff was appointed quay superintendent in March 1943. He was to oversee the reinstatement of the Channel Islands services and was the last GWR manager at the port.

Crews

The safety and success of any ship depends on the skill and knowledge of her crew, particularly in the days before modern navigational aids. During the 1850s legislation covering the seaworthiness of ships, the display of navigation lights, fog signals and a flag signal code become law. From January 1851 examinations for Masters and First Officers became compulsory. In 1862 vessels of over 100 hp had to carry at least one certified Chief Engineer, there also being a qualification for a 2nd class engineer. For the crew, management and discipline was different to that of most railway employees, as employment on a cross-channel ferry came under the laws of the various Merchant Shipping Acts.

Wages were good by the standard of the day, a study of local records showing that seamen serving in local sailing vessels who had a much harder life without the assistance of powered winches and capstans-were poorly paid in comparison with the steam packet men. Below are the wages paid per calendar month to the crew of the *Aquila* during 1878.

	£	s.		£	s.		£	s.
Captain	15	0	1st officer	10	0	2nd officer	6	0
Carpenter	6	0	Chief Eng.	13	0	2nd Eng.	9	10
Able seaman	5	4	Fireman	6	0	Chief Steward	6	0
2nd Steward	5	0	3rd Steward	5	0	Cook	5	0
Stewardess	3	4	Deck Boy	2	8	Cabin boy	2	8

As a comparison, the number of crew required and the weekly wages paid in 1889 for the new GWR vessels against the *Brighton* clearly show the changing scene.

		'Lynx' Class				*Brighton*		
		£	s.	d.		£	s.	d.
Master		3	17	0		3	13	0
1st Mate		2	5	6		2	4	0
2nd Mate		1	11	6		1	10	0
Quarter master	(2)	2	16	0	(1)	1	8	0
Able Seaman	(6)	7	7	0	(6)	7	7	0
Deck boy			10	0				
Chief Steward		1	4	6		1	8	0
2nd Steward			14	0			17	6
3rd Steward			10	6				
Saloon Boy			7	0			7	0
Saloon Stewardess			10	6			10	6
After Cabin Steward			14	0			17	6
After Cabin Boy			7	0				
After Cabin Stewardess			7	0				
Cook		1	1	0		1	1	0
Chief Engineer		3	10	0		3	3	0
2nd Engineer		2	5	6		2	5	0
Greasers	(2)	2	16	0				
Fireman	(4)	5	2	8	(4)	5	8	0
Trimmer		1	1	0	(2)	2	4	0
Total wages		38	17	8		34	3	10
Mess allowance		5	12	0		4	0	6
Total		*44*	*9*	*8*		*38*	*4*	*4*
		Total crew 30				*Total crew 24*		

Added to this a was shore staff consisting of a deputy marine superintendent at £250 pa, one clerk at £70 pa, and a workshop staff of seven on weekly wages thus: 2 fitters 33*s*., 1 boilersmith 33*s*., 1 coppersmith 33*s*., 1 joiner 33*s*., 1 shipwright 30*s*., 1 storekeeper 33*s*.

The master and stewards staff were messed free whilst the ship was running and stewardesses were allowed two dresses per annum, one print and one serge. The chief steward was allowed 10 per cent of the net profit made on the catering of his ship.

It would appear that there was a lack of discipline in Steam Packet Days. It certainly was not up to the standards expected by Captain Lecky, the GWR marine superintendent, as described in a letter sent from him to the Secretary of the GWR on 8th September, 1889.

> Capt. Le Feuvre's excuse for moving the inside propeller against written instructions was the exceedingly lame one that he thought it would not touch the quay, which of course I told him was no excuse at all.
>
> The many mishaps that have occurred to him are the natural results of his being brought up in an indifferent school, as it is well known the late Weymouth & Channel Islands Steam Packet Company's service undoubtedly was. His experience was confined to what may be considered toy vessels, and there was an utter absence of discipline on board of them. I can vouch for this myself from personal observation. According to the statements of the men themselves, though nominally master they were not so in reality, the man having most to say on board being the Chief Steward and after him the Chief Engineer, the Captain playing a very subordinate part. This could only result in their jogging along anyhow, and engendered an indifference to their work and generally speaking a sluggish habit of mind and body.
>
> I was well aware of this when I objected so strongly to their employment at one of the board meetings, and felt certain that until I was able to smarten them up by months of close supervision and get them to take a personal interest each in his own vessel, that we would have trouble and expense. This has come to pass as respects all three captains but I am in hopes that after a while they will appreciate the responsibilities of their position and act accordingly. Meanwhile they have to be treated like children and taught every small thing in connection with their duty, which of course throws upon me an immense amount of additional labour.

Discipline remained strict under Percy Boyle, who insisted that all crew members who had to visit the office, even if it was their day off, had to wear full uniform! However, there was always one who could break the rules, Captain Allan (one of the senior masters), only visiting the office in uniform to collect his pay, and even then he wore a white scarf to hide the fact he had no collar and tie! At sea it is reputed that he often had his flies undone and his boots not laced up, hence he was always kept on cargo vessels, the *Pembroke* being his usual command.

In years past the Great Western had paid a half-yearly bonus of £10 to captains and chief engineers if the period had been free of accident or other problems. More often than not Captain Le Feuvre failed to receive his; he had been master of the *Ibex* when she struck rocks in 1897 and of *Roebuck* when she was sunk in 1911 and he was subsequently dismissed, although he was granted a 21*s*. a week allowance but not a pension! His 40 years' service went back to Packet Company days. In August 1927 the chief officer of *Reindeer* was considered responsible for a minor collision with the PS *Empress* whilst manoeuvring in Weymouth Harbour, and he was retired as a result, whilst two months earlier *St Helier* was fouled by a mooring wire owing to the negligence of the 2nd Officer who was suspended for a week.

From 13th April, 1930 the previous system of paying the masters a 'safe Navigation Bonus' was abolished and a new salary scale introduced. For the masters of passenger vessels it was on increasing increments from one to five years - £470, £490, £510, £530, £550 - whilst masters of cargo vessels received £430, thus giving a weekly wage of between £8 and £10.

Smuggling was a problem for the company; several times the vessels were detained by the Customs until a fine was paid. An example was in January 1901 when tobacco was discovered aboard *Antelope*, the authorities demanding a deposit for the release of the ship. In January 1881 four firemen on the *Cygnus* had hidden 54 one lb. packets of tobacco under boards in the coal bunkers, the fine for this being £45 12*s.* 3*d.* - treble the duty! Shipmates of the accuseds clubbed together to pay the fine.

In November 1900 the chief and second engineers aboard the *Lynx* were charged with smuggling tobacco, the company reducing them to fitters at the Milford workshops, whilst the following year the stewardess of the *Roebuck* was dismissed after cigars and tobacco were found concealed in her cabin. The Magistrates dismissed the case when it was found that 229 keys were in use aboard the vessel, and more than one key fitted the door of her cabin! Indeed, the topic is endless, and many more pages could be devoted to the escapades of both crews and passengers over the years.

The activities of the ships' stewards have often been the subject of enquiry. In November 1891 when Captain Lecky was dealing with smuggling by stewards, the chief stewards' accounts came in for examination. The chief steward of *Antelope* had in comparison with others smaller returns and greater expenses, his percentage of gross profits being the lowest (*Lynx* 95 per cent, *Gazelle* 88 per cent, *Antelope* 67 per cent). Needless to say, a visit from the superintendent took place!

The master of any vessel has the sole responsibility for his ship, her crew, passengers, and cargo, and his skill and knowledge accumulated over the years could at times be stretched to the limit. Likewise the chief engineer has ultimate responsibility for the engine room.

Except for periods of duty as relief masters, captains usually remained with one vessel until appointment to another, their first command usually being a cargo vessel before progressing to passenger ships. Between 1889 and 1966 there were 34 masters at Weymouth, many giving years of faithful service.The following brief outline of the careers of a number of long-serving masters is of interest.

Although several of the masters and many crew members transferred from the Packet Company to the GWR steamers many others were brought in from 'outside'. One such was Captain Joseph Vine, formerly employed on the LBSCR Newhaven-Dieppe steamers, who was appointed a second officer with the Weymouth vessels in September 1889, later to chief officer and master in 1898 and senior master in 1911. He retired in December 1917. One of his five sons,

Reginald Vine, who lost a leg during World War I, became Borough Surveyor to Weymouth Town Council.

Captain C.H. Langdon, a Jerseyman, commenced his career in local sailing vessels, becoming mate of the Jersey Brig *Patruus* engaged in the Newfoundland trade. During a severe gale many vessels were destroyed and *Patruus* was damaged, her captain dying on the homeward voyage. With a jury-rig (temporary makeshift rigging) Langdon took command and brought the vessel back to Jersey. Joining the GWR in 1900 as a second officer his first command was the *Melmore*, and in World War I he commanded the *Pembroke* and then *Ibex*, finally taking command of *St Julien* new from the builders. It was aboard *St Julien* that his career ended when he was found dead in his cabin having suffered heart failure on voyage from Guernsey on 27th September, 1927. He had not been in good health for some time. After seeing his doctor in Jersey he insisted on bringing his vessel back to Weymouth to hand over his command to Captain Richardson. Unfortunately Captain Langdon did not live to see the funnel alterations he had advocated.

Captain William Malhall was born at Waterford and spent his youth in Plymouth, going to sea in sailing vessels before becoming a junior officer for British India Line. He joined the GWR at Weymouth in 1897 as a second officer, and later commanded the GWR steamers between Plymouth and Brest. Throughout World War I he commanded the GWR turbine steamer *St Andrew* whilst she was serving as a hospital ship. In 1921 he was selected to pilot the Royal Yacht when King George V and Queen Mary visited the Channel Islands, and later had command of *Ibex* and *Reindeer. He* was given command of the *St Helier* from the builders. Suffering ill health from the autumn of 1927, Captain Mulhall passed away at his Weymouth home on 17th March, 1928 aged 60 years.

Captain W.Y. Larbalestier joined the GWR as a temporary officer in January 1920 and became a second officer three years later. He was captain of *Roebuck* at the Dunkirk evacuation and the rescue attempt at St Valery. After being involved in convoy work he put the first assault craft ashore in Jersey following the surrender of the German occupation forces. He brought the *Sambur* back to Weymouth after the war and remained with her until his retirement in May 1949. A native of Jersey, he returned to the island and became Harbour Master at Gorey.

Captain Leyghton Thomas Richardson came from a Jersey farming family at Rozel Bay, and as a young boy working on the farm he saw the passing ships and decided that the sea was the career for him. Commencing his apprenticeship at Glasgow, he visited many parts of the world, gaining his master's ticket in 1920. Following the death of Captain Langdon he became master of *St Julien* in September 1927 - the ship he stayed with for the majority of his career. With the invasion of the Channel Islands Captain Richardson's wife and daughters were brought over to England on one of the evacuation vessels. Captain Richardson's expert knowledge of the ports was called for with the liberation of the islands, which he assisted with guidance to the liberating forces in May 1945. Captain Richardson's 49 year sea-going career ended in September 1955 when he brought *St Julien* into Weymouth Harbour for the last time before going into retirement.

Captain Reginald Richard Pitman was born at St Helier on 8th April, 1894, one of three sons of a master mariner. Leaving school at 14 years of age Captain Pitman joined his father and for the next four years was an apprentice with the local pilot cutter. In 1915 he joined an Anglo-French trader as an AB before joining the GWR ship *Pembroke* the following year. He gained his second mate's certificate in 1918 and joined the *Ibex,* being involved in the sinking of a German submarine. Appointed chief officer in February 1926, he became a cargo boat master in the August of the following year. On 21st March, 1928 he became permanent mail steamer master serving in both *St Julien* and *St Helier*, the latter being the ship with which he was most closely associated.

In the early days of World War II Captain Pitman was in command of *St Patrick* whilst trooping between Avonmouth and St Nazaire. Before rejoining the *St Helier* he was awarded the DSC for his services at Dunkirk. When *St Helier* was requisitioned he took command of *St David,* serving in Scottish waters as a hospital ship. He then had a spell with the *Great Western* running between Fishguard and Rosslare before joining the *Sambur* prior to the D-Day invasion. His war service concluded on the *St Andrew* trooping between Harwich and the Hook of Holland, before rejoining *St Helier* to re-open the Channel Islands service in June 1946.

In 1955 Captain Pitman was awarded the MBE for his outstanding services as a master of mail boats, by which time he had become Commodore of the British Railways fleet. It was aboard his beloved *St Helier* that Captain Pitman made his final voyage on 30th April, 1959 before retirement.

Captain Joseph Vine photographed with members of the crew of *Reindeer*. Captain Vine had formerly been employed on the LBSCR steamers before joining the GWR in 1889 as second officer. Master since 1898 and senior master after 1911, he retired in December 1917. *J.D. Ward Collection*

Captain R. Pitman, *third from left*, photographed aboard *St Patrick* on 6th September, 1957. *Extreme left*: R. Long, chief clerk, Weymouth; and *fourth from left*: W.G. Salmon, the last GWR manager at Weymouth. Other officers of *St Patrick's* Fishguard-based crew form the remainder of the group. *The late E. Latcham Collection*

No. 1 Devonshire Buildings, The Esplanade, Weymouth, the offices of the Marine Department between 1928 and 1967. Mr Boyle and his successors could watch operations from their office on the first floor at the end of the building. In this late 1950s photograph the British Railways Marine Department flag flies above the door, whilst in the background at the cargo stage *Sambur* and *Roebuck* unload tomatoes. In the foreground 12 different models of British-built motor cars complete this period scene. *Author*

Captain Victor Newton served his apprenticeship with the Anglo-American Oil Company, and at the age of 24 he gained his extra master's certificate. Later joining the GWR fleet, he served as chief officer of *Roebuck* and was wounded at St Valery. Joining the Royal Navy as a Lieutenant Commander in 1941 he specialised in navigation aboard the larger warships, seeing service on Atlantic and Russian convoys, and the recapture of Guam in the Pacific. At the end of hostilities he returned as chief officer of *St Helier*, becoming master of *Roebuck* in 1950, later having command of *St Julien*, then *St Patrick*, and finally *Caesarea* in 1960. He retired in February 1968 to concentrate on his business of running a fleet of holiday caravans.

Many 2nd and 1st officers held master's tickets awaiting promotion, which usually came in a relief capacity before obtaining command of their own vessels. One who managed to side-step the seniority system was Captain J.R. Imrie who was a comparatively junior officer at Weymouth, but as the only holder of a foreign-going master's certificate he gained command of the *Melmore* and other vessels on the Nantes service. During 1913 he won fifth place out of several hundred candidates for appointment as a Board of Trade marine surveyor at Southampton.

An engineer who saw the development of the Weymouth fleet over a period of 39 years was R.H. Dennis. Sent in 1889 as guarantee engineer for the new steamers by Lairds, he stayed on as chief engineer in various vessels. He stood by at John Brown's yard whilst the *St Julien* and *St Helier* were under construction, and was chief engineer of the former until retirement in 1928.

Captain Richardson stands on the bridge of *St Julien* in September 1955, when he retired after a 49 year sea-going career. *R.C. Clammer Collection*

Coaling & Oil Fuel

Before the tramway opened it has to be assumed that coal brought to Weymouth station was transported to the quay by horse and cart and either tipped or carried aboard the steamers. The tramway made life much easier, the trucks going directly to the quay. Following the take-over of services by the GWR, a siding at the west end of the cargo stage was used to transfer coal into barges by chute for storage and delivery to the ships. In 1898 it was decided to extend the cargo stage and a new siding was laid alongside the Backwater, opposite the end of Lower St Albans Street. There is little doubt that this was not before time, as there had been complaints concerning the coal dust on the quayside. In the event the cargo stage was not extended until late 1904.

Coal from the barges was loaded into the steamers through side doors at main deck level. When a steamer arrived at the passenger stage the steam launch *Armine* would put a barge alongside and as much coal as possible would be loaded into the outside bunker before the ship swung around and backed up to the cargo stage. Any remaining coal required in that bunker then had to be carried across the ship! It was a dirty and hard job, the coal being manhandled in baskets - although the *Roebuck* and *Reindeer* were fitted with coaling gantries for a short period in the early 1900s.

During the summer as much as 350 tons a week could be consumed (35 railway trucks full). Coaling continued on a regular basis until the departure of the *Great Western*. In later years when coal-fired vessels from Southampton were

A view taken before the west extension of the cargo stage in 1905 shows coal being tipped into a GWR coal barge from wagons on the former coal siding on the Weymouth Harbour Tramway. Included in the rake of eight are three steel 'loco coal' wagons.

Author's Collection

The steam launch *Armine* brings a coal barge alongside the *Reindeer* during September 1921. *Author's Collection*

on charter for the season, coal was brought in railway wagons, and shovelled into buckets and swung aboard by one of the cranes. Needless to say, *Hythe, Whitstable, Ringwood,* and *Haslemere* were not popular!

The oil-fired steamers arrived ahead of the arrangements to bunker them, resulting in their fuel being supplied by Portland Dockyard until after October 1925 when agreement was reached with Weymouth Corporation to lay oil and steam pipes under the passenger and cargo stages at a cost of £397. Once these arrangements were in place oil tank wagons were brought down the tramway by goods train. Marshalled amongst the tank wagons was a 10 ton truck stencilled 'To work between Weymouth Quay & Weymouth Goods yard only', which contained a twin cylinder steam duplex pump. Flexible pipes carried in the wagon were connected to the tanks, and from the pump to pipes under the station platform and quay to the ship, steam from the ship being used to pump oil aboard. The two cargo vessels each carried 45 ton bunkers. Even at that early stage there were worries about oil spillage. One Swanage resident wrote to the *Southern Times* concerned that any leakage of fuel would harm the sea birds. He failed to take into account that within two miles was Portland Harbour with a large naval fleet which was mostly oil fired, and large oil storage tanks nearby!

Maintenance Facilities

From remaining records it would appear that the Steam Packet Company locally relied on the railway Motive Power Department at Weymouth for minor boiler and mechanical repairs. So did the GWR steamers after 1878 until the establishment by the GWR of its own yard and workshops at Nothe Parade (on the south side of the harbour) by the purchase in 1890 of the former boat building yard of Mr Ayles. After equipping the workshops and providing a slipway capable of holding coal barges, the workboat, and any of the ships' lifeboats, these facilities served the railway steamers until closure by Sealink.

It has to be assumed that from an early date other minor repairs to both the Steam Packet and GWR vessels were carried out by Messrs Cosens & Company, the Weymouth-based paddle steamer proprietors who also operated a marine engineering and ship repair facility, their assistance being recorded on many occasions. In March 1955 the first complete refit to a steamer was carried out by Messrs Cosens when *Sambur* received her winter overhaul at Weymouth. A further contract was negotiated in October 1955, followed by a five-year contract the following year. In the event Cosens' involvement continued well after the demise of the former GWR vessels, although dry docking and hull work had to be carried out at other locations which had dry docks. Away from Weymouth the GWR carried out repairs, refits and surveys at its New Milford (Neyland) workshops. During the winter months spare vessels would lay up on the Haven until New Milford closed in 1906, workshop facilities then being

The GWR slipway and workshop at Nothe Parade (formerly Hope Quay), photographed in 1971. The sheer-leg type crane was used to lift the bridge section to allow access to the slipway on which a small boat is under repair. Behind stands the corrugated iron workshops. *Author*

provided at Fishguard. Major overhauls and refits were also undertaken at various yards around the Country over the years, the chosen location usually depending on price and availability, resulting in the use of such diverse yards as those on the Clyde, on the Mersey, in South Wales, and at Plymouth or Southampton. The one recorded occasion when a railway steamer was docked locally was on Friday 5th October, 1928 when *St Helier* entered the Admiralty floating dock at Portland, where her hull was cleaned and given a coat of anti-fouling paint before she was floated out on the Monday morning.

Wireless Communication

Before the introduction of wireless there was no means of communication between ship and shore except to fly flag signals when the vessel was within sight of the coast, hence the problems of overdue vessels in earlier days. In November 1911 the GWR Steamship Committee decided that the installation of wireless on three vessels at an annual outlay of £992 was not considered advantageous. The *Reindeer* was equipped with wireless in July 1914, the *Ibex* in January 1915, and during March 1915 it was decided to fit the *Great Western* and *Great Southern* with it because of U boat activity. Surprisingly, *Pembroke* was not so equipped until June 1917! At the time all vessels were equipped with a Marconi ½ kilowatt transmitter and type 31A receiver, powered from the ships' electrical supply, and backed up by a battery-powered emergency set. Wireless had become a standard fitting on all the vessels by the end of World War I.

The next improvement came in October 1926, when it was decided to fit wireless direction apparatus to the *St Helier, St Julien,* and *Reindeer* at £250 for each vessel. In 1938 it was decided to fit Marconi Echo Sounding machines on *St Helier* and *St Julien* at a cost of £450 and the following year both vessels were fitted with improved wireless equipment. The *St David* and *St Patrick* were the first vessels to be equipped with radar, installed when they were built in 1947. The other Weymouth vessels were so equipped during the early 1950s. Prior to that time, and indeed for a short while after, the method of guiding the ships into Weymouth during fog involved members of the shore staff firing maroons from the end of the Old Stone Pier when a ship was due. Having guided the vessel into the bay, a hand-operated Klaxon was sounded and across the harbour on the pleasure pier a bell was rung, the idea being to guide the vessel between the two sounds!

Colour Schemes

Accurate liveries of any form of transport before the days of good colour photography are difficult to determine, especially as everybody's perception of any particular colour varies. However, an early oil painting of *Cygnus* hanging in Jersey museum shows her to have had a black hull, white funnels with black tops, and white-painted masts. The company house flag was a St Andrew's cross with the initials 'WCPC' in red at the four quarters, the vessel's name pennant being white with the lettering in red. A set of paintings of the fleet made during 1885 shows white paddle boxes and upper works, deck shelters and ventilators in brown, whilst the black-topped funnels are deep cream. The GWR ships in the early days also had cream funnels with black tops, the hulls being black and the superstructure white, although as with all ships of the period there was much varnished woodwork and dark paintwork around working areas. With the introduction of the 'Lynx' class in 1889 the funnel colour changed to red with black tops, and the hull plating between the main deck and the bridge was painted white whilst the turtle back was picked out in buff. Raised white beading on the hull at main and promenade deck level enhanced the *Ibex, Roebuck* and *Reindeer*. Up to 1903 the sterns of the vessels were decorated with the company coat of arms and scrollwork together with the vessel's name and port of registry, the last ships to carry this adornment being the *Great Southern* and *Great Western*. Generally this scheme remained until well after World War I, although the cargo vessels displayed less light-coloured paintwork. With the arrival of the new passenger boats in 1925 the majority of the upper works from main deck level upwards were painted white, the bridge and wheelhouse which were of timber construction being finished in varnish. Following World War II white was added to the forecastle head above main deck level. *St David* and *St Patrick,* being of more modern construction, were virtually all white above main deck level. At the Grouping in 1923 the other three railway companies adopted buff as their funnel colour, but the GWR in its usual independent manner retained the distinctive red funnels until Nationalisation in 1948 when they too succumbed to the standard buff.

The house flag of the company was white with a narrow red band at both the top and bottom, the company garter coat of arms without the London and Bristol mottoes in the centre, outlined in yellow and edged with black, with the company name in black letters. The ship's name pennants were red with white letters.

The three vessels of the Packet Company were registered at Weymouth, but after the establishment of the GWR Marine Department with its headquarters at New Milford all vessels were registered at Milford Haven. After 1898 vessels were registered in London, the four regular Weymouth ships *St Julien, St Helier, Roebuck* and *Sambur* being re-registered at Weymouth in September 1929 as an act of local allegiance.

The Weymouth & Channel Islands Steam Packet Company house flag consisted of a white St Andrew's cross on a blue background with the initials WCPC in red at the four quarters.

The GWR house flag, which was plain white with a narrow red band at top and bottom. The garter coat of arms was mounted in the centre, outlined in yellow and edged with black with the company's name in black letters. *Author's Collection*

Chapter Seven

The Weymouth & Channel Islands Steam Packet Company Fleet

Aquila and Cygnus

These were sister vessels although of slightly different dimensions, both being constructed by J. Henderson & Sons of Renfrew in 1854. *Aquila* was completed in August and *Cygnus* in October. Built for the North of Europe Steam Navigation Company Ltd, they were engaged in a service between Harwich and Antwerp. When new *Cygnus* was chartered to convey an official party to Denmark for the opening of the Royal Danish Railway, she sailed from Lowestoft on 19th October, 1854, making the journey in unfavourable weather to Tonning, the coastal terminus of the railway, in 26 hours. Following the opening of the railway on 25th October by King Frederick VII, the king returned to Tonning where he and 60 guests were entertained aboard *Cygnus*.

The Antwerp service only lasted a few months. In 1855 both vessels were chartered by the Eastern Counties Railway to operate an Antwerp service, *Cygnus* arriving back in Harwich on 23rd April and *Aquila* on the 25th. The vessels made three sailings per week from October and a weekly service by *Aquila* only from 12th December until the service was discontinued. Both vessels were laid up in Victoria Dock, London, before being moved to Lowestoft. Early in 1857 the promoters of the Steam Packet Company (which legally did not exist at the time) viewed the vessels and, taking the advice of Captain Joseph Cosens of Weymouth who considered them suitable for cross-channel work, discussed terms with the owners. The asking price was £9,000 for each vessel, or agreed charter terms. The 'as yet to be formed company' decided to charter at £50 per week for each vessel for 18 months, with an option to purchase within six months for the asking price less charter fees already paid.

Following a hurried refit completed on 11th April both vessels underwent trials, during which *Aquila* made a speed of 12½ knots whilst *Cygnus* only achieved 11¼. They departed from the shipyard on 13th April, 1857 proceeding down channel together in bad weather until they were off the Isle of Wight, where *Aquila* set course for Jersey, *Cygnus* arriving at Weymouth mid-afternoon on the 14th. About a mile off Weymouth various Directors, shareholders and invited guests met the *Cygnus*, having sailed out in various small craft and Cosens' steamer *Prince*. In the party was a *Southern Times* reporter who gave the following report,

> As we came alongside we had an opportunity of examining the proportions of the noble vessel. Very 'swan-like' she sat on the bosom of the deep, and glided smoothly through waves. Once on the deck of *Cygnus* one could imagine himself on terra-firma, so entirely free from vibration was her motion. On inspecting the vessel we find she is of considerable length, and her raised quarterdeck affords ample space for a pleasant promenade in fine weather. She has two engines of sixty-horse power each on the oscillating principle, and capable, we are informed, of being 'worked up' to a hundred and fifty-horse power.

> Every requisite for the accommodation of passengers on deck is abundantly provided, and this, in addition to her almost imperceptible motion, cannot fail to render a trip in her very delightful in fair weather, and under any circumstances, nothing less than comfortable. Descending to the steerage quarters we find them fitted up in most magnificent style, reminding us of some 'cosy' drawing room than the cabin of a vessel. The 'State cabin' appropriated exclusively for ladies, is extraordinary in its way, and far exceeds the comfort and luxurious ease of anything we have seen on board a passenger vessel.

Both vessels had graceful clipper bows, the *Aquila* having the carved figurehead of an eagle, the *Cygnus* that of a swan. Constructed with iron hulls, there were slight differences in the dimensions of the two vessels. *Aquila* had a length of 180 ft 4in., a beam of 21 ft and draft of 10 ft 9 in. with a gross tonnage of 264, whilst *Cygnus* had a length of 182 ft, beam of 21 ft 4 in. and draft of 9 ft 7 in. and a gross tonnage of 245. Both vessels were equipped with two-cylinder oscillating engines built by McNabb & Clark of Glasgow, but here again there were very slight differences, *Aquila* had a cylinder bore of 42 in. and piston stroke of 42 in. and developed 110 nhp, whilst *Cygnus* had a cylinder bore of 42⅜ in. with a piston stroke of 42 in., and developed 120 nhp. Two haystack type boilers situated aft of the engines provided steam at 25 psi. Frequent changes of boiler (a common event at that period) and modifications to the engines changed the details of the machinery over the years. The 16 ft 3 in. diameter feathering paddle wheels gave the vessels an average speed of 12 knots.

Despite the glowing reports circulating concerning the two vessels all was not well, there being difficulties with the boilers from the time they arrived at Weymouth. A Court case at the end of April following the dismissal of the 2nd engineer through drunkenness highlighted several problems. The chief engineer stated of the boilers: 'They are the most difficult I have known, and the water will go from the glasses in a minute even if there are seven inches in the glasses. This may be accounted for by the fermentation of the boilers'. These difficulties occurring within a week of the vessel entering service clearly demonstrate there was a serious problem, and it would appear from evidence in the case that the loss of sight of water in the gauge glasses was a common event. *Cygnus* suffered a collapse of the furnace crown of one of her boilers whilst crossing from Weymouth to Guernsey on 7th July, 1857 and on the return sailing the following day the other boiler failed, the vessel having to remain off Portland Bill until morning when Cosens' steamer *Prince* towed her into harbour. The close connection between the Packet Company and the GWR was demonstrated when the *Southern Times* reported that: 'A party of workmen from the Great Western Railway establishment at Swindon has fitted new crowns to her boilers and replaced various tubes and carried out other repairs to render her in all respects equal to a new vessel'. Upon completion of the work a trial trip was undertaken to St Albans Head prior to the vessel re-entering service on 1st September, when *Aquila* was laid up to undergo repairs.

On 1st July, when the Directors had discussed the option of purchasing the vessels, it was revealed that despite the surveyor's favourable report both had given a disappointing performance and required new boilers. The full asking price of £18,000 was excessive in the circumstances, a revised offer of £13,000 being made for the two vessels. In view of the work required and after looking at other options, an independent valuation £14,000 was agreed and the two vessels became the property of the Packet Company on 21st November, 1857. The *Dorset County Chronicle* for 3rd December reported thus:

> The traffic by the superior steam ships employed by this company during the past season, we are informed has been of such magnitude as to induce the company to make a purchase of the vessels. The *Cygnus* made her first trip Thursday last as the property of the Weymouth & Channel Islands Steam Packet Company under the command of Captain A. Munn; the *Aquila* under the command of Captain George Rough sailed on Saturday.

From that moment it can be considered that the Weymouth & Channel Islands Steam Packet Company's service was firmly established, the two steamers giving of their best. As with all forms of transport, the many routine journeys are never reported, and it is only when the unusual happens or disaster strikes that one's attention is brought to the service.

On Wednesday 26th October, 1859 the Portland Coastguard contacted the Packet Company at 1 pm to report that a large steamer was in distress in West Bay and was drifting towards the shore. Steam was raised in the *Cygnus*, which reached the stricken vessel - the *James Dixon* of 1,000 tons bound from London to the Mediterranean with a general cargo - at 4 pm. By then she was only about a quarter of a mile from the Race! After several failed attempts a line was put aboard, but it soon parted. The crew of *Cygnus*, realising the distressed vessel's crew were fatigued, launched a boat carrying the mate and four hands who boarded the stricken vessel on which they found the decks swept clean, the steering gear disabled, the life boats stove in, the fore mast nearly chafed through and the cargo shifted. With a heavy sea running and the ships rolling heavily, ropes were put aboard and the tow commenced, but the ropes parted between Portland Bill and the Race, into which the casualty drifted. *Cygnus* again picked up the tow and by 9 pm had brought the vessel into the lee of the partly-built Portland breakwater. The Packet Company was awarded £10,000 in its salvage claim.

Despite being only six years old *Aquila* received an extensive refit at Southampton during the summer of 1860, when the boilers were replaced. At the same time alterations were made to both the ladies' and main saloons, and the toilet accommodation was also improved. Returning to Weymouth on 28th July the *Dorset County Chronicle* noted, 'the figure-head is replaced by one of an eagle with wings spread, upon which a considerable amount of gold leaf has not been wasted'.

Towards the end of the year *Cygnus* proceeded to Southampton where Messrs Day Summers fitted a new pair of boilers. In running trials on 6th January, 1861 she ran the measured nautical mile with the tide in 4 minutes 35 seconds and returned against the tide in 5 minutes, this giving her an average speed of 12½ knots. The vessel had also been repainted and the hull strengthened longitudinally - as had the *Aquila* in line with new Board of Trade requirements. During a refit at Southampton in May 1867 *Cygnus* again received new boilers, and at the same time new cylinders were fitted to her

Aquila alongside Custom House Quay, Weymouth, prior to 1878. As in the view of *Cygnus* on page 80, more of the vessel has been painted in white livery. *G. Millsott Collection*

A view taken between 1866 and 1878 of *Cygnus* moored alongside Custom House Quay, Weymouth. Over 120 years later the quayside buildings are very little changed. *Author's Collection*

main engine. She received further attention during 1868, when it was reported that the bridge was enlarged, stanchions fitted for awnings, and improvements carried out to the fore cabin.

The *Aquila* had a narrow escape in August 1871 when, proceeding from Weymouth towards Guernsey in dense fog, she struck a rock in the Little Russel Channel. The boats were lowered and the 80 passengers placed in them until it was certain that the vessel was not taking in water, whereupon the passengers reboarded and *Aquila* proceeded on her way.

The *Southern Times* on 30th March, 1873 reported that the *Aquila* had just returned from Jersey where she had been overhauled, the work including the fitting of new engines and boilers by Messrs Stottart of Bristol. An ornamental deckhouse had also been fitted, a similar structure being added to *Cygnus* around the same time.

Leaving Weymouth at midnight on Wednesday 31st July, 1878, *Aquila* suffered engine failure a few miles east of Portland Race, 60 to 70 fathoms of anchor chain being let out to stop her drifting and distress rockets were fired. Fortunately her consort *Cygnus,* steaming towards Weymouth, saw the signals and went to her aid, standing by until daylight and then towing her into Weymouth Harbour. The nature of the breakdown was serious and the following day the crew was discharged, the vessel being out of service for the remainder of the year.

On Monday 7th October, 1878 *Cygnus,* whilst inward bound from the Channel Islands came across the steamer *Diana* flying distress signals about 20 miles SSW off Portland Bill. She was sinking, with her crew in a boat and already boarding a schooner, but owing to the heavy sea it was impossible for *Cygnus* to close in on the waterlogged casualty.

Early May 1879 brought problems for both vessels. *Cygnus* was on charter to the GWR and operating the Cherbourg service on the 2nd when her main shaft failed about 25 miles off Portland Bill on a homeward journey. Flying distress signals it was reported that no less than eight steamers were observed to pass her without coming to her assistance. Eventually the screw steamer *Sappho* took her in tow, bringing her to near the harbour entrance where Cosens' tug *Commodore* assisted her into port. The owners of the *Sappho* made a £1,000 salvage claim. The following day *Aquila* broke down, causing her late arrival at Weymouth, then on the 8th whilst entering harbour her port paddle box sponson was damaged when struck by the *Vulture,* which was entering harbour at the same time.

Whilst on passage from Weymouth at 2.30 am on the morning of 19th September, 1880, *Aquila* went to the assistance of the Eastern Telegraph Company's steamer *Chiltern* of 834 gt which had suffered engine failure about 40 miles SSW of Portland Bill. *Aquila* commenced the tow at 3 am, but owing to the heavy seas the rope parted four times - the fourth time near the Shambles Bank. Eventually at 1.15 pm *Aquila* brought the *Chiltern* with her crew of 75 and cargo of cable into the safety of Portland Roads, the tow having taken 10 hours. *Aquila* returned to Weymouth with her 60 passengers, some of whom declined to resume their voyage, the Packet Company being compelled to pay their claims for deviation and delay and refund some of the fares. Later in the

Admiralty Court the Packet Company was awarded £700 for its services, the Judge in the case remarking on the salvage by a small paddle steamer rendered of a much larger vessel thus: 'The salving vessel was skilfully navigated, and the other vessel was taken out of great peril. Now it is a very serious thing for the Master of a ship with passengers on board to undertake these services'.

The severe gale and blizzard of 18th January, 1881 caused damage to *Aquila* although she was laid up at the time in Weymouth Harbour. A heavy 'run' in the harbour caused the barque *Wallace* of New York to part her moorings and run into *Aquila,* resulting in her also parting her moorings and being blown across the harbour and forcing her bow into the quay wall. Her bowsprit was snapped off as it came into contact with a building, one of her paddles was smashed and her hull was bumped against the wall causing damage both to vessel and wall.

The *Aquila* received a further battering after departing Weymouth at midnight on Friday 30th March, 1883, in what the *Southern Times* described as, 'A Tidal Wave In The English Channel - a very curious and dangerous phenomenon'. The weather was calm and the sea smooth, when about an hour out with the Shambles light still in sight, the steamer was struck violently by successive mountainous seas which swept her decks from stem to stern. Water flooded the saloon, ladies' cabin, fore cabin and engine room, having smashed the glass of various skylights, and one of the paddle boxes was damaged, a rail on the bridge twisted, and various items of cargo shifted, were damaged or swept overboard. Owing to the pump being damaged the cabins had to be baled out with buckets and the skylights were covered with tarpaulins before the vessel proceeded on its way. It was recorded that five minutes after the waves had struck the steamer the sea became perfectly calm.

During 1883 *Cygnus* underwent a major refit, the *Southern Times* reporting on 13th October:

> She has just returned to Weymouth. The repairs consist of her being entirely re-plated, and all weak and defective parts of the hull, machinery and boilers renewed. The old wooden paddle boxes sponsons, bulwarks being replaced with iron, which nearly doubles her strength, and at the same time have added no more weight to the vessel. The hull down to the waterline was renewed in this port, also the repairs to machinery and boilers. The refitting of all cabins, and woodwork was carried out by Mr R.A. Ayles, shipbuilder of this port. The painting and decorating of the vessel, by Mr James Jesty, ship and house decorator, also of Weymouth. The vessel was then taken to Southampton to the well-known firm of Day Summers & Company, who renewed the keel and the whole of the plates below the water line.

Allowing for journalistic licence it is difficult to visualise how the reconstruction was carried out in the order reported, as the plates above water line would have had to be renewed with the vessel afloat, Weymouth having no slipway of her capacity or a gridiron!

The termination of the agreement between the Packet Company and the GWR, and the new service to be commenced on 1st July, 1889 by the latter, was the end for the two vessels. The fact that both had commenced the service 32 years earlier and survived to the end was ample proof of their durability.

Both vessels were sold to Mr A. Tolhurst, a Gravesend tug owner, on 27th June, 1889 for what *The Star* described as a 'nominal sum'. *Aquila* made her last sailing from Jersey to Weymouth on Friday 28th June and departed for Southampton the following day where her crew were discharged and the vessel laid up. *Cygnus* sailed from the islands on the 29th and later followed to Southampton.

Cygnus was quickly resold to Mr T. Holden who intended to operate a service between Preston and Douglas, Isle of Man, running in opposition to the *Great Western* - a superior, faster vessel. He met with little success and in July 1891 *Cygnus* was sold to David MacBrayne - firstly to operate the Loch Fayne cargo service, but she proved unwieldy and was replaced. The following year she underwent an extensive refit, including the construction of a swan bow and new paddleboxes. Her engines were altered by Hutson & Corbett of Glasgow, and Muir & Caldwell, also of Glasgow, supplied two new boilers operating at 25 psi, this resulting in the replacement of her two funnels by one of larger proportions. Her original figurehead was replaced by one of a military gentleman in uniform painted red and gold.

On 8th March, 1892, renamed *Brigadier,* she was placed on the Portree-Strome Ferry mail service, before becoming the Sound of Mull mail boat. In 1894 she became a spare vessel, often working either Oban-Loch Sunart or Portree to the Outer Islands. It was here that she met her end on 7th December, 1896, when she was wrecked on Duncans Rock near Rodal, Isle of Harris. The passengers and crew were all safely landed, before the vessel sank into deep water.

Tollhurst had sold *Aquila* within a month to Onesimus Dorey of Guernsey, who was acting on behalf of the 'Plymouth, Channel Islands, and Brittany Steamship Company'. Re-registered in Guernsey on 6th August, she retained her original name. She was reported as running a service between Plymouth, the Channel Islands and St Brieuc, and was also engaged on local excursions from the Promenade Pier, Plymouth, to Looe, Brixham, and Torquay. A major refit in the early part of 1892 saw her receive a new long foredeck and new boilers, after which her two funnels were placed very close together, although in this revised form she ran only until the end of the 1894 season. On 16th March, 1895 she was sold to John Watkins, a London shipbroker, two days later passing to Joseph Constant - also a London shipbroker - who, on 24th May, sold her to James Jones of Swansea for £1,050 on deferred terms at 5 per cent interest, the ship arriving in Swansea on 29th May, 1895.

Under the command of Captain J. Thomas *Aquila* commenced Bristol Channel cruises on 19th June, her name being officially changed to *Alexandra* on 28th June. The first advertised excursion under her new name took place on 9th July, when a charity trip was run to support a fund for dependants of the crew of the tug *Wasp,* recently lost off the Mumbles. On 26th July, 1895 *Alexandra* made her only excursion to Lundy Island. *Alexandra* still had clipper bows and eagle figurehead, and by that time was completely outdated compared with the fast modern steamers P. & A. Campbell was introducing to the Bristol Channel - a challenge Jones, (and indeed many other small operators) could not match. Jones therefore retired from the excursion steamer business.

Cygnus photographed in St Helier Harbour during 1878. *J. Attwood Collection*

Cygnus photographed in her final years under the ownership of David MacBrayne, when following a refit in 1892 she was renamed *Brigadier*. Her refit had included the reconstruction of her paddle-boxes and the replacement of her two funnels by one of larger proportions. She sailed in this form to the Western Isles until wrecked on 7th December, 1896.
Author's Collection

Alexandra again passed through Joseph Constant's on 21st May, 1896 to a Mr W.A. Paine who was acting for the Hastings, St Leonards, & Eastbourne Steamboat Company with a mortgage of £750. Her name was changed to *Ruby* on 1st June, and on the 17th the mortgage was discharged. *Ruby* entered service at Hastings on the 27th, although she stayed only for seven weeks during which she operated some excursions to Boulogne. Her port of registry was transferred to Newhaven on 27th July, and she was transferred from the ownership of Paine to that of the Hastings, St Leonards, & Eastbourne Steamboat Company - of which Paine was Manager - on 14th August. The company appears to have been in financial difficulties, for on 21st August a loan of £1,000 from Lloyds bank was secured against the ship. Her movements are a little vague after that time, although it was reported that she ran an excursion from Dover to Spithead for the Diamond Jubilee Review on 26th June, 1897.

Sold on 3rd July, 1897, *Ruby* passed into the ownership of Charles Nigel Stewart of Victoria Street, Westminster, and the Lloyds bank loan was discharged on 27th August. At that point the story became somewhat complex. On 1st September James Woodrow Matthews, a City of London insurance broker, advanced a mortgage against the ship, then on 14th October Henry Charles Peach, a solicitor's managing clerk, took up a mortgage for £800. On 20th December her ownership passed to Paul Alfred Boulton, a chartered accountant who was appointed a trustee to the estate of Stewart who had been judged bankrupt. The Custom records show that on 24th December the ownership passed to the Shipping and General Property Company of Cornhill, London, an added complication to this matter being that on 9th February, 1898 the ship passed into the jurisdiction of the High Bailiff of the County Court of Bow on the order of the High Court of Justice, Admiralty Division, dated 24th January, 1898. It was ruled that the same by J.W. Mathews (transaction No. 8) be set aside and that the High Bailiff of the County Court of Bow be empowered to give a Bill of Sale free from encumbrances to Herbert Harcourt Kent of Hillside, Warlingham, Surrey.

On 22nd April, 1898 the ship passed to William Turner Simonds of Boston, Lincs, and the registration of the vessel was transferred to Boston on 8th April. On 20th August she appeared in a list of sailings from Brighton Pier, but the next official reference to the vessel was not until 11th May, 1899, when under survey at Grimsby she was re-registered from 'Schooner, two masts', to 'sloop, one mast'. In July the ship was reported as sold to a subject of France in a letter from the owner dated 24th July, 1899, and her register was closed on 25th July, 1899. A letter on 26th August from the British Consul in Calais reported that the vessel had been sold at that port to a foreign owner, Mr L. Dutillieux of Lille, for the purpose of being broken up. This brought down the curtain on vessels of the Weymouth & Channel Islands Steam Packet Company.

Brighton

Constructed by Palmer Bros of Jarrow in 1857, *Brighton* was a paddle steamer with an iron hull, 193 ft 5 in. long, 20 ft 9 in. beam, and 10 ft draft, her original gross weight being 286 tons. Her oscillating engines - also constructed by Palmer Bros - had two cylinders of 43¾ in. diameter and a stroke of 48 in., developing 140 nhp. Two haystack boilers - one forward and one aft of the engine room - supplied the low-pressure steam that these engines ran on. Originally her funnels had the then traditional bell tops, these being removed by 1870.

Brighton was constructed for H.P. Maples of Shoreham, who operated shipping services between Shoreham and Jersey and Newhaven and Dieppe, his other line of business being that of a ship and insurance broker. Some of the shipping services were operated on his own account, others on behalf of the London Brighton & South Coast Railway which, like the GWR at that time, had no legal powers to operate its own services. A large number of vessels were engaged in the Maples operation. In 1858 financial difficulties caused five of the vessels to be mortgaged to the LBSCR, and others disposed of. Having been cleaned and painted by the LBSCR at a cost of £56 15*s.* 1*d.*, *Brighton* was purchased for a reputed £9,000 by the Weymouth & Channel Islands Steam Packet Company Limited on 23rd July, 1858. She departed from Shoreham three days later, and was registered at Weymouth on 4th April, 1859.

Following her arrival at Weymouth she was placed on the Channel Islands service pending the opening of the new Cherbourg service, her first visit to the Channel Islands being on 31st July. She was, however, no stranger to the islands, having also operated a Newhaven-Jersey service during the Summer of 1857 for her previous owners. With the commencement of the Cherbourg service on 2nd September, *Brighton* took over that run. Although purchased especially for that service, in reality the three company steamers operated both the Channel Islands and Cherbourg services as required, but *Brighton* was always synonymous with the Cherbourg run.

Following the suspension of the Cherbourg service at the end of June 1859 *Brighton* was put up for sale. It would seem there was not much interest in her, for the following year she was withdrawn from sale and retained to assist on the Channel Islands service, as just operating the other two vessels - *Aquila* and *Cygnus* - left nothing in reserve in the event of a breakdown or other problems.

Before taking up these duties in May 1860 *Brighton* had superheaters fitted into her funnel uptakes, the work being carried out by engineers of the Great Western Railway! How efficient the superheaters were is not recorded, but by the end of 1876 the vessel was in need of both hull and engine repairs, estimated to cost £7,000. This work was carried out on the Thames over the next two years. The Victoria Graving Dock Company carried out the hull repairs including the construction of a turtleback deck over the bow section, and the fitting of new paddleboxes, whilst at the same time the internal accommodation was remodelled.

The mechanical work was entrusted to the Thames Ironworks, the details being fully described in a 12 page specification document from the Packet Company's consulting engineer, Frederick Edwards of Leadenhall Street,

London, EC. The boilers were to be replaced by two new boilers of the 'ordinary return tube kind', to be hydraulically tested to 70 psi to withstand a working pressure of 35 psi. The two funnels were to be 27 feet high.

A major rebuild of the engine included two new cylinders, four slide valves, and slide valve jackets (valve chests). A new surface condenser was fitted forward of the engine, this replacing the original and inefficient jet condenser. A new air pump and circulating pump were also fitted as were two new boiler feed pumps. Many other items had to be refitted and machined true, and an engine room telegraph of the 'bell and dial' type was installed.

These improvements gave the vessel a new lease of life, putting her in a class above the *Aquila* and *Cygnus*. Further alterations were made to her engines at the end of 1879 following the failure of an intermediate shaft, which had a crank to work the air pumps. It was decided with the new shaft that both the air pump and circulating pumps would be worked from eccentrics fitted to the new shaft, the necessary alterations taking well into January 1880 to complete.

In February 1879 the close co-operation between the Great Western Railway and the Weymouth & Channel Islands Steam Packet Company again came to the fore when *Brighton* made three runs on the Cherbourg service of the GWR. Between 1st January and 30th June, 1883 she made 32 voyages to Cherbourg compared with 20 to the Channel Islands. However, from the 1st of July until laid up for repairs on 3rd October she operated solely to the Channel Islands, completing 36 round voyages. Later, following the loss of the *South of Ireland, Brighton* was again chartered to maintain the Cherbourg service, carrying out seven voyages during the second half of 1884.

During 1886, her last full year of operation, she sailed 74 times to the Islands. It was on one of these voyages from Weymouth on 11th December that she came across the screw steamer *Bedlington,* which having lost her rudder in a gale, was unmanageable 12 miles off Portland Bill. A tow was connected at 3.15 am and *Brighton* headed back towards Portland Harbour. Owing to the sheering and pitching of the crippled steamer the tow parted and a second hawser had to be made fast, Portland eventually being reached at 12.30 pm after which the *Brighton* proceeded to the Channel Islands. The Packet Company's claim for salvage was heard in the Admiralty Division of the High Court the following March, there being claims for damaged tow ropes, some passengers also having claimed refunds for delays, and claims for delayed cargo and Royal Mail. The Court awarded the Packet Company £600 for its efforts.

Unfortunately as with so many other vessels, fog and the treacherous coastline of the Channel Islands claimed the *Brighton* on 29th January, 1887. Having departed from Weymouth at 12.10 am, under the command of Captain Thomas Painter, thick fog was entered after passing Portland Bill. Approaching Guernsey just after 6.45 am an object was spotted on the port bow. The engines were put to full astern, but before the vessel could be stopped she struck a rock, causing her to rebound. The bow section quickly started to fill with water, the order being given to abandon ship. The 20 passengers and 24 crew quickly got away in the three lifeboats; indeed, so speedy was their departure that many of the passengers were not fully dressed or wearing footwear. About 15 minutes after striking the rock the vessel sank by the head, her stern rising into the air as

The *Brighton* following the improvements of 1878 - an illustration of the vessel presented to Abraham Bishop, Chairman of the Packet Company, from Frederick Edwards the company's consulting engineer.
J. Attwood Collection

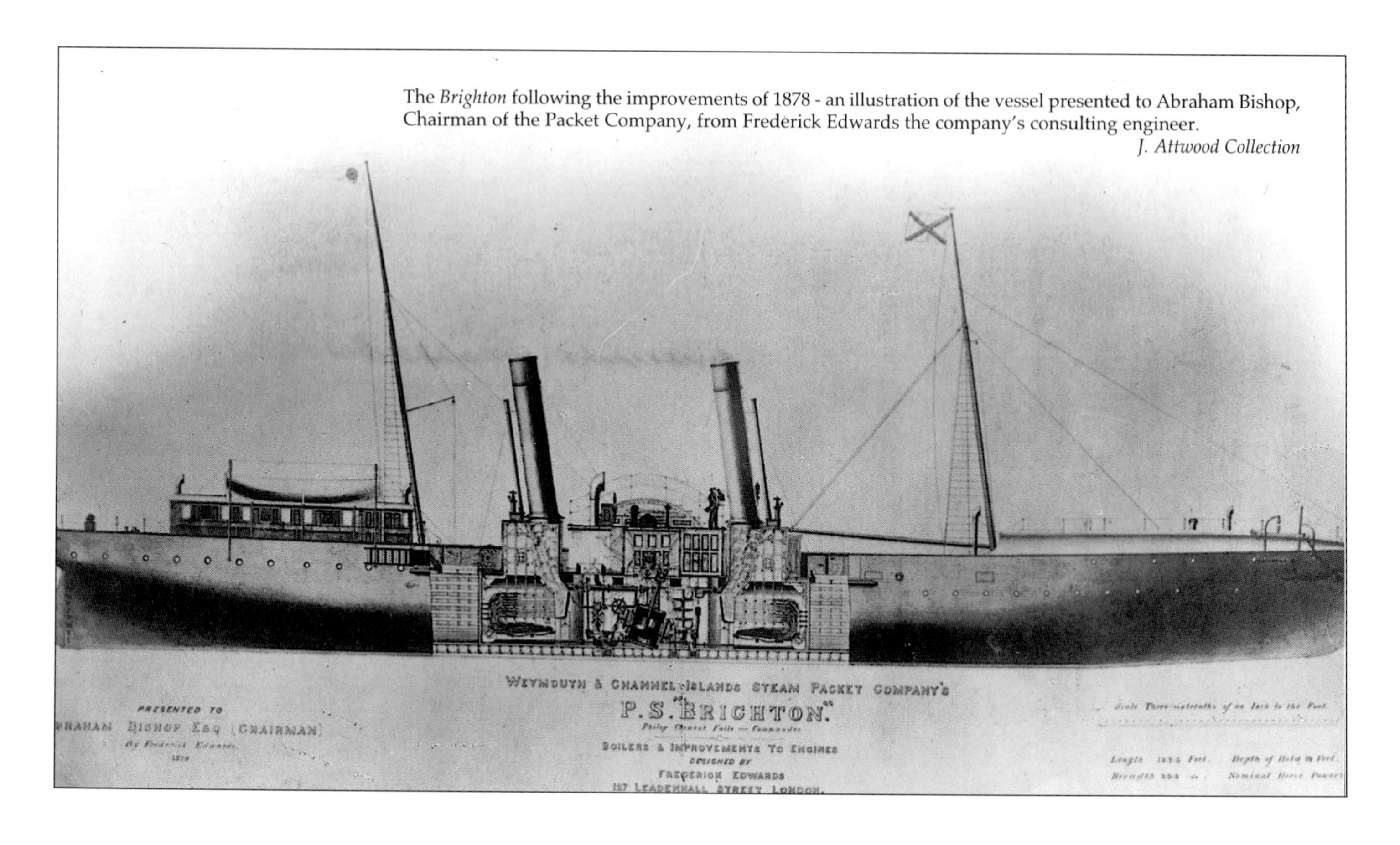

she plunged into deep water. After drifting around for a while in the lifeboats, when the fog cleared the occupants realised they were amongst the 'Braynes' - a group of rocks in the Little Russel Channel off Guernsey. They then rowed to Bordeaux Harbour where they landed at 9.30 am. At the time the exact position of the wreck was unknown. Lost was all the passengers' luggage, about 40 tons of general cargo and 12 bags of Royal Mail, and a coffin containing the body of Miss Marecheaux of Jersey being returned from the mainland for burial, which was later found washed up in Alderney.

An interesting item later appeared in the *Guernsey Mail and Telegraph*:

> We have seen a portion of one of the iron plates of the *Brighton's* hull, and also some rivet heads which have been found by a Pilot on a rock on which the steamer is supposed to have struck. These articles are now in the possession of Mr Sidney Tandevin, the company's local agent, and it is hoped they will lead to the discovery of the spot where the vessel sunk. We are told that a large fragment of the rock, estimated to weigh about two tons, has been broken off, presumably by the steamer's collision with it. The spot where the steamer struck is at present a secret, and a reward of £10 has been offered to any person who can accurately describe the vessel's position, and for this reason the pilot refuses to make known the whereabouts of the unfortunate steamer, in order that he might claim the reward himself.

At the subsequent Board of Trade inquiry held during March, Captain Painter, who had made the voyage 816 times in the past 16 years, stated that the *Brighton* left Weymouth at 12.10 on the morning of the 29th. The weather was rather thick. On leaving the harbour they could not see the breakwater light although they could see the lights on the Esplanade. The sea was quite smooth, and there was no wind. They were bound for Guernsey and Jersey. He was on the bridge on leaving the harbour, and gave orders to go slow, and they went slow until they got abreast of the Portland Breakwater when they went full speed, about 11 knots, which was kept up until they got the two lights of Portland Bill end on, when he reduced her to half speed. She was making about eight knots. He then set course S. by W. which was kept all the way across. The weather was sometimes thick and sometimes clear, and they saw nothing and heard nothing in going across. He was on deck all night, as were also the chief and second officers and three seamen.

It was reported at 6.30 am that the log had run 48 miles. He supposed he was abreast of the Caskets, 14 minutes later the log read 50 miles. He did not see any light or anything to indicate where they were. Shortly afterwards they saw a few heads of rocks around about them. He telegraphed to stop the vessel and to put her full speed astern. These orders were carried out, but the vessel struck the rocks and came off again. He found she was settling down by the head and he consequently gave orders to man the boats as quickly as possible. All the passengers were got into the boats and were rowed about 200 yards from the vessel, which went down in about five minutes.

The engineers gave evidence that the engines were turning at 23 revolutions per minute, but this was merely a calculation as there was no revolution counter fitted to the engine. Captain Painter said he was under the belief that the vessel was travelling at eight knots, but it was later admitted she was going at about

10 knots. Her full speed was 11 knots! The cause of the loss was that the captain kept the vessel going at too great a speed, was kept on the one course for too long a period, and was not navigated with proper seamanlike care. The court found Captain Painter guilty of negligence, and had his master's certificate suspended for six months. The principal reasons given were that he had put too much faith in the distance recorded by the log (at the time these were known sometimes to be 10 per cent inaccurate) and a correct calculation of the vessel's speed was not made.

Not only did the loss of the *Brighton* end the company's 30 year safe record (quite an achievement taking into account the standards of the time) but it also marked the beginning of the inevitable end of the Weymouth & Channel Islands Steam Packet Company.

PS Brighton alongside Albert Pier, Jersey. Although the sailing boat obscures part of the vessel, the turtle-back added in 1877 is clearly shown, as are many other details of the ship. *R.C. Clammer Collection*

Chapter Eight

The Great Western Railway Fleet 1878-1885

Great Western

Built in 1867 by Simmons of Renfrew for Messrs Ford & Jackson to operate their New Milford-Waterford service, *Great Western* had the distinction of being the first ship to be registered at Milford. Her iron hull was 220 ft 4 in. long, 25 ft 2 in. across the beam, with a draught of 12 ft 4 in. and a gross tonnage of 477. Her twin cylinder oscillating engine supplied by her builders had a cylinder diameter of 50 in. and a piston stroke of 48 in. developing 190 nhp.

With the acquisition of Ford & Jackson's services by the railway company *Great Western* became a GWR vessel from 1st February, 1872. Transferred to Weymouth for the commencement of the new Cherbourg service, she departed thence with the first outward voyage on 1st August, 1878 carrying about 40 passengers. Although reported in the local press the inaugural voyage was very low key. 'A considerable number of persons assembled to witness the steamer make her first trip, and in honour of the event the Royal Italian Band played on the harbour staging. No demonstration of any kind was made, not even a cheer being given as the *Great Western* left the harbour'.

Having safely arrived at Weymouth on Tuesday 18th January, 1881 after a very rough crossing from Cherbourg during what was later referred to as the 'Great Blizzard', she lay at her berth only to be struck by the German barque *August,* laden with timber, which was being towed up harbour by the tug *Commodore.* She failed to answer her helm and ran against the *Great Western,* smashing one of her lifeboats situated near the paddle box.

She continued to operate the service until its withdrawal in June 1885 when she returned to Milford as a spare vessel, at times being chartered to the City of Cork Steam Packet Company.

After the loss of the *Brighton, Great Western* was chartered to the Weymouth & Channel Islands Steam Packet Company, making her first voyage to the Channel Islands on 6th June, 1887. The charter was repeated for the following two seasons. Owing to the late delivery of the new steamers for the GWR Channel Islands service in 1889, *Great Western* commenced the new service from 1st July until 4th August when the new vessels became available. Returning then to Milford, *Great Western* was surplus to requirements and was sold for £2,750 on 30th May, 1890.

Her new owner, Mr Nathaniel Miller of the Preston & West Coast Steamship Company, commenced a service between Preston Quay and Douglas, Isle of Man, her first voyage being on Saturday 7th June. The *Manchester Sunday Chronicle* reported that she carried a large number of passengers, and 'the *Cygnus,* a boat belonging to another company, started at the same time, but the *Great Western* passed the *Cygnus* at the bar and reached Douglas at 8.25, the *Cygnus* being some distance behind'. It was indeed the meeting of old friends - although not for long, as the venture was short-lived. In April 1891 *Great Western* was again sold to David MacBrayne, but laid up until 1893 when she

Great Western alongside the original cargo stage in 1878. Behind her stands the imposing building of the Marine Hotel and immediately to its left the offices of the Weymouth & Channel Islands Steam Packet Company. *Author's Collection*

A view clearly showing the deck arrangements of *Great Western* in July 1889. This photograph, showing the vessel laying on the Nothe side of the harbour at a point previously known as the 'Ballast Quay', was taken when *Great Western* commenced to operate the Channel Islands service, the new vessels not being ready. The newly completed passenger landing stage and baggage shed are across the harbour and to the left a dredger is at work. *R.C. Clammer Collection*

underwent a refit during which she was reboilered by Hutson of Glasgow, with one boiler operating at 40 psi, and she reappeared with only one funnel situated in the position of her former aft funnel. Her paddle boxes were also reconstructed, and she was renamed *Lovedale* on 29th May, 1893.

In her modified form she was placed on the Portree-Strome Ferry route. With the extension of the Highland Railway to Kyle of Lochalsh on 2nd November, 1897, *Lovedale* brought 200 excursionists from Stornoway, and also alongside the pier was *Gael* which had brought excursionists from Portree. The new terminal replaced Strome Ferry for steamers on the Isle of Lewis route. On 1st April, 1901 when the Mallaig new harbour station opened, *Lovedale* was waiting to operate the Portree-Kyle-Mallaig service.

During 1902/3 *Lovedale* was running from Glasgow to Islay following the loss of another steamer in the fleet. After a life involved in railway connected work, including the opening of four new services, she went to the breakers during 1904, her register being closed on 29th November.

Kyle of Lochalsh pier on 2nd November, 1897, the opening day of Highland Railway extension. Viewed from the stern is *Lovedale* (ex-*Great Western*) in her later form with only one funnel, waiting to depart for Stornoway. At the pier head lays *Gael*, another former GWR steamer with an excursion from Portree. *David McConnell Collection*

South of Ireland

South Of Ireland was completed at the Renfrew yard of W. Simmons & Company in July 1867, for Messrs Ford & Jackson's Irish Sea services. With the takeover of Ford & Jackson's services by the GWR, *South of Ireland* became a Great Western Railway vessel from 1st February, 1872. Although not a sister ship to the *Great Western* they were very similar, the main visual difference being that the *South of Ireland* was fitted with a single funnel whereas the *Great Western* carried two.

Constructed with an iron hull 220 ft 2 in. long with a beam of 25 ft 8 in. and draft of 12 ft 4 in. her gross tonnage was 474. Her engine, also constructed by her builders, was of the two-cylinder vertical oscillating type, with a cylinder bore of 50 in. and piston stroke of 48 in. developing 200 nhp, her original boiler being replaced during 1882.

With the planned commencement of the Weymouth-Cherbourg service, *South of Ireland* was transferred to Weymouth. A party of GWR officials crossed to Cherbourg aboard her on 15th July, 1878 to make the final arrangements. On the return voyage on the 17th she called at Jersey where the GWR officials dined at the Hotel British with the Directors of the Steam Packet Co. Departing from Jersey at 5 am the following morning *South of Ireland* arrived at Weymouth at 2 pm. The public service commenced on Thursday 1st August. *South of Ireland* made the first crossing from Cherbourg to Weymouth, where she arrived an hour late - not a good start!

Within the month there were further problems. Sailing from Cherbourg at 8.20 am on Saturday 31st August and about 25 miles out, the port side paddle wheel shaft broke inside the bearing. Following disconnection of the failed shaft the vessel proceeded on one paddle wheel, but progress was very slow. She had been due in Weymouth at 3 pm on Saturday, but eventually limped into Weymouth Bay at daybreak on Sunday, Cosens' tug *Commodore* going out to guide her into harbour where she moored at 4 am.

At midnight on Monday 17th January, 1881 *South of Ireland* departed from Weymouth for Cherbourg and shortly after sailing a severe gale developed, Captain Pearn anchoring inside Portland Breakwater until daylight. Proceeding once again, he ran into heavy seas which caused damage to the steering gear and one paddle wheel. Finding it impossible to return to within the Breakwater, he made a run for Weymouth Harbour where a heavy sea running across the entrance made berthing difficult, but good seamanship saved the day. When she entered the harbour she was seen to roll onto her beam end, her keel becoming visible, onlookers thinking she would ram the Pile Pier.

Under the command of Captain William Thomas Pearn *South of Ireland* departed from Cherbourg during the evening of 24th December, 1883. Fog set in during the early part of the voyage and speed was reduced to half. At 12.30 am, the fog having lifted, full speed was resumed, but was soon reduced again and then increased to full, shortly after which a black object was seen ahead. Although the engines were put to full astern, at 1.35 am the vessel ran ashore.

Captain Pearn had misjudged his position and ran ashore east of Lulworth Cove in Worbarrow Bay. It appears that the ship ran over a ledge of rocks and her bows smashed into the cliff. Fortunately the sea was calm and there was only one passenger on board (!). Five of the crew and the one luckless passenger set off along the coast to Weymouth in one of the ship's lifeboats. After rowing for about four hours they arrived at Weymouth Harbour at 6 am, where the non-arrival of the ship had caused no concern owing to the weather. A steam tug and barges were dispatched to the scene, by which time the engine and boiler rooms were flooded and water was starting to seep into the cargo holds where there lay 70 tons of cargo. It was not considered prudent to attempt to unload the cargo in case the bulkheads collapsed to trap men below deck. Instead the saloon was stripped of its furniture and fittings, deck equipment and other movable items were loaded into the barges before returning to Weymouth, the first officer and a boat crew being left to stand by overnight.

The following day steamers brought workmen from Weymouth with timber and equipment to shore up the bulkheads to allow removal of the cargo, the vessel being stripped of everything that could be moved and two-thirds of the cargo was unloaded. The bow section was torn open and trapped on the rocks, and with the rise and fall of the tide the vessel broke in two, but there was hope that the remainder of the vessel could be salvaged. On Sunday 30th two large steam salvage pumps arrived from Glasgow by rail, but unfortunately there was no crane at Weymouth able to lift them so they had to be taken to Portland where they were loaded into barges. The following day the weather became unsuitable to take the barges with the pumps to Worbarrow Bay, but Cosens & Company's tug *Commodore* and a barge went to recover a portion of the remaining cargo. The tug and barge returned the following day when more cargo was saved. On Wednesday 2nd January the weather was more favourable and Cosens' paddle steamer *Queen* towed the barges to the scene, followed by *Commodore* with another barge. Upon arrival the pumps were set to work and in half an hour the engine room, aft hold and saloon were pumped dry. At high tide *Commodore* and *Queen* made a combined effort to tow the remaining section of the ship clear, but it sank into deep water and all hopes of salvage were lost.

The subsequent Board of Trade inquiry determined that the vessel had not been navigated in a proper and seaman-like manner. The second mate in evidence said that, in his opinion, the vessel had crossed from Cherbourg faster than the captain thought. In fact, Captain Pearn was damned by his own admission that he had not heard the Shambles Lightship foghorn, had failed to take lead soundings and failed to consult the 'Patent Log'. The court ruled that for not carrying out these procedures Captain Pearn was responsible for the loss of the vessel, and his master's ticket was suspended for three months. The GWR was less lenient, Pearn being dismissed from its service.

In a lighter vein, the satirical magazine *Punch* alluded to the wreck:

> The Great Western Railway Company notify that the loss of the *South of Ireland* will not in any way interfere with the regularity of the service between Weymouth and Cherbourg! In consequence of this announcement it is probable that the South-Eastern Company will publicly declare that the loss of the whole of Ireland would not interrupt the traffic between London and Paris!

Today the remains of the *South of Ireland* lie in 20 ft of water approximately 100 yards east of the small rocky cove known as Pondfield.

Vulture

Built in 1864 by Aitken & Mansel of Whiteinch, Glasgow her iron hull was 243 ft 2 in. long with a beam of 25 ft 7 in. and draft of 17 ft 3 in. and weighed 793 gross tons. Her twin-cylinder oscillating-engine supplied by her builders had cylinders of 54 in. diameter and a piston stroke of 60 in., developing 200 nhp.

Constructed for the European Trading Company, few records remain of the vessel's early years. Between 1866-1868 she was not on the British Register, until re-registered in Glasgow for William Cameron and others, and engaged in Messrs Thomas Brown's Glasgow-London service.

Acquired by Messrs Ford & Jackson in 1870 as a spare vessel, she was used on the Waterford service when required although she often worked elsewhere; during 1871 it is recorded she was employed by the Government conveying troops!

Following the sale of the other Ford & Jackson steamers to the GWR, the latter was asked if it wished to purchase *Vulture* as a spare. After disagreement concerning the price it was reduced from £10,000 to £9,000 and the vessel became the property of the GWR on 13th April, 1872. During 1876 *Vulture* was used solely as a cattle boat on the Waterford service, thus saving passengers from the unpleasant smells when cattle travelled on the passenger steamer. However this arrangement ceased on 1st March, 1880, by which time *Vulture* had departed from Milford. Following the failure of both the *Cygnus* and *Aquila* on 2nd and 3rd May, 1879, on charter covering the Cherbourg service, *Vulture* was immediately sent from Milford to maintain the service. At the time she was the largest steamer to enter Weymouth Harbour and grounded several times at low water. Within days *Vulture* was in trouble! On the morning of 8th May both *Vulture* - inward bound from Cherbourg - and *Aquila* from the Channel Islands entered the harbour at the same time. *Vulture* ran into the *Aquila*, her bow smashing *Aquila's* port paddle box sponson. This damage, however, did not prevent both vessels continuing with the regular service. *Vulture* was intended to be the spare vessel for the Cherbourg service, but she quickly became disliked by all who were involved with her. She was far too large for both the available traffic and the port facilities and was also slow, making only nine knots, and had a high coal consumption burning 23 tons per return trip.

In a report written during 1883 Captain Lecky stated;

> The *Vulture* is too old, too large, and too slow. It appears that she can carry more than the Traffic Department at Cherbourg are capable of putting into her in the interval between arrival and sailing (unless the sailing be a late one). And the harbour dues paid on her large tonnage, are out of proportion to the freight earned.
>
> I beg to submit therefore that it would be advisable to replace this vessel with one of modern construction which would be more suitable and at the same time less expensive to run.

Although the spare steamer to cover the Cherbourg service, *Vulture* did little to assist in times of need. On 16th June, 1884 a majority of her crew were transferred to the newly arrived *Gael*, and *Vulture* ceased to be listed in the shipping arrivals and departures of the *Southern Times*. Following the loss of the *South of Ireland*, vessels were chartered from the Packet Company until a replacement steamer could be obtained!

Early in March 1885 *Vulture* was called upon to replace the *Gael*. Unfortunately, being in such poor condition, she made only one trip before having to be withdrawn herself. Her boiler, having been replaced in 1875, was well past its best for a vessel of the period, and the decision had been taken the previous month for the vessel's disposal. She had been an expensive failure, spending more time moored in harbour paying dues rather than at sea earning revenue for her owners. By early 1886 *Vulture* was broken up, her register being closed on 16th February, 1886, although no details of her fate are given. It is ironic that in spite of being such a failure part of her still exists. Before she departed Weymouth for the breaker's yard the ship's bell was removed, and later used at the Nothe Parade workshops as the 'time bell'. In 1960 it was removed to the Museum of Transport at Clapham, and today it resides in the National Railway Museum York!

The bell of the *Vulture* on display in the former Clapham Museum. *Author*

Gael swinging in Weymouth Harbour during 1884. To the right the *Vulture* is laid up in the Cove, although officially the relief boat for the Cherbourg service. The *Gael* was purchased following the loss of the *South of Ireland*. To the left is Cosens' paddle steamer *Premier*, which had a 92 year active life from 1846 to 1938.
Late E. Latcham Collection

Gael photographed whilst working in the Scilly Isles, the turtle-back and other details clearly shown.
Author's Collection

Gael

Gael was built by Robertson & Company of Greenock for the Campbeltown & Glasgow Steam Packet Joint Stock Company Limited, especially to operate the Glasgow-Campbeltown service. To gain advantage over other operators a fast vessel was required, and on her trials on 5th April, 1867 she exceeded 16 knots. Her maiden voyage was made on 17th April, and within weeks she was setting new records for the Glasgow-Campbeltown run. A vessel of heavy construction, her iron hull was 210 ft long with a beam of 23 ft 2 in., a draft of 10 ft 6 in. and a gross tonnage of 403. Her oscillating engine supplied by Rankin & Blackmore of Greenock had twin cylinders of 45 in. diameter and a piston stroke of 63 in. developing 150 nhp. As with many steam ships of the period, her engines operated on the 'jet condenser' system which allowed an amount of salt water into the boiler feed tank. The boilers were short-lived, replacements being required in 1874.

When new she also had accommodation for cargo and cattle, and carried a livery of black hull and black funnels with a broad red band. During 1879 it was decided to refit the vessel completely, the work being undertaken by Messrs Inglis at a cost of £14,000. A large deck saloon was constructed on the main deck aft, and the lower cabin was enlarged and converted into a dining saloon. Decks and other fittings were replaced, new paddle wheels were fitted, and two new haystack type boilers installed. The engines were completely overhauled, and most importantly a surface condenser was fitted to replace the jet condenser, thus ending the salt-water contamination problems. In her rebuilt form she underwent trials on 27th June, 1879. Although her owners were pleased with the results, her coal consumption was higher and her speed less. Four years later an up-to-date vessel was ordered from builders and *Gael* was put up for sale. The GWR, requiring a replacement for the *South of Ireland,* purchased the vessel for £3,000 on 8th April, 1884.

Although not exactly the type of vessel required, being found to be 'slight' and tending to take water over the bows in a sea, she was acceptable after Laird's at Birkenhead carried out alterations during the winter. A section of her under deck passenger accommodation was removed and her holds and cargo hatches enlarged to give a cargo capacity of approximately 20,000 cu ft. The revised accommodation allowed sleeping space for 20 first class and 20 second class passengers. The hull was strengthened by the fitting of additional bilge keels, whilst a turtleback constructed of timber over the bow section allowed extra covered stowage and improved her seaworthiness.

Arriving at Weymouth without comment from the local press, she was put into service on the Cherbourg sailings from 16th July, working in conjunction with *Great Western*. During that time she was capable of reaching a speed of only 12 knots. In March 1885 problems occurred with her boiler, and by the time this had been resolved the Cherbourg service had been withdrawn. *Gael,* having spent very little time so employed, became a spare vessel. It was decided that she was suitable for operating a summer service between the railway-owned harbour at Portishead and Ilfracombe, and other destinations on the Bristol Channel. After spending £240 adapting the vessel she commenced sailings on

1st July, 1885 and continued the following season. In the summers of 1888 and 1889 she was chartered to the Scilly Isles & West Cornwall Steam Ship Company until, owing to the delayed delivery of the new GWR vessels to commence the Channel Islands service in July 1889, *Gael* was recalled and sailed direct to Jersey, arriving on 30th June to commence the sailings to Weymouth on 2nd July. She remained on this service until 3rd August when she returned to Milford.

On 24th October, 1889 she acted as tender when the Anchor Line liner *City of Rome* discharged passengers off Milford Haven whilst *en route* to Liverpool. *Gael* landed the passengers at Milford Pontoon and they continued their journey to London by train. This was the only recorded time that tender work took place at Milford, and as most of the passengers were part of 'Barnhams Show' it could well have been a publicity stunt!

A brief return to Weymouth was made on 12th June, 1890 following the grounding of the *Antelope* and to assist with the potato traffic, but with little other work to keep her occupied Captain Lecky recommended she be disposed of. At a meeting on 14th March, 1891 it was decided that *Gael* be placed at auction with a reserve price of £3,500. In April this was reduced to £2,500 but still no bids were received. On 13th May, 1891 it was reported *Gael* had been sold for £1,700 to David MacBrayne for his West Highland services.

The following year her aft cargo hold was removed, and a new saloon extending the full width of the hull constructed aft. At the same time she received her third set of boilers. Once refitted she was placed on the Oban-Gaerloch service. With the extension of the Highland Railway to Kyle of Lochalsh on 2nd November, 1897 *Gael* operated an excursion from Portree, carrying 300 passengers for the opening day. Also at the pier was *Lovedale* (ex-*Great Western*) with a sailing from Stornoway! With the opening Kyle of Lochalsh became the terminal for the steamer services.

During 1901 *Gael* was engaged on the Oban-Skye-Gairloch service, but the following season she usually sailed from Oban to Staffa and Iona. The winter months were usually spent laid up at Greenock. Further alterations took place during 1910 when a steel forecastle replaced the wooden structure, and the ship was generally modernised. With the outbreak of World War I *Gael* was laid up at Bowling Harbour in August 1914 until, following the requisitioning of many Clyde steamers, she was put to work on various Clyde services. During 1915 she operated the Ardrossan-Arran service of the Caledonian Steam Packet Company, and again during 1919.

The main mast, which had been removed in 1892, was reinstated during a post-war refit in 1920 when the vessel was equipped with wireless. Now in the evening of her life, *Gael* spent the winter months on the Mail route to Ardisraig, and the Kyle of Locohalsh-Stornaway Mail service in summer. She was sold early in 1924, spending one night at Campbeltown on her way to the breaker's yard.

Chapter Nine

The Great Western Railway Fleet 1889-1905

Lynx, Antelope and Gazelle

The ordering of these three sister vessels by the Great Western Railway from Laird Bros of Birkenhead in July 1888 was a turning point in the Weymouth-Channel Islands service. At a cost of £35,000 each they were revolutionary at the time, being the first screw steamers constructed for the GWR and the first steamers on any English Channel route to have triple expansion engines and twin screws. It could well have been different, as owing to the shallowness of Weymouth Harbour the company had intended to have paddle steamers constructed for the service, but with Weymouth Corporation's undertaking to dredge the harbour, Messrs Laird in co-operation with the GWR designed a screw ship suitable for the service.

Constructed of steel, the hull had seven watertight compartments and the bow section was protected by a 40 ft long turtleback. The vessels were 235 ft 6 in. long, with a beam of 27 ft 6 in., a draft of 13 ft 1 in., and a gross tonnage of 596. Powered by two triple-expansion engines which were inclined inward to reduce headroom, the high-pressure cylinders were 16½ in. in diameter, the intermediate pressure cylinder 26 in. in diameter and the low-pressure 41 in. diameter, the piston stroke being 30 in. Both the high- and intermediate-pressure cylinders had piston valves whilst the low-pressure cylinder was fitted with a balanced slide valve. The valve gear was driven by Stephenson link motion, screw reversing being operated by a hand wheel. The air pump, feed pump, and bilge pumps, were operated off rocker levers attached to the high-pressure piston crosshead. Centrifugal circulating pumps supplied seawater to the condensers, which were carried on the back columns of the engines.

Two single-ended boilers, each 14 ft 3 in. in diameter and 10 ft 2 in. long, had three furnaces each. The working pressure was 150 psi, the boilers working under forced draught on the closed stokehold system with an air pressure of about ¾ inch water pressure. The coal bunkers held 40 tons. The steam-operated steering engine fitted in the engine room was controlled by a revolving rod from the wheel on the bridge, whilst the rudder was operated by means of chains and rods between the steering engine and stern end. The twin screws were not of the usual type. To allow for the narrowness of the hull and the use of a reasonable size propeller they overlapped, with an aperture within the stem post to admit the overlapping of the 9 ft 6 in. propellers. The electrical equipment, installed by GWR staff, consisted of a Latimer Clark compound wound dynamo coupled direct to a Willans steam engine, requiring 80 psi to operate and taking steam either from the main boilers or the donkey boiler situated on the starboard side of the aft boiler, the dynamo being on the port side.

The local press, the *Great Western Railway Magazine*, and *Engineering* all gave enthusiastic accounts of the sisters, referring to the vast improvements on the previous vessels employed. In the new vessels the main saloon was situated

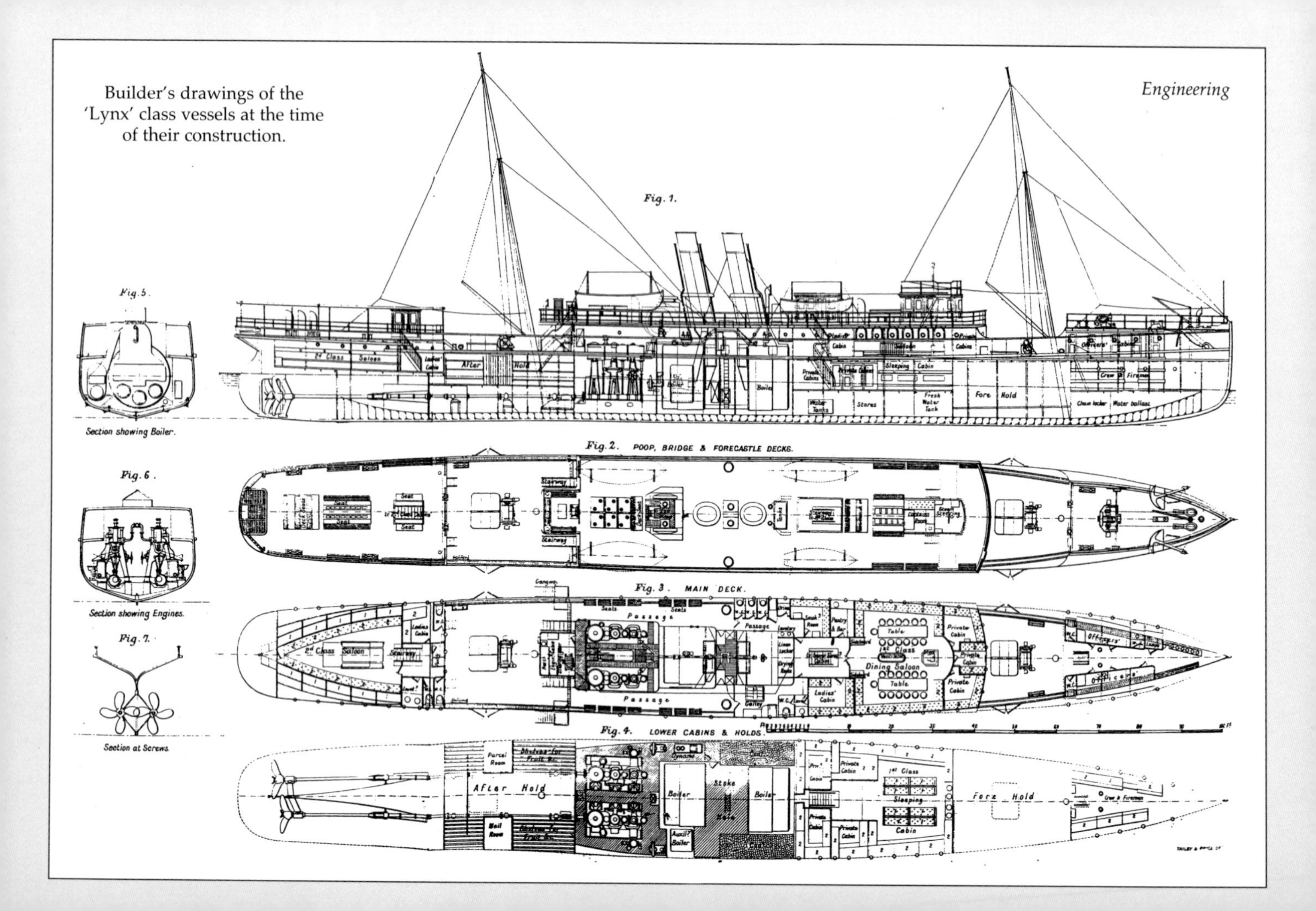

Builder's drawings of the 'Lynx' class vessels at the time of their construction.

forward, and accommodation for second class passengers placed aft, the aft cabin being capable of carrying 139 passengers in 34 cushioned berths of a comfortable character. On one side of the cabin was the toilet accommodation, on the other a ladies' sleeping berth and an adjoining pantry. Between the alleyways was covered accommodation provided with seats for third class passengers.

The accommodation for the 141 first class passengers was described in lavish terms. The companionway leading to the first class saloon was lofty, cheerful, and imposing, handsomely panelled and painted in several delicate tints. The first class saloon was of large size and lofty dimensions, with fittings of bird's eye maple and oak, Venetian mirrors, and crimson velvet upholstery, and the roof painted white with gold panelling. Eight large incandescent lamps furnished a most brilliant illumination. The furniture was of a luxurious nature and included some comfortable revolving arm chairs. Three private cabins at the fore end were available at a small additional charge. Adjoining these was a pantry and a smoking room fitted with an air extractor. Opposite was situated the kitchen (galley) fitted with a double heating range and other equipment. Situated near the saloon entrance was the ladies' cabin, painted white and gold with crimson velvet upholstery and fully carpeted. The first class sleeping accommodation was below the main saloon, containing 76 berths fitted up with sofas and lounges. There were also four private cabins, two with eight berths and two with six. Throughout the ship the lavatories were described as 'models of sanitary science'. The entire ship was illuminated by electricity and steam heated throughout.

The captain's cabin and chart room adjoined the wheelhouse whilst the crew's quarters were at the fore end. The officers' cabins were under the forecastle, and below was accommodation for eight seamen and six firemen. There was also accommodation for parcels and mail, whilst the aft hold had racks for the conveyance of fruit.

Owing to labour troubles at the shipyard there was a delay in construction. *Lynx* was launched on 29th January, 1889 without ceremony, *Antelope* followed on 4th May, and *Gazelle* on 13th June. Further problems were caused by faults in the draughting and ventilation system aboard the *Lynx* which delayed her arrival at Milford until the 6th July - carrying signs of a hurried completion. Rust was already showing through her paintwork and the ship was described as being filthy, resulting in much work having to be done before she could enter service.

Eventually departing Milford on Friday 19th July, *Lynx* arrived in Weymouth at 8 am the next day where she was open to inspection by invited guests and later in the day by members of the public who held a ticket. In the evening the ship was illuminated by electric light, a feature that caused great interest to those present. The *Lynx* made her maiden voyage from Weymouth in the early hours of Sunday 4th August. It was an historic event, the first boat train to run along the Harbour Tramway having departed Paddington at 9.15 pm the previous evening arriving at the new Quay station on time. At 2.20 am, under the command of Captain Le Feuvre, *Lynx* set sail with 175 passengers and several GWR managers aboard. It was reported she made the run from

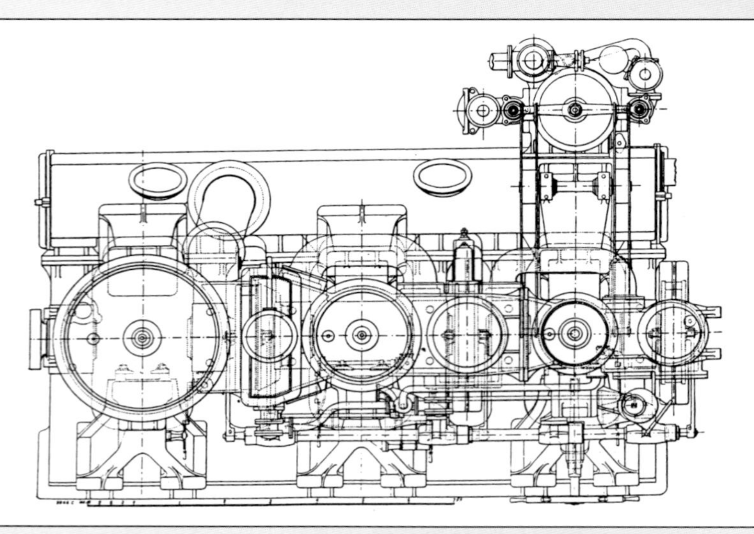

Builder's drawing of the port side of triple expansion engines fitted to 'Lynx' class vessels. Viewed from the cylinder tops. Behind the engine the air pump is illustrated driven by rocker arms from the crosshead of the high-pressure cylinder. *Engineering*

Builder's drawing of the port side triple expansion engine installed in the 'Lynx' class vessels. The high-pressure cylinder is to the right followed by the intermediate pressure with the large diameter low pressure cylinder to the left. *Engineering*

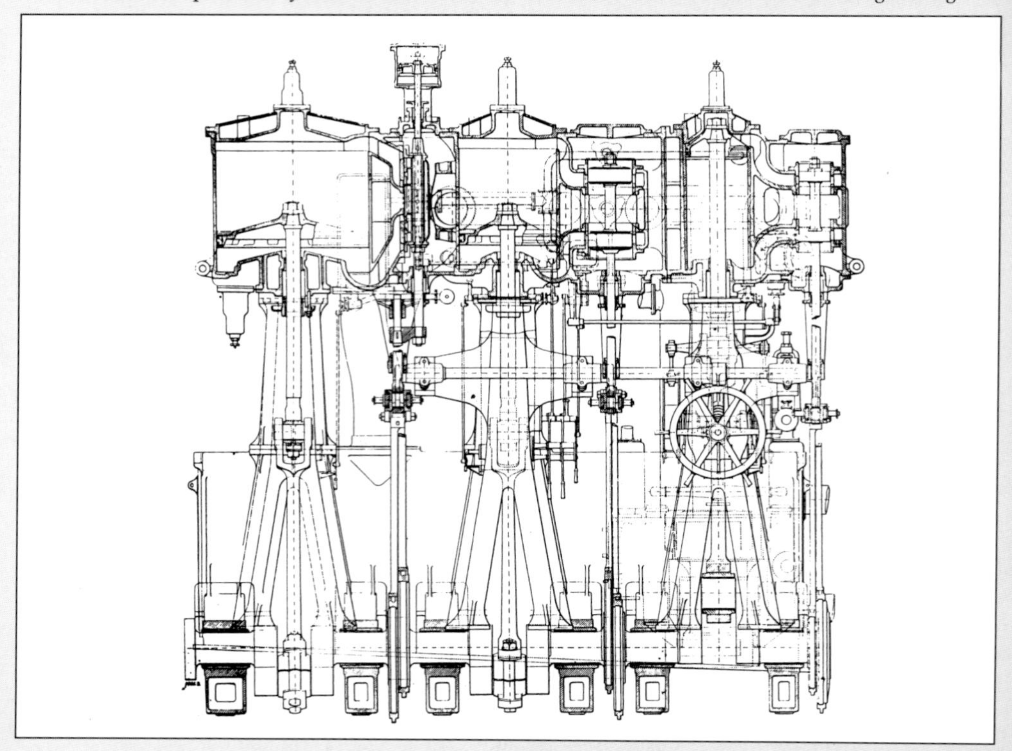

Weymouth to Guernsey in 4 hours 20 minutes - 40 minutes under the advertised time - and sailed between Guernsey and Jersey in 1 hour 35 minutes, also 40 minutes less than advertised.

In the meantime the *Antelope* had sailed from Milford direct to Jersey, arriving on 4th August. On Monday 5th she departed from Jersey at 8 am under the command of Captain Painter, reaching Guernsey in 1 hour 40 minutes, and covered the distance between Guernsey and Weymouth in 4¼ hours. With the connecting boat train, passengers for London arrived at Paddington a few minutes after 8 pm.

Thus the new Channel Islands service had commenced, initially operated by two vessels until the *Gazelle* arrived from Milford on Saturday 7th September, entering the harbour at 10.15 am. She made her maiden voyage the following day, the local press passing little comment on the vessel after their lavish praise of her two sisters. However *Gazelle* received a mention the following week on her return from the Islands on the afternoon of Tuesday 16th September, when passengers boarded the boat train of which the first two coaches became derailed about 200 yds after departing the quay station!

There were slight differences in the performances of each vessel. On their official trials the engines of *Lynx* attained the highest revolution and developed more power than the machinery of the two other vessels, but the speed was less. The *Gazelle*, with fewer revolutions and less power indicated, attained a greater speed. Even in service this was the case her average being 17.4 knots whilst *Lynx* averaged 16.6 knots and *Antelope* 16.4. *Engineering* claimed in the May 1890 edition that 'these vessels are the fastest screw channel steamers on the British coast', going on to say:

> There is no doubt that in wartime the value of such a vessel as the *Gazelle* or her sister ships would be very great. As despatch boats they would prove invaluable. Their small size and great speed would enable them to be at sea when other vessels would be captured. It must not be forgotten that, although under normal conditions they only carry about 40 to 50 tons of coal in their bunkers, yet, by filling their holds with coal, they would be enabled to traverse great distances with safety. It may be remarked that their dimensions are similar to the so-called torpedo boat catchers, and in some vessels now being built by the Admiralty, and engined by Messrs Laird, we believe the type of machinery is similar in all respects, except that the engines are designed to give at least 4.500 ihp.

The *Southern Times* reported:

> The Company also claim for this service that it is likely to be not only the safest but the most regular, the risk of accident and annoying delays being reduced to a minimum by the absence of those fogs which higher up the channel render navigation so difficult.

Within weeks those words had a rather hollow ring! The draughting system in the stokeholds were a cause of complaint from firemen as the heat was unbearable, and deflections were discovered in the furnaces of all three vessels. *Antelope* and *Lynx* both grounded in Weymouth Harbour owing to inadequate dredging, *Lynx* damaging a propeller, and after the arrival of *Gazelle* all three vessels had minor problems with their steering gear.

However annoying these setbacks were to the new service, the incidents of the next 10 years were of a more serious nature and highlighted the problems of running a steamship service in the days before radio and the other technical refinements that are today taken for granted. On the morning of 10th June, 1890 the *Antelope* was approaching Guernsey when fog suddenly descended. Captain Painter reduced speed and soon a rock known as 'The Rouse' was noticed some distance ahead. The engines were put full astern, but as the vessel moved away she sided onto a rock known as 'La Cavale' and stuck there. It was decided to put the 60 passengers onto a nearby rock in case the steamer heeled over. Several local fishermen came to the rescue, the LSWR steamer *St Malo* and the tug *Rescue* also coming out from St Peter Port to take the passengers, their luggage, and other goods to harbour. As the tide rose *Antelope* floated clear and proceeded to St Peter Port where the cargo was unloaded. Damage to the ship's hull was slight: a hole about one foot in diameter in her stern starboard quarter, part of the bilge plate battered, and about 10 feet of plate aft of the engine room pushed in but not holed. *Antelope* returned to Weymouth the following day and after coaling, proceeded to Birkenhead for repairs. The shortage of vessels required the services of *Gael* for a week.

On 5th September, 1890 the *Lynx* was crossing from Guernsey, making good speed about 20 miles off Portland, when the German tanker *Oevelgonne* appeared on the port side steaming up Channel on passage from New York to Hamburg. With both ships in view of each other for a considerable time it was surprising that the tanker failed to steer astern of the *Lynx* as laid down in the rules of navigation, but as the vessels closed upon each other it is even more surprising that the first officer of the *Lynx*, who was on the bridge at the time, took no evasive action! At a range of about 20 yards both vessels altered course but it was too late. The bow of the tanker struck the port bow of the *Lynx* a glancing blow as both vessels attempted to turn away from each other.

The force of the impact caused *Lynx* to roll well to her starboard side, throwing passengers to the deck and those in the dining saloon - including Captain Le Feuvre - from their seats. As the two vessels swung alongside each other about 20 passengers jumped aboard the tanker fearing the *Lynx* would founder. After the vessels had drifted apart and it was certain the *Lynx* was in no danger, a lifeboat from the tanker brought the passengers, including two women and a boy aged 10, back aboard the *Lynx*, which suffered damage to the hurricane deck and crew's quarters as well as bent bows and a leaking plate. But for the grace of God it could have been a major disaster.

Even an event of this nature has its funny side. It appears that following the collision a portly old gentleman made his way to the bridge, demanding to know from the first officer who was going to make good the damage, as he was a shareholder in the company? Having just escaped from death's door, all he could think of was his dividends! Continuing to Weymouth, *Lynx* later sailed to Messrs Day Summers yard at Southampton for repairs, and two months later the tanker was arrested by Admiralty agents. Again no spare vessel was available, so the Isle of Man Steam Packet Company paddle steamer *Snaefell* was chartered for two weeks. It was to be the last time a paddle steamer worked the regular service.

The *Gazelle* assisted in the final abolition of the broad gauge on the GWR in May 1892 on the mornings of Saturday 28th and Sunday 29th when she conveyed the mails and any passengers between Millbay Docks to Fowey and Falmouth. She returned in the afternoon to connect with the up night mail which during the conversion work travelled over the LSWR line as far as Exeter.

Antelope ended up in an embarrassing situation on Saturday 18th November, 1893 when her non-arrival at Weymouth during the afternoon caused concern as there was a gale blowing. At 3 am on Sunday morning Cosens' tug *Queen* put to sea, as it was thought that her fuel had run short and she was sheltering under the lee of Portland, but the *Antelope* was nowhere to be seen and the tug smashed a paddle box and side houses in the heavy sea. Just after the tug returned to harbour at 9.30 am a telegram was received notifying that the *Antelope* was at anchor off Swanage, short of coal. Immediately another Cosens' paddle tug, *Albert Victor*, had 10 tons of coal loaded onto her deck and sailed for Swanage, *Antelope* eventually arriving at Weymouth during the afternoon!

Lynx encountered the perilous rocks around the Channel Islands on Saturday 20th March, 1897. Having departed from Weymouth just after 2 am thick fog was encountered, causing the vessel to lay off Guernsey for three hours. She later proceeded towards Jersey, but when near the Corbière the steamer grazed a rock. A passenger later spoke of feeling a strong jarring sensation, which was twice repeated, as if the vessel struck then grazed again. The lifeboats were loosened ready for lowering, but the steamer kept on her course without making water. After arrival at St Helier the hull was examined at low tide, it being found that she had sustained only slight damage to two plates below her tanks amidships, although two blades were broken off the port propeller. This was replaced by one of the spare propellers, the vessel then returning to Weymouth before proceeding to Milford for repairs. The *Lynx* had a lucky escape. Ironically it was *Lynx* that on Good Friday 31st March, 1899 picked up two lifeboats with 34 survivors from the LSWR steamer *Stella* and conveyed them to Guernsey, also being the medium of conveying the news of the fearful catastrophe which had taken place off the Casquets.

On 16th February, 1900 *Lynx* on a cargo service from Weymouth off Portland Bill found the dismasted schooner *Levant* of Fowey on voyage to Antwerp with china clay. Her lifeboat had been smashed, but a lifeboat from *Lynx* with volunteer crew headed by Mr Hughes the 2nd officer succeeded at considerable risk in rescuing the crew of six. Efforts were also made to take the schooner in tow before it foundered. It would appear that the idea of earning the odd fee from salvage was not above the company's consideration. The Steam Boat Committee minute books note that on 27th/28th December, 1900 Spanish steamer *Enecori* drove onto Portland breakwater during a gale and steam was raised on *Lynx* with a view to salvage, but unfortunately before she could be reached the vessel heeled over and sank.

Apart from the normal wear, tear, and corrosion that any ship suffers, the lightweight construction of the trio was starting to show. In 1901 it was reported that all three vessels required renewal of boiler room floor frames, as the originals were of a flimsy nature. During 1905 several of *Gazelle's* frames and reverse bars were found to be corroded and essential repairs were required to

Lynx entering Weymouth Harbour during 1895, flying from the fore mast the ship's name pennant, the GWR house flag from the aft mast, and the Red Ensign from the stern. When built she was considered one of the finest cross-channel boats afloat, but by 1895, only seven-years-old, she was already outclassed by *Ibex*, and two years later totally eclipsed by *Roebuck* and *Reindeer*, such was the progress in ship design. *SE&CR Society*

The *Antelope* departing from Plymouth for Brest on 27th July, 1907. *R.C. Clammer Collection*

One of the 'Lynx' class boats off the beach at Looe whilst operating an excursion from Plymouth.
Allan Kitteridge Collection

One of the 'Lynx' class boats on the River Fowey with Polruan in the background whilst operating a cruise from Plymouth. *Allan Kitteridge Collection*

Gazelle goes astern into Weymouth Harbour. A railway container lies above the aft hold, whilst other cargo sheeted-over with tarpaulins can be clearly seen under the lifeboats lying on the promenade deck. *(Both) The late E. Latcham Collection*

the boilers. In fact the 'Purves' type furnaces fitted to all the vessels as built had caused trouble. In 1903 the *Antelope* developed a crack in the port forward furnace. This being replaced by one of the 'Fox's' corrugated type, as were the other two 'Purves' furnaces remaining in the vessel.

The introduction of the joint service with the LSWR in 1901 caused a reduction in the number of ships required to operate the winter service, to some extent making the three original vessels surplus to requirements, although, being more economical than the *Ibex, Roebuck,* or *Reindeer,* they continued to operate the winter service until 1903, after which they concentrated on the conveyance of the seasonal fruit and flower traffic except when required for relief duties.

At the time the GWR was expanding the liner trade at Plymouth, where passengers, their luggage and the mails had to be brought ashore from Plymouth Sound by tender. To supplement the elderly small tenders previously used the *Gazelle* was employed for the purpose during 1900. To enable her to embark passengers from the side doors of liners her forward lifeboats were removed from her boat deck and portable gangways were carried. The *Lynx* served at Plymouth the following year, and from 1903 the *Antelope* virtually became a Plymouth-based vessel putting in few appearances at Weymouth. When not employed on tendering work the vessels would operate short excursions to Looe, Fowey and Falmouth during the summer season, but they would appear on the Weymouth-Channel Islands service if required. The GWR were always looking for new trade and during 1906 *Lynx* and *Antelope* were chartered to a French strawberry growers' association to convey their produce from Plougastel (near Brest) to Plymouth, the season lasting about six weeks from the middle of May. The vessels were hired out at £360 per month, the charterers paying coal and port charges, this contract being retained for several seasons. In the July and August of 1906 *Lynx* was chartered by a Jersey syndicate operating cruises around the island and excursions to Sark and France. A totally unexpected contract occurred in March 1907, following the grounding of the White Star liner *Suevic* off the Lizard, *Antelope* being employed in landing passengers' baggage and the removal of much cargo from the stranded vessel, and later carrying workmen and the equipment required for the salvage of the aft section.

At Weymouth the Channel Islands fruit traffic was growing yearly - so much so that it required both the existing fleet and chartered vessels to handle it. It was decided that one of the 'Lynx' class vessels be converted into a cargo boat. The *Gazelle* duly arrived at Messrs Cammell Laird in February 1908 for conversion, the saloon and most of the passenger accommodation being removed at a cost of £4,900. Alterations were completed by May, when *Gazelle* returned to Weymouth for the summer season.

Although the Plymouth-Brest service had operated originally as a charter, from July 1908 it became a regular service run by the GWR - usually by the *Lynx* or *Antelope*. In July 1910 the Weymouth-Nantes service was transferred to Plymouth, a summer move to relieve congestion at Weymouth. The ponderous *Melmore* made a few crossings from Plymouth, but the work was usually undertaken by *Lynx* or *Antelope*. However, the ending of the French services the

Lynx serving as *HMS Lynn* at anchor off Mudros in the Aegean Sea. *Imperial War Museum*

The *Gazelle* on war service in the Mediterranean, the gallows used for minesweeping fitted over the stern. A crows nest for the look-out on the fore mast and the overall grey paint portrays the seriousness of the situation. *Imperial War Museum*

following year again left the *Antelope* and *Gazelle* without employment. *Gazelle* was sent to H. & C. Grayson of Liverpool towards the end of 1911 for conversion into a cargo boat, but problems were encountered which doubled the estimated cost of the work to £13,112, added to which the replacement of the two boilers by Rollo & Son cost a further £2,000, before the vessel returned to Weymouth in March 1912.

The *Antelope* found employment on charter during the 1912 season, shipping French strawberries from Plougastel to Plymouth, after which she became a spare vessel. In November brokers acting for foreign buyers approached the GWR who offered to sell her for £7,000 but the asking price was too high - although in August 1913 she was sold to a Greek company, Navigation à Vapeur Ionienne, for £4,500 and renamed *Atromitos* with Yannoulatos Bros as managers. In 1929 the owners were restyled as Hellenic Coast Lines, the *Atromitos* being broken up in Italy during 1933.

Following the outbreak of war the two remaining sisters *Lynx* and *Gazelle* were requisitioned by the Admiralty on 22nd October, 1914, and two days later Great Western crews delivered them to ship repairers at Millwall, on the Thames, where both were converted into minesweepers. Commissioned into the Royal Navy as HMS *Lynn* and HMS *Gazelle* they departed from Millwall for Portsmouth on 1st December.

Unfortunately warships did not maintain war diaries, so only the logbooks of *Gazelle* survive to give an outline of her wartime activities. Early in December both *Gazelle* and *Lynn* were carrying out minesweeping trials in the Solent, where on the 8th they collided with each other, resulting in *Gazelle* entering dry-dock. Following repairs and gunnery practice *Gazelle* sailed from Portsmouth on 22nd December calling in at Portland, Devonport, Falmouth, Pembroke Dock and Fishguard, where she arrived on the 30th. The following day in company with *Lynn, Gazelle* proceeded to Holyhead, and by 12th January, 1915 she had reached Longhope, Scapa Flow.

Arriving at Gibraltar on 2nd April *Gazelle* took on coal before sailing the same day for Malta, where she moored alongside *HMS Clacton* on 6th April. Although both *Gazelle* and *Lynn* were fitted out as a minesweepers their reasonably high turn of speed - 16 knots - made them more valuable for other duties. Minesweeping could be undertaken by fairly slow vessels. It appears *Gazelle* was used as a stores transport and patrol boat between Mudros and Kos Island, and other places in the Aegean Sea. These activities resulted in an incident on 21st May; whilst investigating a schooner snipers opened fire, whereupon she steamed out of range and employed her 12 lb. gun. The ship's log refers to workmen at Mudros being engaged in extending the mine platform on 25th May and the following day the crew were loading mines whilst workmen were putting up protection for mine laying. There were references the following month to mine laying, patrol and examination work. On 6th and 7th July *Gazelle* was patrolling the Meylini Channel, and on 16th she was fired upon by snipers in the Gulf of Gal-Baghehe. The following day she delivered a torpedo to *Ben-My-Chree* (an exceptionally fast (24½ knots) steamer from the IOM Steam Packet Company's fleet, requisitioned by the Admiralty in 1915 as a seaplane carrier), and the latter part of the month was occupied with mine laying, whilst checking Greek ships was undertaken during August. This general type of duty interspersed with other work - including the mail run - continued well into 1917, when on 17th June the ship's log notes that the vessel carried the Japanese Naval Attaché and five ratings as passengers.

Back at Malta that August she escorted a convoy on the 8th before returning to the dockyard for a refit on the 14th. After trials she sailed to Suda in convoy on 18th October. The following day whilst astern of the convoy at 10.40 pm, the *Eliston* was torpedoed, the *Gazelle* later putting shots into the vessel as she became a hazard to navigation. On 13th December *Gazelle* was involved in searching for a seaplane, which she found at 2 am, and towed the plane to Suda - arriving there 11¾ hours later.

Both *Gazelle* and *Lynn* served for the remainder of the war in the Mediterranean area, but the oft repeated story of *Lynn* stopping and arresting her old sister ship *Antelope* (*Atromitos*) was dismissed as untrue by Captain H. Bond who had commanded *Lynn* during the war.

In May 1919 the GWR applied to the Admiralty for the return of the two ships. In July *Gazelle* arrived at Devonport, and by October it was reported that both vessels were under refit in the dockyard. During reconditioning it was discovered that the boilers in *Gazelle* were beyond economic repair, two second-hand boilers being obtained and fitted. *Lynx* returned to Weymouth on 10th March, 1920, *Gazelle* arriving on 12th April. Returning to the Channel Islands service they continued to handle the majority of cargo traffic. *Lynx* grounded on the Mixen outside Weymouth Harbour on 16th July, 1923, being pulled clear by Messrs Cosens PS *Albert Victor*. The reason given for this unfortunate incident was that as her forward winch was away for repair, she had swung outside the harbour. On 31st December, 1924, whilst on passage between Jersey and Guernsey during a severe gale, mountainous seas swept over her and smashed in the front of the wheelhouse, damaging the compass and steering wheel and also causing damage to the bridge rails.

With the two new cargo boats nearing completion, *Gazelle* and *Lynx* were offered for sale, but the best price the company's brokers could offer was £2,960 each, less commission. Within a month the offer had dropped to £4,800 for both vessels, less £120 commission! *Lynx* made her final crossing from Weymouth to Jersey on 16th March, 1925, and after discharging her cargo she sailed direct to Plymouth where she laid up. *Gazelle* laid up at Weymouth at the end of March, sailing for Plymouth on 17th April. The Alloa Ship Breaking Company Ltd purchased both vessels for £2,500 each from the brokers in May. *Lynx* arrived at Charlestown on the Firth of Forth on 15th June and demolition commenced 10 days later, whilst *Gazelle* arrived on the Forth on 29th June with demolition commencing on 8th August. By the end of 1925 the two vessels had passed into history.

Ibex

Of the first generation of GWR cross-channel steamers, *Ibex* was the most popular and best-remembered vessel. Ordered in August 1890 from Laird's of Birkenhead, she cost £57,000. She was not launched until 6th June, 1891, there being some delay in obtaining steel plate because of industrial unrest in the steel industry.

The completed vessel underwent trials on 24th August, an average speed of 19.17 knots being achieved. At the end of August she was delivered to Milford and immediately sent to Jersey and Guernsey for inspection by invited members of the public. Departing from Guernsey on 7th September, she made the crossing in a new record time of 3 hours 35 minutes - which must have impressed the officials of the company headed by Deputy Chairman Viscount Emlyn and his invited guests. As *Ibex* steamed into Weymouth Harbour the 'Season Band' played 'Rule Britannia' and 'God Save the Queen', after which she was again open to inspection by ticket holders. She made her maiden voyage to the Channel Islands on Wednesday 9th September, 1891.

In general the *Ibex* was an improvement on the 'Lynx' class. The steel hull, 256 ft long, was divided into 10 watertight compartments, with a beam of 32 ft 6 in., draught of 14 ft 2 in., and a gross tonnage of 1,160. The propelling machinery consisted of two sets of triple-expansion engines. The high pressure cylinder was 22 in. in diameter, the intermediate of 34 in. diameter and the low pressure 51 in., the piston stroke being 33 in., developing 282 nhp. Steam was supplied by two double-ended return tube boilers, each with six furnaces. The boilers were placed side by side and forced draught was maintained by the enclosed stokehold system. An auxiliary boiler was provided, capable of providing steam to the fan engines, electric light dynamo engine and winches. The two three-bladed propellers were 10 ft in diameter. The Great Western themselves fitted the electric light installation, there being 196 lights throughout the ship. DC current was supplied at 80 volts from a dynamo room placed amidships.

The first class accommodation, placed forward of the boilers and engines, consisted of a ladies' deck saloon, ordinary deck saloon, and smoke room. On the lower deck beneath the grand saloon, which extended the full width of the vessel, were situated both the gentlemen's and ladies' sleeping cabins, each approached by separate stairways. The second class accommodation in the poop was of a far higher standard than usual, there being private cabins, ladies' private retiring rooms, and a ladies' sleeping saloon, plus a spacious general saloon, below which was situated the gentlemen's sleeping saloon. The entire ship was heated by steam. When built the vessel carried a certificate for 600 passengers, full sleeping accommodation being provided for 210 of which 140 were for first class. Crew accommodation was forward. Two large holds, one forward and one aft, were fitted with shelves for the carriage of fruit and vegetables, and originally five lifeboats were carried.

All went well; good time keeping, reliability and comfort were her hallmarks until confidence was shaken on Good Friday 4th April, 1897 when an 'accident waiting to happen' took place. Being the Easter weekend both the Weymouth and Southampton boat trains arrived late owing to a congested railway system,

Above: *Ibex* beached in St Aubin's Bay, Jersey on 4th April, 1897 following her striking Noirmontaise Rock. Clearly shown is the port side propeller shaft with all four blades missing. *Below:* Workmen prepare to construct a cement box to cover a hole in the starboard side below the bilge keel before the vessel was towed to Barrow for repairs. *(Both) Author's Collection*

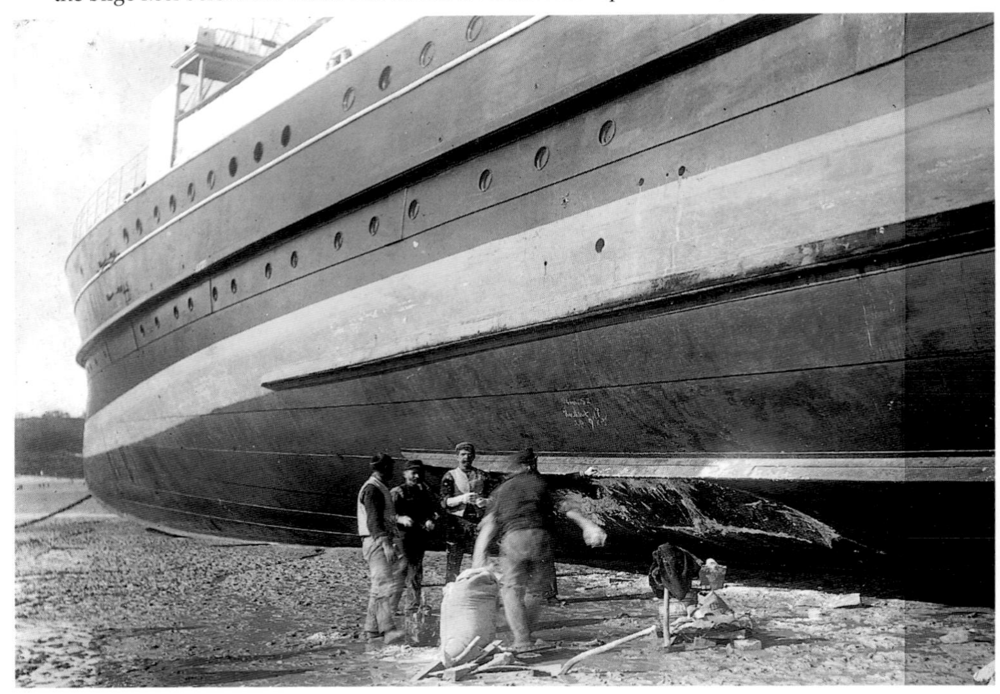

this having a knock-on effect to the ships of both companies. Departing Weymouth at 2.55 am, 45 minutes late, *Ibex* arrived at Guernsey at 7.32 am and quickly discharged and embarked passengers and some cargo. At 8.05 am she was on her way, heading for Jersey. The LSWR steamer *Frederica* departed 10 minutes later. Both ships had to arrive at St Helier before 9.45 am after which time there would not be enough water, but as only one vessel could enter harbour at a time and swing round with the falling tide, the other would have to anchor outside for five hours!

Both vessels proceeded at full speed of around 19 knots, *Frederica* being slightly faster gradually gaining ground and coming up on the port quarter of the *Ibex,* both captains having decided to take the short cut between the headland at La Corbière and the Noirmontaise rock (which was submerged at high water) to save both time and the strength of the tide. Having set his course aboard *Ibex,* Captain John Le Feuvre noticed *Frederica* closing on his port quarter and gradually overtaking, although she was about 450 feet distant, having just turned slightly to port. Fearing a collision he turned to starboard - and immediately *Ibex* struck the submerged Noirmontaise. With water entering the vessel, she was steamed towards Portelet Bay escorted by the *Frederica.* The fore saloon quickly filled with water, the occupants having to make a speedy departure wearing only their night clothes, whilst water rising in the stokehold drowned the centre fires of the boilers before the vessel reached the beach. When she did so there was five feet of water in the boiler room. The 261 passengers were put ashore in the ship's lifeboats and those of the *Frederica.* Assisted ashore by local fishermen, groups of passengers then made their way over the hill to St Aubin's station and completed their journey in special trains provided by the Jersey Railway to St Helier. The passengers' luggage was then taken ashore in the boats, whilst the mail was transferred to a tug.

On the high tide of Friday evening *Ibex* refloated and the Guernsey tug *Assistance* attempted to tow her towards St Helier, but the tow line parted several times and the strength of the current proved too much for the tug. In deteriorating weather conditions the tow again parted and, drifting westwards towards the Corbière the anchor was lowered. With both boiler room and fore saloon flooded *Ibex* rode out a rough night which said much for her construction. Early on the Saturday morning, towed by the *Gazelle* and steered by the *Assistance,* she was brought into St Aubin's Bay and beached. The extent of her damage was then visible. All the blades of the port propeller and three of the starboard propeller were broken off, and there was a 13 ft gash torn in her bottom which opened up two compartments. Workmen were brought over from the mainland and the Plymouth tender *Sir Francis Drake* arrived. At low tide on Sunday the leak was plugged and during the evening when the tide rose, with the *Assistance* towing, *Sir Francis Drake* supporting her starboard side, and *Gazelle* astern to assist steering, *Ibex* was moved into St Helier harbour where the undamaged cargo was removed. Following further patching to her hull *Ibex* was towed to Barrow where repairs costing £2,202 were carried out, whilst 48 claims for loss and damage to luggage and personal injury cost a further £897 8*s*. 4*d*.

The Board of Trade inquiry placed the blame fully on the master who, having set too fine a course to pass inside the Noirmontaise, ported his helm in immediate proximity to the Noirmontaise Rock, which he would otherwise have cleared. According to eye witness accounts quoted in the press at the time passengers on both vessels were watching progress and taking a keen interest in what appeared to be a race; indeed, if not being intent on arriving ahead of the other vessel is not a race, what is? In any case Captain Le Feuvre had his master's certificate suspended for six months.

Racing was of course officially denied by all parties, but the final paragraph of the official report makes interesting reading:

> It so seldom happens that the two vessels reach St Helier practically together that the court sees no reason for suggesting any alteration in their times of starting from Southampton and Weymouth, and considers that the occasions when the first vessel arriving at St Helier prevents the later one from being berthed are so rare, that the semblance of racing with the object of first arrival is practically inappreciable. The difficulties and inconvenience for delivery of the Government mails and conveyance of passengers, if the times of starting the vessels from Southampton to Weymouth were made to depend on the tide at St Helier, appear to be so great that the court does not think that it would be advisable to make any alteration, especially as the depth of water in the harbour at St Helier is being increased by dredging.

With *Ibex* returned to service and the pooling agreement in operation following the *Stella* disaster, the most serious accident to befall a Great Western ship on the Channel Islands service took place on 5th January, 1900. *Ibex,* under the command of Captain Thomas Baudains, had left Weymouth at approximately 2.30 am with 42 passengers and 31 crew and having a clear passage was approaching Guernsey and entering the Little Russel Channel heading for St Peter Port at about 6.20 am. Baudains decided to check his course from the Casquets light, which lay astern, instead of by the leading lights for the Little Russel. Owing to the obstruction of the wheelhouse and funnels the ship was turned to port to allow the Casquets light to be seen, and once the bearing had been taken the quartermaster returned to the original course. Unfortunately it appears that the vessel then went too far to starboard, but when the Master ordered the vessel turned to port to correct the course it failed to answer to the helm immediately. In the confusion the St Peter Port lights went out of view and the ship struck the submerged Fougere Rock. She immediately bounced off the rock, and owing to the inrush of water through the torn starboard side the captain decided to head for Herm where there was a convenient spot to beach the vessel. However, as water entered and flooded the boiler room causing falling steam pressure, an attempt was made to reach Guernsey. About 2¾ miles north of St Peter Port near the Gant Rock the stricken vessel turned a half circle to starboard, and with her bows facing north-east, sank on an even keel.

After the lifeboats pulled away seaman Randell was seen clinging to the flagpole at the stern of the vessel. One of the boats returned to his assistance, but being unable to swim and frightened he would not jump, and eventually owing to the risk of the boat being dashed against the sinking ship by the swell or dragged down in the vortex when the ship sank, it was forced to pull away. Two of the lifeboats proceeded to St Sampson's, the other to St Peter Port. The actions of the officers and crew came in for much praise from the passengers -

especially one of the two stewardesses, Miss Lowman, who was later presented with a gold watch subscribed to by the grateful passengers.

Later a letter appeared in the *Guernsey Evening Press* from a passenger, calling attention to problems in launching the lifeboats, and complaining,

> . . . of the delay and difficulty which occurred for a quarter of an hour before they could be moved. I have always heard that a boat could be lowered into the water on any Atlantic liner in less than five minutes. Another point - surely each boat has or should have, its appointed officer in command. Then how come it that one of the starboard boats was forced, through having no officer in command to navigate, to make a long row of what was well over an hour to St Peter Port Harbour, with women and children on board suffering bitterly from the cold. When this same boat was got over the side of the ship it swung helplessly in the air for some time, and twice crashed into the *Ibex* with such force that everyone thought it would stove in. I might mention that at this time all the other boats were well clear, and even then we could not get free as the ropes refused to run through the blocks and had to be cut at each end with knives before finally we got away.

For one passenger, Mr James of the Vautelets, St Andrews, it was the third time he had been shipwrecked within a year! A survivor from the *Stella* disaster, he was also a passenger on the liner *Paris* when she was wrecked on the Manacles.

The GWR tug/tender *Sir Francis Drake* arrived from Plymouth at 8.45 am on Saturday 6th, with two divers on board. Later in the morning the tug visited the scene of the wreck, although no attempt was made to inspect it. During the afternoon the *Alert* went alongside on the falling tide and salvaged a miscellaneous collection of items including lifebuoys, cushions, tables, and furniture from the deck cabin. Some St Sampson's fishermen recovered one of the lifeboats from its davits that the crew was unable to remove at the time of the sinking.

A gale during the Saturday night caused both the funnels to be carried away, and other items were washed up on Herm. The *Sir Francis Drake* assisted by the local steam launch *Charlotte,* sent a diver down on the 8th who found the doorway of the mailroom obstructed. The German salvage steamer *Neva* arrived on Wednesday 10th, sending divers down to examine the wreck on the 15th, but after seeing the position of the vessel the contractor declined to make a salvage offer and *Neva* departed on other business.

Work continued with the *Sir Francis Drake,* assisted by the *Charlotte,* on the recovery of mail and other items. On 23rd divers discovered a body lying in a bunk in one of the cabins. It was identified as that of George De Ste-Croix of Jersey, a sailor returning on leave from *HMS Excellent.* Having searched what parts of the vessel they could and recovered a majority of the mail. In all 42 mail bags were recovered and, after drying, the letters were delivered, some bearing a hand-stamp indicating that they were from the *Ibex*. The *Sir Francis Drake* returned to Plymouth on Thursday 25th January.

The subsequent Board of Trade inquiry into the sinking took place the following month, Captain Baudains was judged to have navigated his vessel negligently and his master's certificate withdrawn for six months, Captain Baudains resigning from the employment of the GWR.

Ibex lying in the Little Russel Channel within days of her sinking in January 1900. Already the tides have carried her funnels and other deck fittings away. Her lifeboats are being used together with the local steam launch *Charlotte,* to salvage anything possible from the vessel. *J. Attwood Collection*

During January a number of salvage organizations inspected the wreck but showed little interest. In March the North German Salvage Association offered a £15,000 'No cure no pay' Agreement, and preliminary work commenced on 4th May.

The first attempt to raise *Ibex* took place on Monday 9th July, 1900.The tug *Sea Adler* had arrived from Cuxhaven and together with the local vessel *Assistance*-was employed in keeping other vessels at a distance. The tugs *Reiher* and *Mowe* were alongside two hulks, which were placed one each side of the wreck, the cables having been tightened up as the tide fell allowing the wreck to be lifted on the rising tide. Unfortunately although the bows were lifted some 15 feet the stern rose only a small amount, and as there was the risk of the wreck slipping out of the cables as soon as towing commenced the wreck was lowered to the bottom to allow adjustments to be made and await further neap tides.

There was a further attempt to lift *Ibex* on Friday 20th July, but it had to be abandoned. However, at 3 am the following morning preparations were made for another lift which commenced at 7.15 am when the pontoons were pumped out and the *Ibex* started to lift. With the tug *Sea Adler*, the hulk *Arethusa* and pontoon *Nordsee* on her starboard, and the tug *Albatross*, hulk *Friedrich der Grosse* and pontoon *Ostsee* on the port side and the tug *Reiher* on the stern, and the tug *Mowe* at the head, *Ibex*, with the tattered remains of her name pennant flying from her foremast, was slowly moved towards St Peter Port. The harbour entrance was reached at 11.30 am and at 2.30 pm *Ibex* was allowed to lie on the seabed. The lifting hulks and pontoons were adjusted at low water for a further lift on the rising tide the following morning to bring *Ibex* into the harbour, where she remained surrounded by the hulks that lifted her ashore. The Great Western took charge of the vessel and gangs of men were employed to clear away the seaweed and other debris that covered the vessel, whilst divers and workmen made temporary repairs. The full extent of damage to the hull could also be examined. There were two indentations to the starboard side, one 40 ft by 8 ft wide the other 6 ft by 4 ft wide. The bilge keel was torn off for a considerable length and the smashing in of plating and frames very severe. There was also damage to the port side forward, close to the keel, which appeared to have been caused by the point of a rock. Throughout the entire vessel, in the holds, cabins, stokeholds and engine room, there were tons of decomposed matter that had to be removed, as well as the remaining cargo.

A reporter from the *Guernsey Evening Press* described the scene thus:

The appearance of the *Ibex* herself is most weird. Everywhere is seaweed of various kinds, sand and water. The cabins are of course filled with water, even at low tide, but the interior may be seen through such of the ports as were open at the moment the vessel struck the rocks. Through these ports can be seen doorways without doors, water washing quietly in and out of empty bunks, and here and there small articles floating from one side to the other with the wash of the water. On deck the scene is also strange. All doors and windows have been washed away by the strong tide of the Russel, leaving ugly gaping holes. Rails on the deck have been bent and broken, and the force of the water has bent even the strong wheels and blocks over which the rudder chains pass. A rapid transformation is however being effected. Work was first commenced on the bows of the vessel, and here all the seaweed has been scraped away, and the deck washed clear of sand.

On the 27th July the opportunity was taken to move *Ibex* further up harbour to within a few yards of Victoria Pier, and by the 29th sufficient repairs had been carried out to enable her to be moved to St Sampson's. The two pontoons were moved away and the hull, supported by two hulks and two tugs, departed from St Peter Port at 7 pm, with the *Albatross* towing ahead, St Sampson's being reached an hour later. *Ibex* was taken to a spot near the South Quay, and further repairs to make the vessel seaworthy were carried out, the smaller holes being repaired with steel plates. The main hole was patched with timber secured with steel plates all riveted and further secured with steel bands - much of which was prepared beforehand and fitted into numbered positions. Four vertical boilers were installed in the well between the boat and after decks to power steam pumps should the need arise. A long narrow funnel was erected where once one of the main funnels stood and the donkey boiler had been brought back into use to operate the vessel's own pumps to assist with keeping the water level down, and her steam winches were put into working order. On 11th August advantage was taken of the spring tide to move *Ibex* about 200 ft towards the quay at Crocq, after which a long gangway was erected to the bows of the ship alleviating the necessity of using boats to reach her. The *Guernsey Evening Press* reported on 29th August that the hull of *Ibex* was being painted and that workmen were working by night with lamps to complete work on the vessel.

The propellers had been unshipped, the anchors swung into position and the lifeboats returned to their davits. A skeleton crew came from St Sampson's under the command of Captain Burnand and also aboard were Captain Hemming, the deputy marine superintendent of the GWR, and Mr Harris, the chief engineer of the company, along with several boiler makers and mechanics. It has to be assumed some form of accommodation was provided for the 500 mile voyage! With the temporary funnel painted red and flags flying from the foremast *Ibex* left St Sampson's at 6 pm on Sunday 9th September for Birkenhead towed by two German salvage tugs, *Sea Adler* and *Albatross*. She arrived in the Mersey at 11.25 pm on the 12th, having travelled at an average speed of 8 knots.

Work was immediately put in hand and the refurbished vessel was floated out of dry dock early in March 1901. There has always been contention that the cost of the extensive refitting of the vessel was high compared with the construction of a new ship. Laird's original estimate had been between £20,000 and £22,000; however, the final bill came to £32,000, as extra work included a new propeller shaft, and rudder stem, and new frames under the boilers. The third class

Above: Safely beached alongside Victoria Pier, St Peter Port, in July 1900, *Ibex* is still surrounded by lifting hulks with the tugs *Mowe* and *Reiher* at her fore end. *Below:* Viewed along the remains of the starboard boat deck, showing the destruction wreaked by six months' subjection to the tides and weather of the Little Russel Channel. Much of the woodwork has disappeared, as have ventilators, the two funnels and many deck fittings. *(Both) J. Attwood Collection*

Ibex in St Sampson's Harbour at low water. The propellers have been removed and the ship prepared for the tow to Birkenhead. One of the temporary vertical boilers for working pumps and other equipment can be seen in the well between the promenade and the poop deck.
J. Attwood Collection

Afloat and equipped for the tow to Birkenhead and with flags flying *Ibex* prepares for the journey.
The late E. Latcham Collection

With the tug *Albatross* on her starboard side and *Sea Adler* on her port side *Ibex* is guided out of St Sampson's, Guernsey, on 9th September, 1900 at the beginning of the three day tow to Birkenhead and restoration for 25 further years of service. For the GWR her salvage had been a very expensive affair. *J. Attwood Collection*

A view of *Ibex* after her return to service during 1901, alongside the landing stage at Weymouth. A coal barge is alongside and a boat train stands in the platform. A local tug heads out of harbour, whilst the sweep of buildings on Weymouth Esplanade form a backdrop. *Author's Collection*

accommodation was also altered, reducing her net tonnage by 77, thus saving the company £6 5*s*. 11*d*. in harbour dues each trip! The refit was completed on 16th March and a trial run made on the Mersey the same day. She proceeded to Milford to load stores before returning to Weymouth where she replaced the *Roebuck* on the evening run on 24th March, 1901. It was indeed a miracle that the *Ibex* returned at all, certainly under her original name. At an earlier Board meeting it had been suggested that in view of her unfortunate reputation it was desirable to change her name, *Elk, Fawn, Roe, Eland, Koodoo* and *Moose* having been proposed.

It certainly seemed that the *Ibex* was dogged with bad luck, for on Wednesday 16th August, 1911 she departed from Weymouth at 1.40 pm with about 100 passengers and cargo for the Channel Islands, and on passing the Shambles Lightship the low pressure cylinder cover of her starboard engine smashed - luckily without causing injury to the engine room staff. Signals were sent to the Grove Point signal station and Cosens' paddle tug *Helper* was dispatched to assist *Ibex* back to Weymouth slowly using her port engine only.

Fate again struck in the early hours of Wednesday 18th April, 1914. Under the command of Captain Vine, she had just departed from Weymouth when she collided with the three-masted schooner *Hannah Croasdell* which was sheltering from a westerly gale under the east side of Portland. The wooden vessel had her bows smashed in, but fortunately the damage was above the waterline. The *Ibex* stood by until the Portland tug *Petrel* arrived to tow the schooner into Weymouth Harbour.

The outbreak of World War I soon left *Ibex* as the only vessel available to maintain the service. Following a refit at Plymouth in November 1916, during which she was fitted with a 12 lb. gun for defence, the Admiralty withdrew the embargo on daylight sailings. She returned to service on 28th November. Two days later, on 30th, whilst on passage from Guernsey to Weymouth she was chased by a U boat, but her superior speed allowed her to escape. The shortage of vessels was a problem for two weeks at the end of February 1917 whilst *Ibex* was laid up for maintenance, the passenger service having to be suspended.

The U boat menace was never far away, and in March 1917 - whilst on passage to Guernsey - *Ibex* narrowly missed being torpedoed. From 25th May, 1917 the Admiralty insisted that all Weymouth sailings be made at night. On the night of 18th April, 1918 she encountered a U boat on the surface. The crew of *Ibex* opened fire with their gun, hitting the hull of the submarine which then submerged, although it was considered to have been sunk, the Admiralty awarding £500 for distribution between the officers and crew in appreciation.

The luck of the *Ibex* again ran out on 19th September, 1917 when on voyage between Guernsey and Weymouth and about 20 miles south of Portland Bill, *Ibex* ran into the coaster *Aletta,* also on voyage from Weymouth to Guernsey. To add insult to injury this vessel was on charter to the GWR to assist *Ibex*. The *Aletta* quickly sank, her crew boarding the *Ibex* which had sustained some damage including damaged belting and two dented plates above the waterline. The starboard lifeboat was badly damaged, and the port side one lost, a second-hand one being later purchased as a replacement.

In the spring of 1918 *Ibex* was requisitioned at short notice to serve as a troopship between Dover and Calais, and again between 17th and 30th January,

Ibex approaching the landing stage at Weymouth, photographed just before World War I. The funnels were fitted with the cowl-type tops at that period. *The late E. Latcham Collection*

1919 she was employed as a troop transport between Le Havre and Weymouth, before sailing to Plymouth for overhaul. Upon return she was again employed as a troop transport from 25th March to 5th April.

With the loss of *Roebuck,* the *Ibex* together with *Reindeer* were the principal passenger vessels covering the service. During a refit at Liverpool in 1922 her shelter deck was extended by 50 ft.

With the impending arrival of new vessels, *Ibex* made her last sailing from the Channel Islands on Tuesday 14th April, 1925. A crowd gathered on the quay at St Helier to watch the final departure of the vessel which had for many months of the war saved the Islands from complete isolation from England. Before her departure the St Helier Harbour Master, Captain F.J. Renouf (who had been her first captain), placed a wreath on board. The final voyage was under the command of another Jerseyman, Captain Charles Langdon.

After removal of stores at Weymouth, *Ibex* retired to lay in the Cove. At 11.40 am on Thursday 7th May she sailed from Weymouth for the very last time. Despite her early accidents no other vessel could approach the *Ibex* for an eventful, useful and loyal career. To many watching her departure the Channel Islands service without her was almost unthinkable. Steaming down harbour she sounded her siren many times, and as she disappeared around the Nothe her successor, *St Julien,* gave a farewell blast on her siren. Following lay-up at Plymouth she was sold for £4,750, sailing under her own steam to arrive at Sharpness on the River Severn on 30th November, 1925, having been purchased by schooner owner Capt. Cotlow, who had started to dismantle vessels at Sharpness at that period. Of the three large vessels that were dismantled, the gunboat *Tribune,* the *Jujurat* and the *Ibex,* the latter was the largest to be broken up at this small Gloucestershire port. She was stripped to the waterline on the foreshore behind North Pier, where a railway line was laid down to assist with the work, and many local men were employed for several years cutting up and removing the scrap. Thus ends the story of one of the most interesting vessels ever to have operated the cross-channel service.

In the evening of her life *Ibex* departs from Weymouth heading for the Channel Islands, which she had served with distinction during World War I - much of the time alone - being the only link with the mainland. Despite the problems in her early years, she had been reliable and many mourned her passing. *(Both) The late E. Latcham Collection*

Roebuck and Reindeer

To operate the new daylight service commencing in the summer of 1897, two vessels, both larger and faster than the *Ibex*, were ordered from the Naval Construction & Armaments Company of Barrow-in-Furness (later Vickers Armstrong) at a cost of £110,000 as yard Nos. 256 & 257.

Constructed with steel hulls 280 ft in length with a beam of 34 ft 5 in. and draft of 16 ft 8 in., and a gross tonnage of 1,281, both ships were powered by two sets of vertical triple expansion engines constructed by the builders, inclined inwards to reduce engine room height. Developing 900 nhp and giving a speed of 20 knots, the diameter of the cylinders were 23 in., 36 in. and 56 in. and the stroke was 33 in. The high-pressure and intermediate-pressure cylinders had separate cast-iron liners and were worked by piston valves whilst double-ported flat valves operated the low-pressure cylinders. The valves were worked by double eccentric 'Stephenson'-type link motion, the reversing engines being of the direct-acting steam and hydraulic type. Each engine had an air pump of 20 in. diameter and 16½ in. stroke worked by levers from the high-pressure cylinder crosshead, whilst the two condensers had centrifugal circulating pumps each driven by an independent steam engine. Other fittings included two Weirs boiler feed pumps complete with filters and feed water heater, a Weirs fire and bilge pump, a sanitary pump, and a duplex pump for bilge and ballast and supply water to the Lees ash ejector. The two propellers were of solid cast manganese bronze, each with four blades.

Placed side by side the two boilers, each 20 ft long and 15 ft 2 in. diameter, were of the Scotch type, having six furnaces in each, three at each end, worked at a pressure of 175 lbs psi. Howden's forced draught system supplied air to the boilers the two fans being driven by independent steam engines. The steam steering engine was situated in the engine room, control being transmitted by chains and rods to the rudder. The entire ship was illuminated by electricity generated by two steam-driven dynamos, two sets of wiring being so arranged that if one failed alternate lights only would be extinguished.

The promenade deck ran the full length of the vessels, and in general the hulls had a sleek appearance, but unfortunately the two funnels were finished with cowl tops, fitted horizontally across the tops and not angled to match the rake of the funnels. Indeed whereas the GWR had perfected the chimneys on its locomotives, on the marine side the good looks were sadly lacking!

The hull was fitted with 10 watertight bulkheads and three complete decks, lower, main, and promenade, the latter extending fore and aft, except for the well aft in connection with the cargo hatch. At that point there were cargo-gangway doors in the vessel's side, which were hinged in the upper part, but the lower sections were sliding so they could be kept shut until the vessel was alongside the wharf.

The six lifeboats - three each side - were carried in davits above the promenade deck, on which was the ladies' sitting room, smoking room, and the first class entrance with a broad staircase to the dining saloon and ladies' retiring room on the main deck, and to the state rooms, gentlemen's and ladies' sleeping cabins on the lower deck. The first class accommodation was amidships forward of the boiler rooms, berths being provided for 150 passengers. The dining room ran the full width of the ship and was capable of seating 50 passengers comfortably. The saloon was lighted by large portholes and a large domed skylight which rose in the centre to the top of the promenade deck house, this being decorated by stained glass and surrounded by electric lights. The furniture was finished in walnut and upholstered in green velvet, whilst the sides of the saloon were covered in Japanese wallpaper and decorated with mirrors and photochromes. The ceiling was panelled in white relieved with gold.

The first class entrance and smoking room were upholstered in dark green leather, the sides being in mahogany with Chippendale panels. The staterooms were of oak and mahogany, the ladies' and gentlemen's sleeping apartments were panelled in satinwood with rosewood mouldings, and the ladies' sleeping cabin and retiring rooms were upholstered in peacock blue with gold relief. Sleeping accommodation was provided for 76 second-class passengers on the main and lower decks, provision being made for 30 people to dine at once. The lower deck was reserved for the ladies' sleeping cabin, whilst the dining saloon, ladies retiring-room, pantry and toilets were situated on the main deck, as were most of the officer's quarters. The engineers and captain were accommodated on the boat deck, with the chief officer on the promenade deck. Petty officers were accommodated in separate cabins on the main deck forward whilst the crew were berthed on the lower deck forward. The accommodation throughout was heated by steam and ventilation was provided by trunking under the decks with branches into cabins at floor level, with ventilators being provided in the ceilings. Electric bells were provided for communication with stewards.

The first of the sisters to be launched was *Roebuck* on 6th March, 1897, the launching being performed by Mrs Bryce, wife of Mr J. Annan Bryce, one of the Directors of the Naval Construction & Armaments Company. At the after-launch luncheon Mr A. Adamson, Managing Director of the company said 'I hope the successful way in which the new ship has taken the water will be a happy augury of her future success', then proposed a toast: 'Success to the *Roebuck*'. Following fitting out, her speed trials took place on the Clyde and on four runs between The Cloch and Cumbrae Lights she averaged a speed of 20.217 knots.

Following her acceptance trials on 1st June she proceeded to Weymouth, her first duty being to convey the GWR Directors and other officials to the Naval Review at Spithead on 25th June. Her first voyage to the Channel Islands was on 1st July when the new daylight service started. Leaving Weymouth Quay 10 minutes late at 1.40 pm she arrived in Guernsey at 4.56 pm, departing again at 5.28 pm, and arriving in Jersey at 6.43 pm, clipping 17 minutes off the booked time to create a new record! Unfortunately for *Roebuck* success was always overtaken by fate! On 10th July she suffered a fractured steam pipe and had to proceed to Milford for repairs, not returning to Weymouth until 23rd August. In the meantime *Reindeer* had arrived from the builders. On Bank Holiday Monday 2nd August, 1897 she carried returning day excursion passengers from Guernsey to Jersey, the following day commencing her regular service with the morning sailing from Jersey/Guernsey to Weymouth. A month later, on 3rd

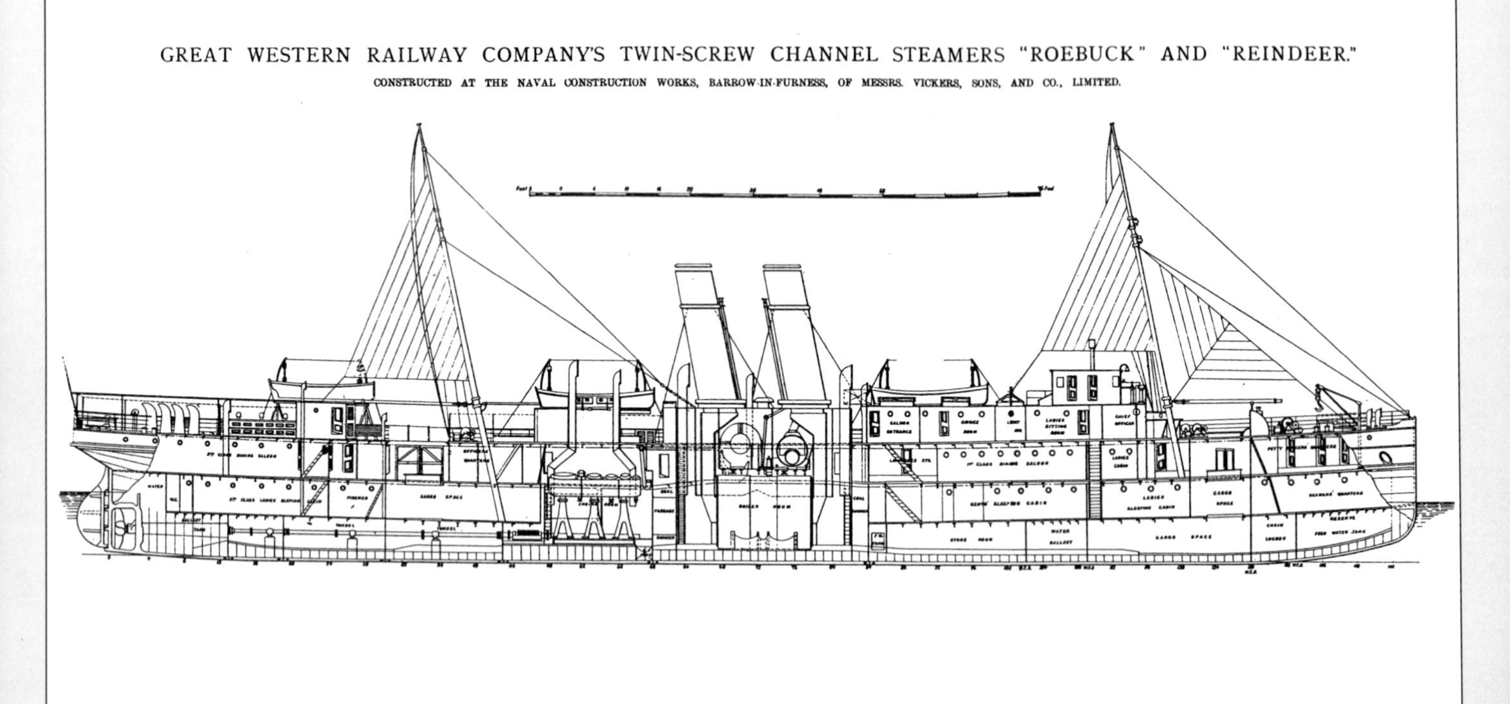

Builder's drawing of the *Roebuck*/*Reindeer* at the time of their construction. *Engineering*

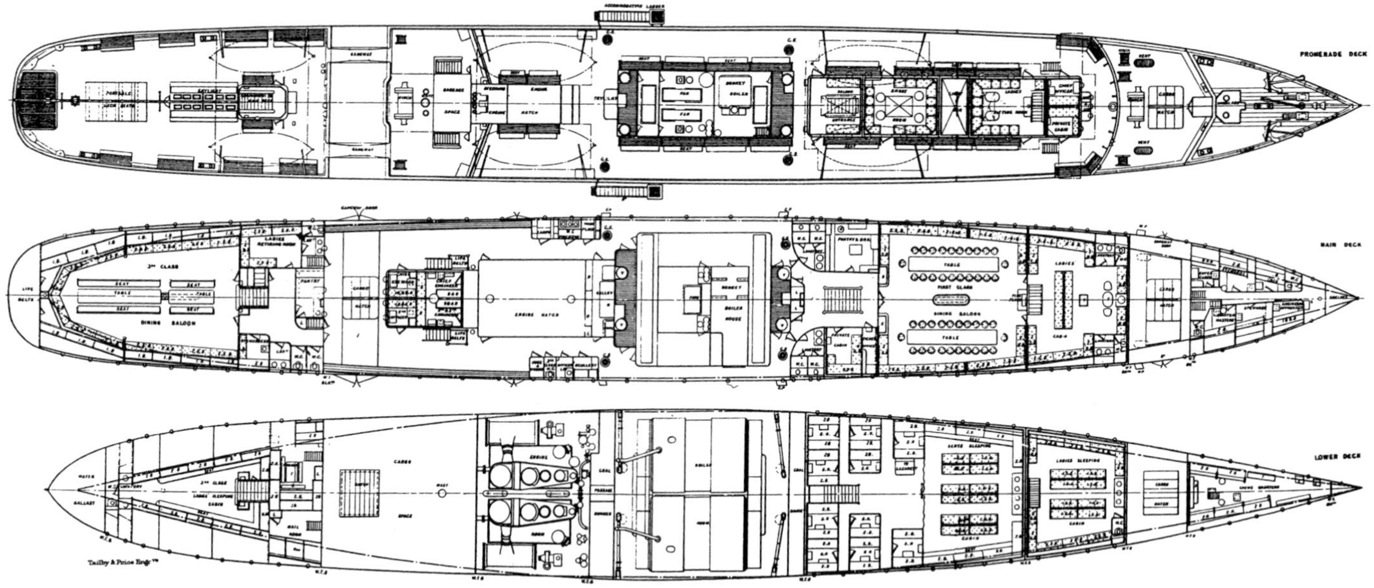

Builder's drawing of the *Roebuck/Reindeer* at the time of their construction. *Engineering*

Above: A pre-1914 view of *Roebuck* entering Weymouth Harbour. The funnels at this period had the tops angled to the horizontal, which detracted from the otherwise graceful outlines of the vessel. *Below:* The starboard side of the vessel viewed from the Pile Pier. Note the anchor chain trailing from the hawse pipe up onto the deck where it was attached to the anchor which had to be man-handled over the side with the assistance of the davit fitted on deck.

The late E. Latcham Collection

September, whilst entering Weymouth Harbour on a low tide, the vessel 'smelling the ground' failed to answer the helm and ran into the paddle steamer *Brodick Castle*, damaging the port side sponson and demolishing the gents' toilet. Luckily a passenger using the facility escaped with severe bruising!

Once working together the sisters were untouchable, being the fastest steamers on the Channel Islands run. Like many lightly constructed vessels with powerful engines they suffered from vibration at speed, this being overcome towards the end of the year when their hulls were strengthened around the amidships area. Their speed brought them to the attention of the Spanish Government who at the time were engaged in the Spanish-American war, and in April 1898 offered to purchase both vessels at valuation plus £30,000, an offer the GWR declined.

Minor mishaps occurred to both vessels during 1900. On 19th July *Reindeer* struck the wall in Guernsey Harbour owing to a misunderstanding between the bridge and the engine room, the vessel having to proceed to Day Summers of Southampton for repairs costing £335, whilst Mr Elliot the engineer lost his £7 10*s*. annual bonus. Captain Breach of *Roebuck* lost his bonus following an incident whilst leaving Guernsey on 19th September when his vessel fouled the anchor of the LSWR vessel *Honfleur*, carrying away five stanchions and rails.

There were also problems with the boilers on *Reindeer*, it being found that six of the 12 furnaces had become distorted by over ⅝ in., and two of the back tube plates were leaking at the riveted joints connecting them to their respective furnace ends. The marine superintendent stated:

> . . . it is impossible to run the *Roebuck* and *Reindeer* at their original speed of 20 knots, as the boilers will not endure the intense heat generated by Howden's system of forced draught, which has been applied to these vessels to obtain that high speed, and, with a view of preventing further trouble, it is recommended that the forced draught pressure be reduced so as to assimilate it to that in use in steamers worked on the closed stoke-hold system. This will reduce their speed to about 17½ knots.

On 23rd March, 1901 whilst on passage from Weymouth to Milford for refit *Roebuck* was in collision with the *Lady Mostyn* 13 miles off the Longships lighthouse. Both vessels were steaming on the same course and running parallel when *Lady Mostyn* sheered towards *Roebuck*. As the rule of the sea is that the overtaking vessel keeps clear, the *Roebuck* was at fault. At the time the captain was taking a meal, the first officer Mr Hughes being on the bridge. Repairs cost the GWR £675. The Directors considered Hughes an unsuitable person to be in charge of one of the company's vessels and he was given a week's notice!

Having high coal consumption, in their early years the sisters operated the Channel Islands service only during the summer months, the off-season sailings being carried out by the *Ibex* and *Lynx* class boats. The winter months were occupied operating either the Plymouth-Brest or the New Milford-Waterford service whilst other vessels were under refit, or they laid up at Milford where special moorings were laid for them in Barn Lake Pill. It was during a winter lay-up at one of the fish jetties at Westfield Pill, on the night of 26th January, 1905 that *Roebuck* caught fire. A steward named Harwood was left in sole charge, but at 7.30 pm he decided to 'nip ashore', returning two hours later to see smoke and flames coming from the saloon. The GWR fire brigade were quickly on the scene and soon had four high pressure hoses at work, their efforts being hampered by the ice lying on the ground that freezing night, and the Royal Naval Dockyard across the Haven sent their fire ship *Alligator* to assist with her powerful pumps. It took three hours to bring the fire under control. The heat had caused the glass in many of the port-holes to break, and the vast amount of water pumped into the vessel to quell the fire caused the vessel to list to port, causing more water to rush in through the broken port-lights. As the tide rose water flowed over the decks and flooded the remainder of the ship, but by good fortune she settled on an even keel. The following day divers commenced the work of sealing the holes in the hull. With the aid of the pumps of *Alligator* and pumps obtained from the Mount Stewart Dry Dock Company at Cardiff *Roebuck* was refloated on 4th February, when the full extent of the fire damage could be seen. It had destroyed the saloon and the 1st class accommodation. After being cleaned out and prepared for sea, *Roebuck* returned to the builder's yard at Barrow, where £11,000 was spent on repairing the interior damage. The following year *Roebuck* returned to South Wales to operate the Fishguard-Rosslare winter service from September.

Fire again struck *Roebuck* on 3rd October, 1910 when in mid-channel whilst inward bound from the Channel Islands, a fire was discovered in the fan room. Speed was reduced and the blaze tackled by the crew who succeeded in quelling the outbreak within 45 minutes, allowing the vessel and her 241 passengers to proceed to Weymouth, where *Roebuck* was taken out of service to allow repairs to be carried out.

Fate again struck on the morning of Wednesday 19th July, 1911. Shortly after leaving St Helier for Weymouth fog descended, and *Roebuck* ran onto the Kaines Reef near the Corbière lighthouse on the south-west coast of Jersey. A majority

Roebuck sunk alongside the fish jetty at Westfield Pill, New Milford, following the fire on 26th January, 1905. She was raised on 4th February, and refitted at a cost of £11,000.

Author's Collection

of the passengers were at breakfast when the vessel struck, the impact throwing plates and crockery from the tables. *Roebuck* had been badly holed, water rapidly flooding the forecastle and the fore hold, the vessel having sunk almost to deck level. The lifeboats were lowered and the 200-odd passengers, with the aid of the pilot vessel and various fishermen who went to the scene, were landed at La Creux Harbour, and later taken to St Helier, being brought back to Weymouth in the early hours of Thursday by the *Reindeer* which made a special journey over for the purpose. The following morning a 500 ft cine-film of the passengers being rescued from the stricken vessel, and other footage taken at various states of the tide during the day, was shown at the Alhambra Cinema.

Roebuck remained firmly wedged between two clusters of rock, and with the massive rise and fall in the tides off the Channel Islands, she was perched high and dry at low water. The Svitzer Salvage Company sent their *Em Z Svitzer* to carry out salvage operations, but several efforts at refloating the vessel failed and a pessimistic view of salvaging *Roebuck* was prophesied. On Friday 28th July a second salvage vessel from Hamburg - the *Albatros,* a powerful tug with extra steam pumps - arrived. Some of the pumps were transferred to the forward part of the *Roebuck,* and as the tide rose the pumps were put to work. With those alongside also pumping, the tugs *Albatros* and *Duke of Normandy* attached towlines whilst the *Sir Redvers Buller* stood by. With the pumps hard at work *Roebuck* lifted with the swell and the salvage vessels moved her off the rocks. With her decks barely above water she was swiftly towed to the safety of St Brelades Bay, and within 40 minutes was beached on the sand. At low water the extent of the damage was revealed! Forty to fifty feet of her port bilge was torn open with another large hole further aft and also one on the starboard side. Later patches were fixed to the hull before moving her into St Helier where further work was carried out. She was towed to Southampton on 29th August, arriving two days later, where repairs were carried out by Harland & Wolff at a cost of £20,000, and *Roebuck* returned to Weymouth in January 1912. During her refit the cowl tops had been removed from her funnels, the *Reindeer* having her's removed the same year.

At the subsequent Board of Trade inquiry it was decided that Captain Le Feuvre had not verified his position off Noirment Point, had set too fine a course and was proceeding too fast in foggy conditions. The court decided that owing to his long record as an unblemished character, his master's certificate be suspended for only three months. However, as he had been the master who put the *Ibex* ashore in 1897, the GWR disposed of his services and granted him an *ex gratia* pension of a guinea a week.

Under the command of Captain Joseph Vine on 6th May, 1913, shortly after leaving Guernsey, *Roebuck* took the schooner *Thetis* - which had lost her sails - in tow back towards the Island and handed her over to a tug.

With the outbreak of World War I both vessels made trips with troops to the Channel Islands, and between Jersey and Le Havre. *Roebuck* made her last trip from the Channel Islands on 30th September, 1914 then, requisitioned for Government service, she was converted into an armed cruiser. Her last visit to the South coast was in November when she was at Portland. Officially renamed HMS *Roedean* on 19th January, 1915, she never sailed under her new name! On 13th January whilst moored in Langhope, Scapa Flow, for boiler cleaning, a severe gale

The extreme tide range of the Channel Islands is clearly demonstrated by these views of the *Roebuck* perched upon the Kaines, off Jersey in July 1911. In the lower photograph the salvage vessel *Em Z Svitzer* stands by the stern of the stricken vessel. *(Both) J. Attwood Collection*

Another picture of the *Roebuck* perched upon the Kaines, off Jersey, in July 1911.
British Railways

The salvage vessel *Em Z Svitzer* prepares to tow the *Roebuck* clear of the Kaines, the vast tidal range making such a salvage possible. *J. Attwood Collection*

Salvage operations on the *Roebuck* in July 1911, with the salvage vessel *Em Z Svitzer* alongside and the States of Jersey tug *Duke of Normandy* and the War Department vessel *Sir Redvers Buller* standing by as *Roebuck* is towed in a waterlogged condition away from the Kaines.

J. Attwood Collection

The tidal range in St Brelades Bay allowed the *Roebuck* to be towed in a sinking condition to this spot near the shore. When the tide had receded onlookers could walk around the vessel with ease.

J. Attwood Collection

Roebuck departing from Weymouth shortly before World War I - an event from which she was never to return. Having survived potential disasters in 1906 and 1911 she met her fate at Scapa Flow in January 1915 before she had chance to confront the enemy.

Author's Collection

developed which resulted in her mooring cable parting. Without power she was driven broadside across the ram bow of the depot ship HMS *Imprerieuse*, and badly holed, she drifted down the side of the depot ship in a sinking condition. Her crew abandoned her before she drifted away and sank in five fathoms of water with her masts still showing, lying 6⅓ cables, 303 degrees from Hackness Martello Tower, her bows facing west, north-west. With the difficulties of war and the lack of salvage vessels it was decided not to raise the wreck, but she was a hazard to vessels approaching the nearby pier. Divers recovered her ammunition, and by October 1915 it was reported that much of her gear had been removed including deck winches. Owing to there being only about 8 ft of water above her wheelhouse her upper-works were demolished to give a greater clearance over her, this being further increased during the 1950s. Her remains still lie on the bottom of that notorious Scottish anchorage. *Roebuck* was the first railway steamer to be lost on war service, and as a result of the GWR rejecting the first compensation offer of £20,712 16*s*. 7*d*. by the Admiralty, following further negotiations it was agreed that after such a loss a competitive tender for a new vessel on the original specification be sought, then depreciation of 4 per cent per year from the date of building be deducted less any large alterations (such as reboilering). These improved terms established a benchmark for later cases.

Reindeer was transferred to Fishguard on 18th August, 1914 to replace a requisitioned steamer on the Rosslare service until she herself was requisitioned on 2nd October, equipped for minesweeping and sent to the Mediterranean. When HMS *Majestic* was torpedoed by U21 off Cape Helles on 27th May, 1915 *Reindeer* stood by and was the last ship to leave before *Majestic* sank. Ten days later whilst acting as a troop transport, *Reindeer* departed from Mudros at 8 pm on June 12th with A and B Companies of the 4th Battalion of the Royal Scots. Two hours later whilst steaming at 17 knots through a calm sea, *Reindeer* ran

Above: *Reindeer* as *HMS Reindeer* lies at Malta Dockyard following her collision with the Great Central Railway's *Immingham* on 12th June, 1916. The damage to the bows is clearly shown. Drab grey has replaced her splendid GWR livery and the trappings of war litter the vessel. A crows nest for the lookout man is fitted up the fore mast. *Below:* Following the reconstruction of her bows *HMS Reindeer* lies at anchor off Mudros. A false bow wave is painted above the water line forward - an idea designed to give the impression of speed and confuse the enemy!

(Both) Imperial War Museum

A stern view giving details of the aft deck of *Reindeer*. The vessel's name and port of registry 'Milford' are picked out in gold whilst in the centre the crest of the Great Western Railway surrounded in decoration, is also picked out in gold. The vessel is laid up in the Cove in Weymouth Harbour. Alongside is Cosens' paddle steamer *Empress* (1879), which, although a much smaller vessel, often undertook day excursions across the channel before World War I.
Author's Collection

Reindeer entering Weymouth Harbour during the 1920s. Note the burning of the funnel paintwork, a sign that the vessel had been steaming hard. *The late E. Latcham Collection*

into the Great Central Railway's *Immingham* (1906) on service as a supply ship. The *Reindeer* became embedded in the side of the *Immingham*, which fortunately only had her crew aboard. They all scrambled aboard *Reindeer*, which managed to free herself before *Immingham* sank, and later the Great Central was awarded £45,000 by the Admiralty for the vessel's loss. *Reindeer* had severely damaged bows and a gash just above the water line, but by moving the troops and their equipment around the ship to trim her she was able to keep afloat, and steaming astern, slowly returned to Mudros Bay where she was vigorously bombed by a hostile aeroplane - which fortunately failed to register a hit. *Reindeer* sailed later to Malta Dockyard for repairs. The new bows fitted allowed the use of stockless anchors, so her anchor crane was removed.

Upon return to England she spent a while as a troop transport between Weymouth and Cherbourg. At the time her funnels were patched as a result of the hard steaming she had undertaken, it being suggested that they should remain as a memento of her war service. However, as this impaired her draughting arrangements the funnels were replaced during a refit by Thornycroft's at Southampton in late 1919. Returning to Weymouth on 30th January, 1920 reconditioning continued, the upholstery being fitted by workmen from the Carriage & Wagon Department at Swindon. She made her first run to the Channel Islands on 8th February, 1920. During a refit at Birkenhead three years later she was fitted with a shelter deck between the bridge and funnels and various interior alterations took place.

It was surprising that *Reindeer* was refitted at all following war service in view of a report by the marine superintendent and consulting marine engineer dealing with the work carried out by the Admiralty on the *Roebuck* and *Reindeer*. It appeared that the alterations were of such an extensive nature, they thought that both boats would not again be able to resume their normal working as passenger vessels on the Channel Islands service.

With the arrival of the new turbine steamers in 1925 *Reindeer* became a relief steamer sailing mainly at weekends. On 18th November, 1925, whilst steaming between Guernsey and Jersey in heavy weather, *Reindeer* took the *SS Corbiere* in tow, that vessel having run short of coal, handing her over to the Jersey States tug once in calm water. A second rescue took place on 19th March, 1926 whilst proceeding to Liverpool for repairs, *Reindeer* picked up three men in a boat, the crew of the ketch *Denbighshire Lass* which had foundered in the vicinity of the Smalls. This voyage was for the purpose of having repairs carried out after striking the pier head at St Helier on 11th March whilst relieving the *St Helier*, which had struck the same pier head the previous day!

On 18th November, 1926 *Reindeer* again went to the assistance of the steamer *Corbiere* which had engine difficulties off Jersey, towing the vessel towards St Helier where a local tug took over. On 4th August, 1927 whilst manoeuvring in Weymouth Harbour she struck the paddle steamer *Empress* causing damage estimated at £138. Chief Officer Bell was considered responsible for the mishap and was retired.

Reindeer, now outclassed by the new vessels, was nearing the end of her days, and on 23rd February, 1928 she left the Channel Islands for the last time, being laid up during that summer. She was later towed to the Briton Ferry breaker's yard of T.W. Ward, arriving on 30th November, 1928, and by April 1929 she had been dismantled.

Chapter Ten

The Great Western Railway Fleet 1905-1925

Melmore

Melmore was constructed in 1892 by Messrs D.J. Dunlop of Port Glasgow. Her steel hull was 156 ft 2 in. long with a beam of 25 ft 8 in., a draft of 11 ft 3 in. and a gross tonnage of 412. She was powered by a triple expansion engine supplied by her builders with cylinder diameters of 15 in., 23 in. and 38 in. and a piston stroke of 27 in., developing 96 rhp, steam being supplied by one single-ended three-furnace Scotch type boiler.

Her original owner was the Earl of Leitrim, who operated a service between Glasgow and Northern Ireland, and at one period he placed her on charter to David MacBrayne to operate West Highland services. Meanwhile, the Great Western was looking towards purchasing a vessel to assist with the Jersey potato traffic and reduce their dependence on chartered vessels, and authority was given to purchase *Melmore* for a sum not exceeding £9,000. Terms were agreed, and £8,650 was paid - the bill of sale being dated 4th May, 1905. She was insured for only half her value, the premium being £214 19*s*. 4*d*. *Melmore* made her first voyage for her new owners on 13th May. When not employed with the potato traffic Melmore would carry general cargo - usually to Jersey, operate between Plymouth and Jersey, lie at Milford as a spare vessel for the Waterford service, or be laid up.

The passing of the GWR Steam Vessels Act on 16th August, 1909 provided work for the *Melmore*, and on 4th September, 1909 she made the inaugural voyage on the weekly Weymouth-Nantes service. The first flush of success on this route with cargo traffic soon receded, and passenger numbers at times failed to reach double figures, so plans to insulate the fore hold and fit ice tanks for the perishables traffic were dropped. For the Summer season of 1910 the service was transferred to Plymouth, which brought about a slight increase in the traffic carried. On 6th June, 1911 the final sailing was made from Weymouth, and following its summer transfer to Plymouth it ceased altogether after 30th September. Although unsuccessful, the place of this service will always be marked in railway cross-channel history as being the longest journey - 352 miles taking 36 hours - and the only one to sail beyond 'Home Trade Limits'!

With the conversion of *Lynx* and *Gazelle* to cargo vessels there was no place for *Melmore*. As the only single screw vessel in the Weymouth fleet she was slow at 10 knots, and sometimes unreliable. Those who knew her referred to her as 'A bit of an old tub', and following three trips to Jersey in May 1912 to assist with the produce traffic she sailed to Plymouth for lay-up. Already a decision to sell the vessel had been taken, the asking price being £5,000. However, she was sold on 10th June, 1912 for £4,200 to Charles Forbes, within weeks passing to H. Whitworth of Glasgow. Newspapers reported the vessel as being prepared for a trip to the Cocas Island to attempt the recovery of £20,000 worth

Melmore alongside Custom House Quay Weymouth. The ship is dressed overall, the top flag on the aft mast being the GWR house flag. Flags are also flying from other buildings, suggesting that the ship itself is not the reason for the celebrations. *R.C. Clammer Collection*

Melmore departs from Weymouth Harbour with her bulwark doors still open. Although the jib has been removed, the steam operated deck crane remains sheeted over, clearly shown halfway back along the fore deck. *Author's Collection*

of gold and jewels. *Melmore* sailed from Barry on 25th September arriving at Panama on 13th February, 1913, having called at Cocas Island *en route*, but no details about the recovery of the treasure are known. Sailing through the Panama Canal she arrived at Vancouver on Friday 13th June, at which point she appears to have been reprocessed by J. Constant, the shipbroker. Following several subsequent moves in 1914, she was sold to the Melmore S.S. Company of Vancouver, Canada - this being a newly formed subsidiary of the Union S.S. Company of British Columbia. The *Melmore* had been purchased to replace a vessel seized by United States coastguards for illegal trading. The following year, when the impounded vessel was released, *Melmore* passed into the ownership of G.E. Leith, and was registered at Callao in Peru under the name of *Santa Elena*. She was sold again during 1936 to the Peruvian Government Ministry of Marine and renamed *Contdestable Celendon*. Her last known entry was in the 1946-47 Lloyds Register, after which date her fate is unknown.

Pembroke

Constructed in 1880 by Messrs Laird Bros of Birkenhead, *Pembroke* was the largest and last paddle steamer built for the Great Western Railway, and the only one constructed of steel. Her length was 254 ft, with a beam of 30 ft 9in., a draft of 15 ft, and a gross tonnage of 760. She was powered by a compound oscillating engine with cylinders of 51 in. and 91 in. bore with a stroke of 84 in., developing 400 hp giving a speed of 15 knots. A surface condenser with an air pump operated off the main engine was fitted, as was steam steering gear. Two double-ended return tube boilers, each with three furnaces at each end supplying steam at 75 psi were installed aft of the engines, and a donkey boiler was also installed to operate the winches when the main boilers were not in steam. Constructed especially for the Milford-Waterford service, she was equipped to carry passengers, cargo, and cattle and had 10 stalls for the conveyance of horses.

Whilst approaching Waterford on 16th March, 1895 the piston rod on the low-pressure cylinder failed, damaging that side of the engine beyond repair. Stranded off Hook Point, two tugs were hired to tow the vessel into Waterford, but owing to dense fog she could not be taken up river and one of the tugs took the passengers and mails to Waterford. Later *Pembroke* was towed to Liverpool for repair at Messrs Laird Bros, but as replacement of the remaining paddle steamers in the fleet was being considered, it was decided to convert *Pembroke* into a twin-screw vessel there and then.

The reconstruction was carried out by Laird's at a cost of £30,000. The two triple expansion engines each had cylinder diameters of 19 in., 30 in. and 46 in. with a cylinder stroke of 30 in., developing 650 nhp. A new boiler was also fitted operating at 175 psi. The engines developed 3,500 ihp, and on her trial trip she obtained a speed of 17½ knots. Her revised gross tonnage was 976.

Pembroke returned to service at Milford on 17th May, 1896. Her first appearance at Weymouth was in June the following year when she assisted with the Guernsey fruit traffic, and that July she took over the passenger service

The cargo stage in the years following World War I with *Pembroke* alongside. Astern lies either *Gazelle* or *Lynx* with a coal barge alongside. In the background is the Marine Hotel by that time renamed 'Hotel Edward', in the foreground are the ferry steps, and to the extreme left a ferryman conveys a passenger across the harbour to the Nothe Gardens. *Author's Collection*

Pembroke departing Weymouth for the Channel Islands during the final years of her life. Originally built in 1880 as a paddle steamer for the Irish service, and later converted to a screw steamer, she faced an uncertain future, before becoming invaluable, serving at Weymouth until 1925. *The late E. Latcham Collection*

following the failure of the new steamer *Roebuck* until being returned to Milford on 3rd August. Other relief work included covering the Wexford-Rosslare-Bristol service for the *Voltaic* during 1898.

On Saturday 13th February, 1899 *Pembroke* departed from New Milford at 2.06 am under the command of Captain John Driver with 28 passengers and about 20 tons of cargo aboard. At 6.19 am dense fog was encountered and speed was reduced, and just nine minutes later a black outline was seen and the engines were put to full astern, but before the ship lost way she struck rocks just off Saltee Island - about three miles off the south-east coast of Ireland. Lifeboats were lowered and the passengers and mails were put ashore on the island as the vessel flooded in all compartments forward of the boiler room. An officer was sent ashore to the nearest point on the mainland at Kilmore Quay to send a telegram reporting the accident and requesting assistance. The GWR agent at Waterford arrived the same day in a hired tug and took on board the passengers and mails, the parcel post hampers and other small packages from the ship and conveyed them to Waterford.

Upon examination it was found that the fore part of the vessel was firmly fixed on the rocks and plates on both sides were fractured. The stern was overhanging in deep water and there was the risk of her sliding off into it and sinking or that she would break her back. A salvage contractor transferred all the cargo to a tug on the Sunday, after which weather conditions deteriorated and it was not until the following Wednesday that it was possible to get the diving and pumping plant and timber to shore up bulkheads on board the stricken vessel. Work proceeded apace and on Thursday the ship was hauled off the rocks by the hired tug *Flying Fox,* the GWR tug *Palmerston* and Plymouth tender *Sir Richard Grenville,* and towed to the Waterford River where she was safely grounded.

After patches of wood and cement were placed over the damaged plates, *Pembroke* left Waterford for Birkenhead on 4th March under her own steam, escorted by the Plymouth tender *Sir Richard Grenville* (1891). Rough weather caused the convoy to run for shelter at Holyhead before proceeding to Messrs. Laird's yard the following day, the repair bill coming to £6,230 15*s*. 1*d*.

At the subsequent Board of Trade inquiry into the stranding it was disclosed that the vessel was about six or seven miles off her proper course. There was, however, evidence that there were abnormal tide conditions following a storm in the Atlantic. The Court ruled that the vessel had not been navigated in a proper and seamanlike manner, but owing to the Captain Driver's long and unblemished record it was decided not to suspend his master's certificate. The Great Western thought otherwise, and for a period of a year he was reduced to shore duties at New Milford which included the shifting of vessels under repair from berth to berth and the control of the crews employed upon them.

Pembroke was rapidly becoming dated with the introduction of newer vessels, and it must be said that conditions aboard *Pembroke* were far from ideal. During 1903 eighteen head of cattle died whilst on voyage, an investigation revealing that improved ventilation in that part of the vessel was required! However, owing to the new turbine steamers not being completed on time, *Pembroke* ceremonially opened the Fishguard-Rosslare route on 21st July, 1906, and upon arriving with the Great Western officials, Directors and other guests, ran aground on Holden's Bed sandbank, being refloated on the rising tide.

Pembroke was used as required on tendering duties to the visiting liners at Fishguard, and early in 1910 she received damage when tendering to the Cunard liner *Campania*. The following year a fire broke out on board whilst on voyage from Liverpool to Fishguard following refit, fortunately the crew managed to extinguish it before it took hold.

The introduction of the new steamer *Waterford* on the Fishguard-Waterford service in May 1912 displaced the ageing *Pembroke*. Early the following year *Pembroke* was converted into a tender by the workshop staff at Fishguard, with a certificate for 665 passengers within the three-mile limit. The Fishguard port of call for ocean liners was not successful, so *Pembroke* spent her time as a cargo vessel or laid up. In January 1916 it was decided to sell the vessel if a suitable offer was received

With only the *Ibex* operating from Weymouth during World War I various cargo vessels had to be chartered at a time when ships were in short supply. *Pembroke* was therefore taken out of lay-up at Fishguard and refitted as a cargo vessel especially for the Channel Islands service, arriving at Weymouth at the end of March 1916 to replace the *River Crake* which was on hire from the Lancashire & Yorkshire Railway.

As a cargo vessel she could only carry 12 passengers, but when the *Ibex* was not available a special licence was granted by the Board of Trade allowing 40 passengers to be carried. The threat of U boat attack was always a problem, and on 24th September, 1916 *Pembroke* was attacked by gunfire from U37 on the surface 22 miles north of the Casquets. As a precaution daylight sailings ceased, and a gun for defence purposes was fitted at Portland Dockyard during January 1917, the vessel also being camouflage painted. Wireless equipment was installed in that June. Whilst *Ibex* was serving as a troop transport in the spring of 1918, *Pembroke* maintained the entire service. Likewise early in 1919, when *Ibex* was engaged in trooping followed by a refit, *Pembroke* again carried out the entire service.

However, with the war over and the return of other vessels, in July 1920 it was again decided to sell the *Pembroke* on the most favourable terms. In August 1920 she sailed to Plymouth for a well deserved lay-up. In 1921 her Board of Trade Load Line certificate was renewed for two years, and from then on she was mainly employed only during the summer season with the produce traffic. Replaced by the two new cargo vessels, she made her last sailing from Guernsey on 4th July, 1925 and was laid up again, being sold through Constant's to Alloa Shipbreaking for £3,125. She left Weymouth under tow on 4th August for Charlestown, on the Firth of Forth, arriving there on the 8th. Breaking up commenced on 19th August, 1925, thus ending the career of a vessel that had changed out of all recognition over the years, and had on several occasions been considered superfluous, but in the event had proved invaluable in keeping the Channel Islands service open.

Great Western and Great Southern

To replace the older vessels on the Milford-Waterford service two new vessels were ordered from Messrs Laird Bros of Birkenhead in early 1901, and construction commenced by early April. Miss Laird, a member of the builder's family, launched the *Great Western* on 12th December, 1901, and in early January 1902 the ship was in dry dock for the boring out of her stern bushes, her masts, engines and boilers having already been placed into the hull. *Great Southern* was launched by the daughter of Mr MacIver, a Director of the Great Western Railway, on Saturday 25th January, 1902.

The official trials of *Great Western* took place on 17th April, 1902 when six runs were made between the Bar and the North West lightship on the Mersey at full speed, resulting in a mean speed of 16.2 knots with a steam pressure of 174 psi and engine speed of 160 rpm. Handed over to her owners, she made her maiden voyage from Waterford to Milford on 1st May, 1902. *Great Southern* underwent trials on 15th May and entered service on 4th June. With the two new ships in service an accelerated service could commence, both vessels being very successful. On 9th July *Great Southern* made a record passage from Milford to Waterford in 5 hours 49 minutes.

Of steel construction with a length of 275 ft 8 in., a beam of 36 ft 3 in. and depth of 15 ft 2 in., they each had a gross tonnage of 1,339. The cargo space consisted of two holds forward, and accommodation for 500 head of cattle in spaces that were ventilated by electric fans. The main engines supplied by the builders were four-cylinder triple expansion with a high-pressure cylinder diameter of 19 in., intermediate-pressure cylinder of 29½ in. and two low-pressure cylinders of 33 in. diameter. The piston stroke was 30 in. developing 3,250 indicated horse power and 228 nominal horse power and their speed was 16 knots. Steam was supplied by two coal-fired double-ended Scotch type boilers with a working pressure of 180 psi, working under slight forced draught on the closed stokehold system. An unusual feature for the time was the forced draught being supplied by electrically driven fans. The two dynamos that supplied power to the vessel were driven by compound steam engines situated in a room on the main deck, electric lighting being fitted throughout the vessel, including the masthead, side, and stern navigation lights.

Their accommodation was more modest than the *Ibex*, *Roebuck* and *Reindeer*, but could accommodate 680 passengers. The dining saloon was placed at the forward end of the bridge deck, panelled in walnut and satinwood with decorative panelling in ivory, the ceiling being decorated in white and gold. The upholstery was in Utrecht velvet. Measuring 36 ft by 24 ft, the saloon extended the full width of the vessel and could accommodate 40 passengers per sitting. A smoking room panelled in light oak and upholstered in Moroccan leather was placed amidships. A ladies' cabin on the starboard side panelled in walnut and light oak was equipped with sofas, which formed berths for 12 passengers, and there were nine state rooms each capable of accommodating four first class passengers. On the poop deck aft, a large deckhouse provided accommodation for female steerage class passengers and cabins for the ship's officers. Male steerage class passengers were accommodated on the forward part of the main deck where a cabin was also provided for cattle dealers. The engineers' cabins were situated on the main deck near to the engine room; the firemen were

Great Western goes stern first into Weymouth Harbour during the 1920s, her decks loaded with troops. It was the usual practice for the troops of the Island garrisons to be transported via Weymouth. *The late E. Latcham Collection*

Great Western alongside the jetty at St Peter Port, Guernsey, in June 1925. *Author's Collection*

Detailed views of the fore deck of the *Great Western,* whilst employed as a baggage tender to the RMS *Mauretania* at Fishguard on 30th August, 1909. *(Both) Author's Collection*

Great Southern steaming across Weymouth Bay towards the harbour entrance, during the summer of 1924. Of the two sisters *Great Southern* only appeared at Weymouth for 12 days during the summer of 1916 and during the summer of 1924. *The late E. Latcham Collection*

accommodated on the main deck aft and seamen in the forecastle under the main deck. Steam radiators supplied heating to all accommodation.

Neither vessel was requisitioned during World War I, except *Great Southern,* which was requisitioned by Admiralty for several short periods between 26th April, 1916 and 17th May, 1917. Otherwise they continued their service across the Irish Sea, although because of U boat activity it was decided to equip both vessels with wireless in March 1915.

The first appearance of the sisters at Weymouth was during the shipping shortage of 1916, when *Great Southern* replaced *Ibex* for 12 days during July and August and undertook four sailings to the islands. The *Great Western* first served as a relief vessel at Weymouth between 22nd June and 16th October, 1922. Following the withdrawal of the older cargo vessels *Great Western* returned for the 1924 season, an arrangement that continued until 1932. The withdrawal of *Reindeer* after the 1927 season put added pressure on *Great Western* as a relief passenger boat; a slower vessel than *Reindeer* her accommodation was far below the standard of the two new 'Saints'. However, the introduction of *St Patrick* for the 1930 season resolved the problem, although *Great Western* appeared at Weymouth up until 1932, her large holds being invaluable for the seasonal traffic. In June 1929 the decision was taken to replace both vessels. *Great Western* was chartered by the Shetland Agricultural Improvement and Discussion Society for 17½ days from 29th August, 1932 at a net rate of £313 10*s*. per week.

In October 1932 the General Manager stated that the age and condition of both *Great Western* and *Great Southern* made it desirable that the vessels should be replaced. The Board discussed the possibility of purchasing a second-hand cargo vessel as a replacement. However good sense prevailed and a new general-purpose vessel was ordered. Launched on 24th August, 1933 she was named *Great Western,* her predecessor being renamed plain *GWR No. 20*. This was not to be for long, as early in 1934 she was sold to Cashmores at Newport for £1,925 and broken up, her register being closed on 13th March. *Great Southern* followed, her certificate expiring on 20th January, 1934. The new *Great* Western replaced her on the Waterford service on 22nd March. *Great Southern* was sold to Cashmore's for £2,500, proceeding to Newport where she was broken up, her register being closed on 8th September, thus bringing to a close the life of two unremarkable but reliable sisters.

Chapter Eleven

The Great Western Railway Fleet 1925-1947

St Julien and St Helier

The requirement for new vessels and the design of them was under serious consideration during 1923, and by November Leonard Peskett, Naval Architect to the Cunard company, had been requested to prepare detailed drawings and specifications which resulted in two new steamers being ordered from the yard of John Brown & Company of Clydebank in March 1924 at a cost of £248,000. *St Julien* was launched on 23rd February, 1925, *St Helier* following on 26th March. On trials over the measured mile both ships averaged 19½ knots, although in service a more sedate 18 knots was usually required. With a length of 282 ft 2 in., a beam of 40 ft, a draught of 16 ft 3 in. and gross tonnage of 1,885 they eclipsed all previous vessels. Built to Lloyds highest specification, the steel hull was divided into 11 watertight compartments with a straight stem and cruiser stern. Two capstans forward on the focsle for mooring and anchor purposes were powered by a vertical steam engine situated below, a steam driven warping capstan being provided on the promenade deck aft. The steering engine was housed in the steering flat aft and was attached to the rudder post, winding itself along a geared quadrant, control from the bridge being via hydraulic telemotor. Six lifeboats supported by 'Quadrant' type davits were housed on the boat deck. The two cargo holds, one forward and one aft of the main superstructure, had a combined capacity of 23,500 cubic feet. On the bridge a single lever controlled the closure of all watertight doors in an emergency and the captain could speak directly to many parts of the ship via a Laryngaphone system. Electric navigation lights controlled from the bridge were fitted to the masts and ship's side. The galley was equipped with the latest equipment of the day, including oil fired ranges, electric fish fryers, egg boilers, and electric toasters.

Originally certified to carry 1,004 passengers, the accommodation was far superior to that of previous vessels. The first class accommodation was placed amidships, the deckhouse housing six cabins for two persons each at the aft end, forward of which was the galley and pantries followed by the dining saloon panelled in mahogany with seating for 44. Ahead of this was the ticket office, ladies' room, lavatories, and two four-berth cabins. The bar and first class smoking room panelled in French walnut, was at the forward end. Below was a 46 berth open sleeping compartment for ladies and another for gentlemen with 40 berths. There were also a further 16 berths for ladies and a compartment with 48 open berths for men, six cabins for two persons each and four cabins for four persons each. Promenade space was provided each side of the deckhouse, the forward 40 feet being enclosed behind glazed side screens, and seating was provided alongside the deckhouse. Second class accommodation was aft, housed in a deckhouse on the promenade deck, with a saloon panelled in oak, smoking room, bar and pantry. The top of this deckhouse formed a poop deck

THE CROSS-CHANNEL STEAMSHIPS "ST. JULIEN" and "ST. HELIER."

Built and engined by Messrs. John Brown & Co., Ltd., Clydebank.

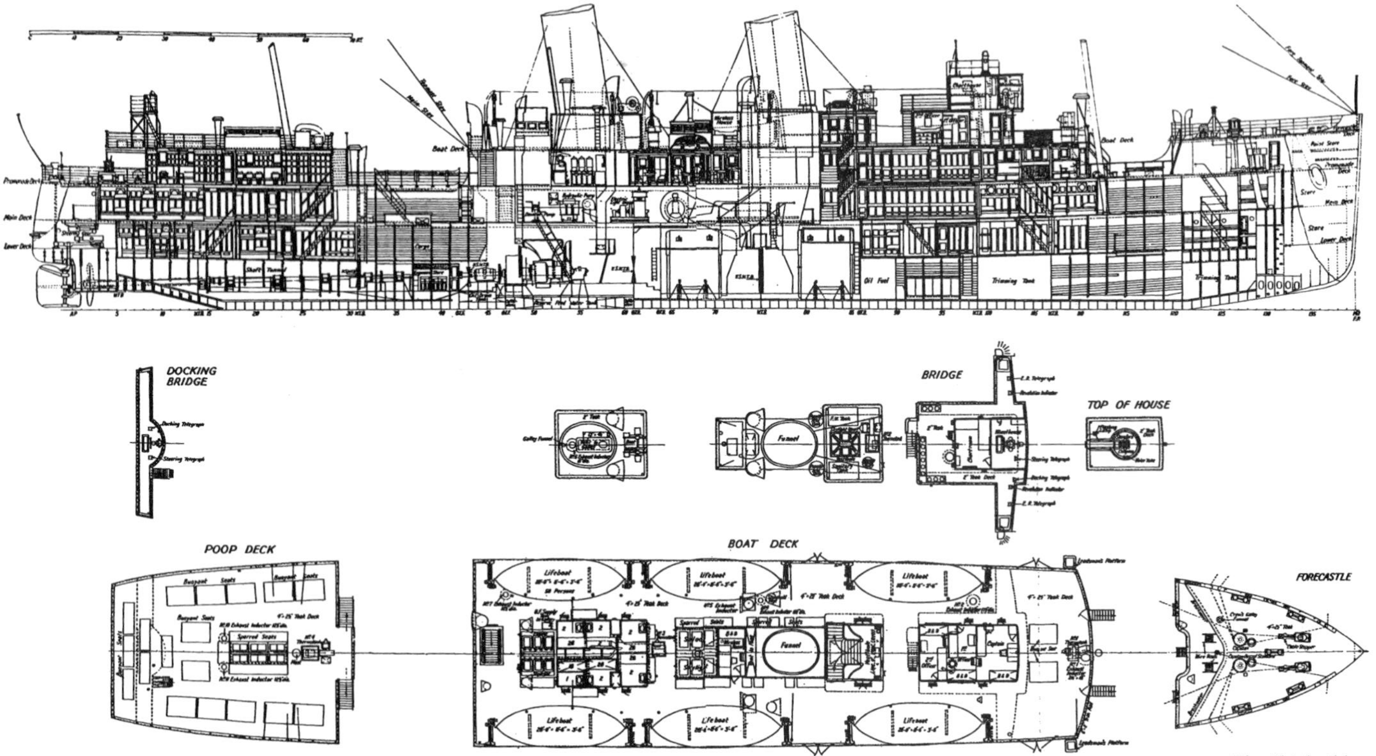

Promenade Deck
Main Deck
Lower Deck
Boat Deck
Shaft Tunnel
Oil Fuel
Trimming Tank
DOCKING BRIDGE
Docking Telegraph
Steering Telegraph
BRIDGE
TOP OF HOUSE
Funnel
POOP DECK
Buoyant Seats
Sparred Seats
BOAT DECK
Lifeboat
FORECASTLE

The Shipbuilder

THE CROSS-CHANNEL STEAMSHIPS "ST. JULIEN" and "ST. HELIER."

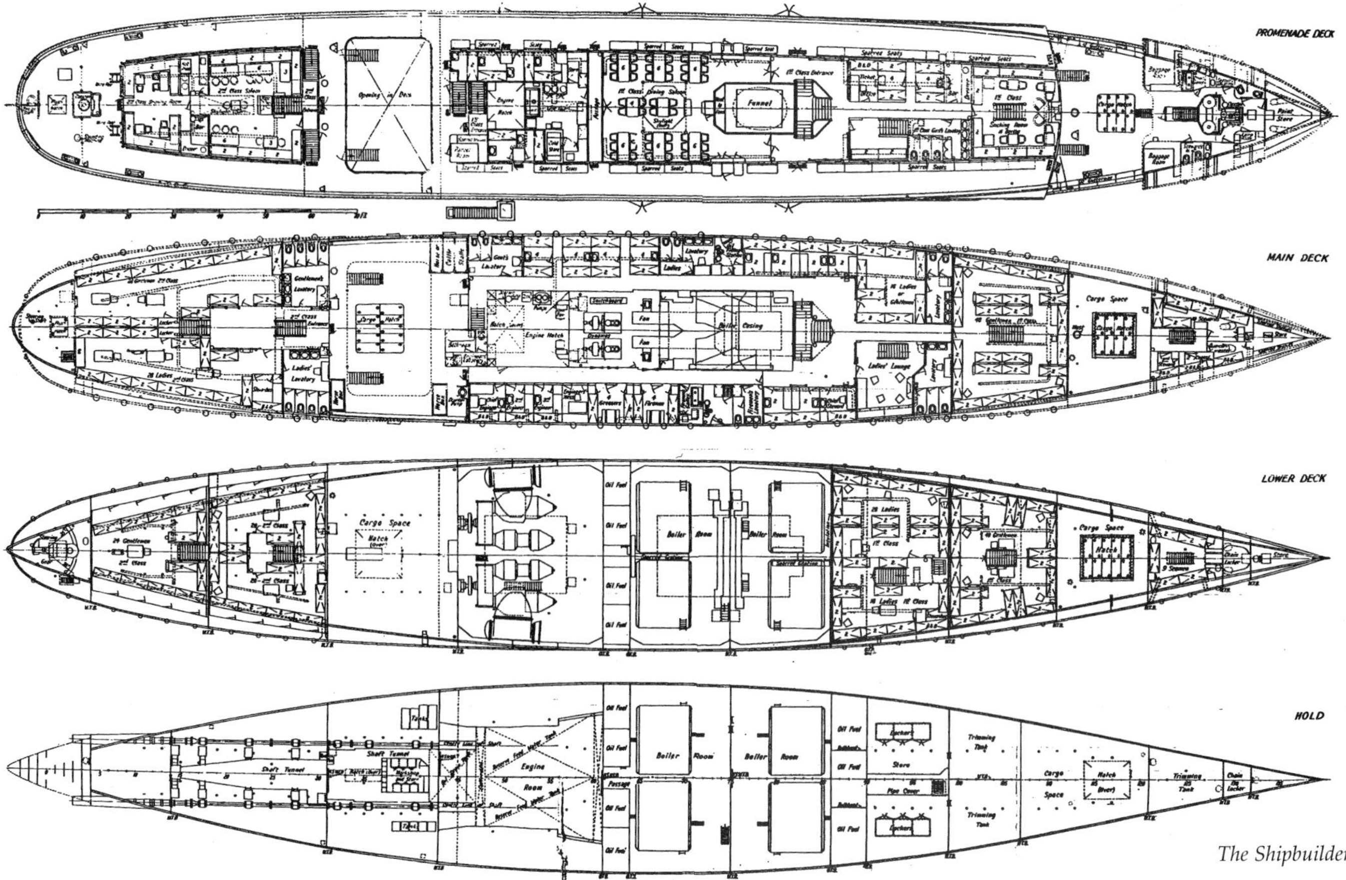

PROMENADE DECK

MAIN DECK

LOWER DECK

HOLD

The Shipbuilder

St Julien lying in the fitting-out basin at John Brown's yard, Clydebank, early in 1925, clearly showing the detail of the starboard side of the upper decks. *University of Glasgow*

St Julien whilst fitting out, showing detail of the forecastle - including the twin capstan drums and the small hatch of the fore hold. In the background sister vessel *St Helier* is also fitting out. *University of Glasgow*

which was a promenade deck for second class passengers on which was provided a number of buoyant deck seats. Below the saloon were three open-berth compartments, one for 24 passengers and the other two each holding 20.

Crew accommodation for the captain and officers was situated on the boat deck. Engineers', firemen's, and greasers' cabins were situated on the starboard side of the main deck, seamen being housed in the focsle on the lower deck. Ventilation and heating throughout the vessel was provided by the Thermo-tank system.

Both ships were powered by two sets of Parsons compound turbines through single reduction gearing giving a combined horse power of 4,350 to the twin screws. Electric power at 110 volts DC was supplied by two Bellis and Morcom high speed enclosed steam engines, direct-coupled to dynamos situated with the switchboard in a dynamo room at main deck level. Steam was supplied through four single-ended Scotch type return tube boilers, oil-fired on the Howden forced draught system and providing steam at 230 psi. The fuel oil was stored in bunkers situated between the engine room and aft boiler room which reached up to the main deck and three bunkers reaching up to the lower deck situated ahead of the forward boiler room.

St Julien sailed from the Clyde to arrive in Weymouth Bay at 9 pm on Monday 4th May, 1925, where she lay at anchor overnight, fog having delayed her arrival. She berthed in Weymouth Harbour at 7 am the following morning, where officials and Directors of the GWR who had travelled with her disembarked. At the time she was the largest vessel to have entered the harbour and created much interest, the local press describing her as 'like a small liner'. On board were about 80 workmen from Clydebank who were putting the finishing touches to the vessel. On Friday 22nd May officials of the GWR, members of Weymouth Town Council and other invited guests enjoyed a channel cruise to the Isle of Wight and back.

Great interest was shown in *St Julien's* maiden voyage, departing from Weymouth on Sunday 24th May with the overnight service under the command of Captain Langdon. On board were various officials of the GWR and the Lieutenant Governor of Jersey. A large crowd gathered at Guernsey to witness her arrival, and one lady, a regular GWR passenger, presented the ship with a large floral horseshoe. Again at Jersey large crowds had gathered for her arrival. However, celebration was to turn to embarrassment. When entering the harbour during a heavy squall the wind caught her broadside on and forced her against the steamer *Continental Trader* which was moored at the Albert Pier slipway, causing damage to the coaster's bridge. On moving forward, the *St Julien's* companion ladder was damaged when it came into contact with the anchor fluke of the Southern Railway steamer *Vera*. *St Julien* had to drop her port anchor to check her progress, this having to be weighed before the vessel could berth and land her 452 passengers.

St Helier arrived at Weymouth on the 7th June and took over the service from *St Julien* on the 17th. She commenced the summer daylight service on Monday 29th June, 1925 the event being marked again by the presence of many GWR officials and representives of the press. The boat train consisted of new articulated restaurant car stock, the improved service giving a journey time

The control platform in the engine room of *St Helier*, looking towards the starboard turbine controls and telegraph, below which is the astern throttle control wheel with the ahead control wheel slightly lower to the right. To the left of the telegraph is the revolution and direction indicator, the box below being the revolution counter. Above are the various pressure gauges required to indicate the boiler and engine conditions. *C.W. Hurworth*

St Helier going astern out of St Peter Port, Guernsey, shortly after entering service in 1925. This view showing her cruiser stern and upperworks clearly demonstrates the improvements from her Victorian predecessors. *The late E. Latcham Collection*

St Julien during the first three years of service, with her two funnels, lays alongside the quay at St Peter Port, Guernsey. The quayside crane is not exactly the latest model, but far superior than anything Weymouth could offer at that period. *Author's Collection*

St Julien departs from Weymouth about 1929. The ship is dressed overall and appears to be packed with passengers, but the original photograph bears no details of the occasion. *Kestin/Caddy Collection*

Damage to forward boat deck bulwarks of *St Helier* caused by heavy seas whilst crossing from Weymouth to Guernsey during a gale on 29th December, 1929. It was estimated that permanent repairs would cost about £400. The workman in the light coloured overalls is Frank Midgley the boilermaker employed at the GWR slipway in Weymouth. *(Both) J. Attwood Collection*

from Paddington to Guernsey of 7 hours 55 minutes and to Jersey 9 hours 45 minutes.

An unusual charter took place in the November 1925, when the shipping magnate Sir Robert Houston (who had been in ill health) wished to cross from Southampton to Jersey and elected to charter either the *St Julien* or *St Helier* at any cost - despite the fact he owned a luxury yacht! A party of 10, including eight servants, sailed aboard *St Helier*, and it is understood the cost of this charter was about £450. A second charter took place when *St Julien* appeared on the silver screen in the film *'Q' Mystery Ships*, made by New Era Films, in which she became a passenger ship stopped by a German submarine, the filming taking place off Portland on 3rd December, 1927.

The two vessels quickly settled into the new service, their top hamper compared with the old vessels gave problems when docking during high winds. At the time of their introduction the GWR produced a jigsaw puzzle of *St Julien*, it being reputed that Captain Langdon often put this puzzle together omitting the aft funnel. This matter was resolved during 1928 when the aft funnel and docking bridge of *St Helier* were removed during refit, the Marine Committee reporting on 24th March that 'it was considered a decided improvement', and a similar alteration was later made to *St Julien*. Other minor interior alterations were carried out at the same time, including the enlargement of the second class dining saloon into the smoke room. The aft funnel had weighed four tons, but it was virtually a dummy and had carried only the outlet from the galley stoves. Removal had no effect on the running of the vessels, but did destroy the symmetry of the design, the two funnels having been perfectly balanced in regard to their position on the vessels. The one remaining funnel therefore appeared to be a trifle too far forward of the position it would have occupied had they originally been designed as single funnel vessels.

In the autumn of 1936 *St Julien* received extensive reconditioning and overhaul costing £22,140, plus £5,805 7*s*. 10*d*. for unspecified extra work. Upon her return in February 1937 *St Helier* received a similar refit costing £21,900. With both ships a number of internal alterations took place. The windows of the sheltered promenade deck which were prone to weather damage were reduced many being replaced by port-lights, and the first class smoke room was reconstructed to take it the full width of the ship. The sleeping and seating arrangements of both classes were improved, cabins rearranged and extra bar facilities installed. External appearance was also altered, the remaining funnel which looked out of proportion was shortened by five feet and a naval type cowl added, this remaining on *St Helier* throughout her war service although removed from *St Julien* upon her conversion into a hospital ship.

War clouds were gathering during 1938 as Naval activity increased in the Portland area. On 30th June whilst outward-bound *St Helier* had to take avoiding action 14 miles south of Portland Bill when a submarine surfaced ahead of her. On the return sailing she had to alter course to avoid a submarine exercise that was taking place.

The outbreak of World War II brought the passenger service to a swift conclusion as the holiday trade abruptly ended. In anticipation of U boat activity mail steamers began steering zig-zag courses from 3rd September. *St Helier*

St Helier, following the 1937 alterations including the fitting of a cowl top funnel, lies alongside at St Peter Port, Guernsey, on 29th August, 1937 with a day excursion from Weymouth on which the photographer travelled. Departing Weymouth at 9 am, and returning at 10.30 pm the fare was 10*s*. 6*d*. *The late R.H. Rickett Collection*

St Helier alongside at St Peter Port on 29th August, 1937, looking forward from the deck above the second class saloon along the starboard side. The recently fitted cowl funnel top is clearly shown. The seats in the foreground are classed as 'buoyant apparatus', inside the framework are air tanks to enable the seats to float clear in the event of the ship sinking.
The late R.H. Rickett Collection

St Helier entering Weymouth Harbour prior to 1937. The wooden structure on top of the wheelhouse was part of the wireless direction apparatus. *Kestin/Caddy Collection*

brought 125 passengers home on Saturday 9th September, and four hours later the *St Julien* returned empty to Weymouth. On 12th September *St Julien* sailed for Avonmouth, from where she carried out two troop sailings to St Nazaire, before sailing to Southampton on 5th October for conversion into a hospital ship. The *St Helier* was laid up at Weymouth until 19th September when she sailed for Fishguard to replace the *St Andrew* on the Rosslare service, remaining on that duty until 16th November. The following day she sailed for Southampton where she underwent survey in preparation for Government service.

From that point both vessels and their crews performed duties far in excess of anything they were designed to undertake. First, an account of the war service of *St Helier*, which on 24th November commenced conveying troops and mail between Southampton and Cherbourg. Her second of these voyages - on the 30th could well have been her last. As she lay awaiting convoy instructions anchored in Spithead without lights in a south-westerly gale, at 8.45 pm the destroyer HMS *Kelvin* struck the *St Helier* a heavy blow on the stern, and there was danger of the destroyer's depth charges being smashed against the side of *St Helier* as it crashed down along her side before striking the starboard bow, holing it above water, before she cleared and came to anchor. After inspecting the damage *St Helier* returned to Southampton, where she disembarked the troops before proceeding into the Empress dock for repairs that were completed on 6th December.

Between 8th December, 1939 and 28th January, 1940 *St Helier* made 13 crossings to Cherbourg with troops - usually accompanied or in convoy - although three crossings were made alone. This pattern of operations continued throughout February and into early March. On the 16th March sailings commenced to Le Havre and up to the 20th April nine such voyages were completed, two without escort. Even sailing in convoy was not without danger as on 13th April, when proceeding 15 miles from the Nab, the Commodore's ship altered course and stopped for a westbound vessel without indicating his intentions to the other ships in the convoy, resulting in all ships having to take immediate action to avoid a series of collisions. Luckily everybody managed to extract themselves from a dangerous situation. Towards the end of April *St Helier* was laid up for boiler cleaning and the fitting of de-gaussing equipment which would give protection against magnetic mines. However, the compass adjuster failed to allow for the de-gaussing gear, which affected the steering compass, the next voyage to Le Havre on the 14th May being completed by simply following the ship in front!

Events in France were taking a turn for the worse, *St Helier* being ordered to Folkestone on 21st May to await orders for what was to become the evacuation of Dunkirk. From that point the records vary, the official naval report for the day stating that *St Helier* made a crossing to Dunkirk to repatriate 600, mostly RAF, personnel. However, Captain Pitman's log tells a different story.

> At 4.30 pm 21st May, 1940 ordered to proceed to Calais to embark British troops. No destroyer escort available. Twenty-two fighter planes accompanied us across channel. Arriving at Calais at 6.15 pm at low water, on seeing the results of bombing, ships sunk alongside the quay and buildings in ruins, decided to swing ship ready for hurried departure if necessary. Whilst still swinging was attacked by three enemy planes. Bombs fell both sides of the ship but no hits were made.

On 23rd May she is recorded as bringing back 1,500 persons from Dunkirk, but abortive crossings were made on the 25th and again on the 27th, being ordered away from Dunkirk on the second occasion without picking up any troops. At 8 pm on the 30th she went alongside and embarked 1,013 French servicemen, departing two hours later. Whilst proceeding west of Dunkirk, the destroyer *Sharpshooter* cut across her bows, the *St Helier* ramming her in the side, resulting in the steamer going slow ahead in the side of the destroyer for 40 minutes until the tug *Foremost 22* could take the destroyer in tow. In the confusion shortly after this *St Helier* was struck on the starboard bow by the Red Funnel paddle steamer *Princess Helena* (1883). Proceeding to Folkestone *St Helier* then struck an underwater wreck before arriving in port at 6.45 am the following morning. When she was returning to the French coast later that morning an aircraft dropped four bombs ahead of her and nine 20 yards off her port bow, but despite all these difficulties she embarked 1,250 troops before steaming to Dover, which was reached early on 1st June.

She was back again the next day, entering Dunkirk at 3.30 pm, where she endured a seven-hour stay alongside under fire from shore batteries whilst loading 1,334 troops, in the process of which three crew members were injured. In the evening of 2nd June she returned again to Dunkirk, arriving alongside at 10.15 pm and embarking 1,227 troops before sailing for Folkestone. On 4th June *St Helier* sailed to Southampton for repairs.

According to the official GWR records *St Helier* made one trip to Calais and seven successful trips to Dunkirk and brought back approximately 1,500 evacuees and 10,200 troops. For their efforts Captain Pitman, First Officer H.D. Freeman, and Second Officer F.E. Martin were awarded the Distinguished Service Cross, whilst Quartermaster C.J. Walkey received the Distinguished Service Medal.

During the evening of 11th June *St Helier* departed from Southampton and headed for St Valery-en-Caux to rescue the beleagured 51st Highland Division, arriving off the French coast at 11.55 pm. A naval vessel was supposed to make contact, but *St Helier* circled around for two hours under the threat of low flying enemy aircraft without result. At about 1.45 am the following morning several boats full of people and showing bright lights approached, Captain Pitman hailing one of them to enquire their business. The fact that they were obviously foreigners, and the lack of other boats in an otherwise deserted sea made him suspect treachery, and speed was increased until a safe distance was reached. As no naval vessel had appeared by 2 am *St Helier* returned to Southampton. In view of the later incident involving the *Roebuck* and *Sambur*,Captain Pitman's actions were fully vindicated.

The following day *St Helier* departed Southampton for St Malo loaded with 600 French troops for repatriation, and on the 15th she brought back 800 refugees of mixed nationality including British, French, and Belgian. She returned to St Malo the following day where it was found most of the lights on the fairway buoys had been extinguished and the pilot boat was nowhere to be seen, but at 12.40 am on the 17th the pilot did come aboard, reporting that the

The boat deck of *St Helier* viewed from the starboard bridge wing, looking aft during the period in 1939-1940 when the vessel was engaged in transporting troops from Southampton to France. Note the troops are wearing their lifejackets and the lifeboats are swung out in the ready to lower position - such was the danger from mines and U-boat attack. *G. Millsott Collection*

port was virtually occupied by the Germans. The pilot was thought to be behaving strangely, and upon entering the dock he was deposited at the lock, Captain Pitman berthing the ship unaided. Although there were enemy planes overhead no attack was made whilst the 2,545 British and French troops were embarked before departing for Southampton at 7.25 am.

Sailing from Southampton again at 4 am on 18th June *St Helier* proceeded down channel and received an un-decodeable message from Land's End Radio. Following several requests for a repeat her course was altered for Plymouth where she anchored in the Sound at 4.30 pm. Receiving further orders, *St Helier* set sail again at 10.30 am on 19th June. The following passage from the captain's log describes the situation confronting the crew.

> Passed 20 miles west of Ushant. Huge fires observed at Brest, the smoke from which extending 30 miles south. Frequent SOS calls from ships being attacked by aircraft and submarines in the Bay of Biscay, during this passage, which, considering enemy activity was without incidents. Arriving at position off La Palice, reported to HM ship, and was instructed to anchor at 9.20 am and await further orders regarding embarkation of troops. Many ships of various nationalities were anchored in vicinity including steamer *Lady of Mann** engaged as HM trooper. At 3.15 pm this day I was called out by the Chief officer who informed me that all the ships except the *Lady of Mann* had been ordered to sea and that La Palice was in flames. About 3.45 pm aircraft was distinctly audible overhead, and thereon ordered the crew to stand by the guns ready for action, still having six bren guns on board from Dunkirk. Saw HM ship approaching from La Palice at full speed, shorted in cable ready for emergency. About 4.10 pm HM ship close alongside two planes observed coming from astern flying very low and fast. Immediately opened fire. The leader singled out *Lady of Mann* and the other concentrated on *St Helier*. My crew put up a splendid show preventing the planes from flying over either of the ships. One bomb was dropped very near *Lady of Mann* but happily missed her, and *St Helier* was machine gunned by the second plane, HM ship being helpless to act in time as planes were shielded by *St Helier*. Once clear, HM ship opened fire and soon smoke was pouring from tail of second plane as he flew away towards land. Whether it reached the land or not we had not the satisfaction of knowing. When the air was again clear HM ship ordered us to heave up and proceed to sea.At 4.46 pm anchor away following astern of HM ship as instructed, *Lady of Mann* signalled me that his compasses were rendered useless by the bomb explosion and that he would have to keep station on me throughout the passage. At 6.30 pm whilst steering westwards off the land, HM ship hoisted alarm signals, and altered Course to starboard, instructing us to maintain our original course and speed. She proceeded at full speed to a position on our starboard quarter, circling this position for a short while. She returned and took up her station ahead of us. A few hours later an SOS from a torpedoed ship ½ a mile from the position circled by HM ship was picked up by our radio officer. Severe electrical storm was experienced for many hours. At about 5.30 am on 21st of June thought de-gaussing wire burnt out causing the ship's compass to become erratic and useless.

Eventually at 5.35 pm *St Helier* anchored in Plymouth Sound. The above narrative was typical of the events of the period, highlighting the situation facing the crews of steamers which in peace time just simply crossed the channel on a regular basis. Here was a situation where Masters and crew-with no formal training in naval warfare - were literally thrown in at the deep end.

* IOM Steam Packet Co. steamer, 23 knots, 3,104 tons.

On 24th June *St Helier* sailed for Liverpool where repairs were carried out at Gladstone Dock before she anchored in the Mersey. During July two voyages were made to the Isle of Man with internees before sailing to Gourock, arriving there on the 20th. She then made several trips disembarking troops from liners before anchoring in Gareloch, where she remained until 25th October. On that date she sailed for Penarth for survey before being handed back to her owners, arriving at the dock on 28th during an air raid. Whilst at Penarth *St Helier* was taken over by the Admiralty and commissioned as *HMS St Helier* on 7th November. She was required for combined operations duties, later sailing with troops to Milford Haven to undertake training exercises before going to the Clyde on 8th December to act as a tender at Inveraray. Moving then to the River Dart she took over as Combined Operations Base and Accommodation ship at Dartmouth from 9th February, 1941, remaining moored in the river for 13 months.

After that she returned to the Clyde and underwent conversion into an infantry landing ship, moving to Inveraray on completion of conversion work on 4th September, 1942. Whilst working in that area she received damage when entering dry dock at Troon in October 1943, and was damaged again when leaving Preston docks in January 1944. Finally departing from the Clyde on 1st February, 1944 she headed for the South Coast forming up in the Solent prior to D-Day. She departed on 5th June as part of Convoy J10, landing her troops at Juno beach the following morning, returning to Plymouth for further reinforcements and loading at Southampton from 1st July, thence to Newhaven and crossing to Dieppe from 1st November.

On 29th January, 1945 *St Helier* arrived at Tilbury to operate a forces leave service to Ostend. In the restricted waters of the Thames estuary she grounded on the Nore Sands on 5th February and on the 24th was in collision with tug *Tid 90*.

It was very fitting that *St Helier* was one of the vessels chosen for Operation Nestegg - the liberation of the Channel Islands. Steaming from the Thames on 4th May to Plymouth, she prepared to sail to Guernsey on the 11th, anchoring off St Peter Port. From there she returned to Southampton, then back to Jersey on the 16th with reinforcements before returning to Tilbury on the 22nd to continue the Ostend ferry service. At 12.30 am on the night of 16th July the cargo ship *Lightfoot* ran into her causing severe damage to her port side aft. With her shaft tunnel flooded and engines unusable the tugs *Stoke* and *Persia* towed her up river firstly to Gravesend and then to dry dock at Blackwall where she was paid off as a Royal Navy vessel in September. Sailing under the Red Ensign she reached Harwich on 15th November and commenced a trooping service to the Hook of Holland three days later. Her work completed, she arrived at Harwich for the last time on 15th March, 1946 before sailing to Newport for refit.

Much work had to be carried out to restore the vessel to her pre-war condition before she was able to return to Weymouth on Thursday 13th June, 1946 where she received a hero's welcome. The cargo steamers *Roebuck* and *Sambur* and other vessels in the harbour were dressed overall, flags were flying from the pier and sirens of ships in Weymouth Harbour and the home fleet in

St Helier whilst serving as an infantry landing ship during World War II. The landing craft which were carried suspended over the ship's side from hoists had not arrived when these photographs were taken. It is clear to see the structural alterations including the removal of the bridge wings that had to be carried out to enable the vessel to operate in its new role.

(Both) Imperial War Museum

Portland Harbour sounded as *St Helier* berthed. At 2 am on Sunday 16th June, 1946 with 350 passengers she departed on the first post-war voyage from Weymouth to the Channel Islands under the command of Captain Pitman DSC, with Mr E.R. Hawkyard as first officer and Mr C.H. Griffiths as chief engineer.

During her refit the cowl had been removed from the funnel although the top band of black remained narrow, this being rectified at a later refit. Proudly displayed on the reconditioned ship in the entrance to the first class accommodation were two plaques commemorating her service at the D-Day landings, a shield of ebonised wood bearing a large maple leaf carved from Canadian maple with a small silver shield in the centre inscribed 'Normandy June 6th 1944' with a silver plate at the base which read 'Presented to the officers and men of HMS *St Helier* by Captain George Malcolm as a token of appreciation for kindness and comradeship shown to Canadian soldiers on D Day', and the other a simple piece of oak carved with the single word 'Dunkirk' fitted unofficially at some stage during her service.

St Julien went to war as hospital carrier No. 29. She was painted white with distinctive Red Cross markings. Alongside her normal crew she carried an army medical staff of 37 and was equipped to carry 78 patients in swing cots and 152 walking wounded in berths. Taking up her duties at Newhaven on 2nd November, 1939, she proceeded to Dieppe two days later where she lay until 11th December before returning with 153 wounded. On 12th May, 1940, 217 casualties were conveyed from Boulogne to Southampton, a second sailing later being made.

Proceeding to assist with the evacuation of Dunkirk she arrived during an air raid just before 9 am on 24th May and was ordered from the area. She returned at 4.40 pm and embarked 220 casualties from both ambulances and a hospital train, departing at 8.15 pm and coming under fire from shore batteries as she steamed clear. Fortunately when her Red Cross markings were illuminated the firing ceased. Other crossings were made on the 26th, 27th and 29th when she picked up more casualties. On the third crossing towards the French coast she came under bomb and machine gun attack causing damage to the vessel. Taking aboard 21 naval personnel to assist the crew *St Julien* departed Newhaven just after 5 am on 31st May arriving at Dunkirk at 8.50 am. By that time the conditions ashore were rapidly deteriorating and the injured had to be carried a considerable distance but in just over two hours 247 casualties had been taken aboard before she returned to Newhaven.

On 9th June, 180 casualties and the nursing sisters from an army hospital were taken from Cherbourg to Newhaven before *St Julien* proceeded to Plymouth, from where she made a sailing to Brest on 18th June, but with air attacks taking place she was ordered back to Plymouth. On 12th July she sailed for the Clyde, where she lay until 3rd December when she moved to Scapa Flow to operate a hospital ferry service to Aberdeen. In March 1941 whilst moored at Aberdeen the ship was visited by King George VI and Queen Elizabeth. In September 1941 she sailed south to Newhaven where there was to be a proposed exchange of wounded prisoners of war via Dieppe, but the negotiations failed and the plan did not proceed. She than arrived in

St Julien as Hospital Ship No. 29 lies alongside the quay at Dieppe in the weeks preceding the fall of France. *The late E. Latcham Collection*

St Julien as Hospital ship No. 29 alongside at Newhaven shortly before the dramatic events at Dunkirk and the fall of France. *Imperial War Museum*

Belfast Lough on 22nd January, 1942, and the following day moved 223 patients from Bangor Pier to Liverpool. With little other employment, she moved to Loch Eve on 28th August where her staff dealt with the sick either aboard their own vessels or were taken aboard the *St Julien*. On 11th November she moved to the Clyde where she was equipped with an operating theatre, whilst four of her lifeboats were replaced by life rafts and special electrically operated davits to carry six water ambulances each capable of carrying five or six stretcher cases. Upon completion the vessel moved to Orkney until returning to the Clyde on 22nd May, 1943 when, following training exercises in Faslane Bay and with the water ambulances aboard, in company with *St Andrew* she sailed for the Mediterranean and the Italian campaign on 25th June.

Departing from Malta on 10th July she steamed to the Sicilian Bark West beachhead, the following day moving in to take off casualties with her water ambulances. On 17th she departed for Tunisia with 91 stretcher cases and 39 walking wounded, this being the beginning of a series of sailings to the North African coast. On 17th August her water ambulances rescued injured from a torpedoed ship, and on the 20th August 205 hospital personnel were transported from Tunisia to Augusta in Sicily.

On the second day of 'Operation Avalanche' 219 casualties were moved from Salemo Bay. On 23rd January, 1944 whilst she was anchored five miles off the Anzio beachhead, her water ambulances took medical supplies ashore. The damage caused by a collision in the Gulf of Naples on 2nd February was insufficient to prevent her conveying three American surgical teams from Naples to Anzio two days later. It is calculated *St Julien* steamed 30,000 miles in the Mediterranean and carried over 90,000 patients. Following dry docking at Taranto to rectify collision damage, *St Julien* departed for Penarth on the 8th April, 1944 arriving on the 20th.

Having completed her refit at the end of May she proceeded to Milford Haven to await orders to sail to the Solent from where she departed towards the French coast on 7th June. But she struck a mine which exploded under the starboard bow, flooding her forward hold and one of her hospital wards. She was settling by the head, the trawler *Switha* and tug *Jaunty* taking her in tow stern first to Southampton which was reached the following day. In dry dock it was a discovered that a hole in excess of 10 ft square had been made from the waterline down to the keel, which was also damaged, along with some of her deck plates.

Back in service by the end of the month, on 29th June she brought 175 casualties away from the Juno beachhead. Further damage was caused just before midnight on 21st July whilst at anchor off the Isle of Wight, when a vessel collided with her port side and opened up her plates from the boat deck to just above the waterline. She was in drydock again until mid-August, after which she went to Arromanches on 3rd September, Cherbourg on the 28th and Dieppe on 13th October.

In an ever varying role, *St Julien* was transporting American casualties from Boulogne to Dover in March 1945, by June visiting Le Havre and later Ostend in the August, firstly from Tilbury and later Southampton, taking German

Above: *St Julien* being towed up Southampton Water on 8th June, 1944 after her starboard bow had struck a mine whilst the ship was heading towards the French coast. *Below:* In dry dock at Southampton, receiving repairs to the damage caused by the exploding mine.

(Both) The late E. Latcham Collection

prisoners of war on the outward sailings and returning with British and Canadian troops. She made her final crossing on 30th-31st December, 1945, later sailing for Penarth where she underwent an overhaul before returning to Weymouth on Friday 29th November, 1946, making her first crossing to the Channel Islands on 1st December.

Although the war was over there were still dangers at sea, which now included floating mines that had been missed by the mine clearance programme. The crew of *St Julien* sighted one floating off Corbière in January 1948.

Apart from the change of ownership to the British Transport Commission little disturbed the regular sailings of the two sisters, and it was not until the announcement in November 1955 that two new vessels would be constructed for the service that the days of *St Julien* and *St Helier* were numbered. They were then 30 years of age but still in first class condition and thoroughly reliable. Although their accommodation belonged to a past era they performed well until the end, with only minor problems, such as the failure of the port propeller shaft of *St Helier* requiring a visit to dry dock in September 1956, interfering with their regular sailings to the Islands.

St Helier returned from the Islands on her last regular run on Monday 12th September, 1960. Her last passenger sailing of all was a day excursion from Torquay to Guernsey on Wednesday 14th September. The following week she moved to a buoy in Portland Harbour to await her fate, which came in December. Returning to Weymouth Harbour she made her final voyage on Saturday 27th December when the Dutch tug *Schouwenbank* towed her away, as she had been sold to breakers Et Van Heyghen Freres SA of Ghent, where she arrived two days later.

St Helier about to depart from Weymouth in September 1959. The wire stretched across the harbour in the foreground was at times used to pull the bows of the vessel clear of the quay wall if another ship was moored directly ahead. In the background the framework of the new Pavilion Theatre under construction. *Author's Collection*

St Julien departs from Weymouth for the final time on 10th April, 1961 in the tow of the Dutch tug *Martine Letzer*. The final port of call will be Antwerp and the breaker's yard, ending a major chapter in the history of the Channel Islands service and two vessels that served their owners and country with distinction in both peace and war. *Dorset Evening Echo*

Below left: The bell of the *St Julien* on display at the Weymouth Museum, Brewers Quay, Weymouth.*Courtesy Weymouth Museum*

Below right: A lifebouy from *St Julien* on display at *STEAM: Museum of the Great Western Railway* in Swindon. *J.D. Ward*

St Julien made her final sailing from the Channel Islands on Tuesday 27th September, 1960, but before departing from St Peter Port Captain J.P. Goodchild presented her name pennant to the Castle Cornet Museum. Leaving the islands for the last time the vessel was dressed overall, but high winds prevented the flying of flags upon arrival at Weymouth. Laid up in the Cove at Weymouth she was put up for sale through ship brokers Kellock & Company, being sold in March 1961 to Et Van Heyghen Freres of Ghent. She departed from Weymouth under tow behind the Dutch tug *Martine Letzer* on 10th April, 1961, arriving at Ghent two days later. This, however, was not the end. Described as 'unrigged', *St Julien* was used as a workers' hostel by the Royal Dockyard 'De Schelde' Flushing, under the name *Massnymph*. By 1970 it was reported that the vessel had been dismantled, thus bringing to an end the story of the two most popular and reliable ships ever to have sailed between Weymouth and the Channel Islands.

Roebuck and Sambur

The GWR accepted the tender of £90,000 for two vessels to be constructed by Swan, Hunter, & Wigham Richardson of Newcastle-upon-Tyne. The first to be launched (yard No. 1204) on 24th March, 1925 was named *Sambur*, sister vessel (yard No. 1206) named *Roebuck* following on 9th April. They were 201 ft 2 in. long, had a beam of 33 ft 7 in., and draft of 15 ft 3in., with a gross tonnage of 776.

They were powered by two sets of vertical triple expansion engines supplied by the builders with cylinder diameters of 14½ in., 23 in. and 38 in. with a piston stroke of 27 in. developing 226 nhp giving a speed of 12¼ knots. Steam at 185 psi was supplied by two single-ended three-furnace Scotch boilers oil fired on the Howden forced draught system, and the two vertical steam fan engines were situated at shelter deck level in the forward part of the engine room. The steam-driven 110 volt DC dynamo was in the centre of the engine room floor aft of the main engines.

Whereas before the Great Western had relied on second-hand or converted ships for cargo work *Roebuck* and *Sambur* were the first and only Great Western vessels built purely as cargo vessels. Both were constructed with high-sided hulls, the main deck running from the straight stem to the cruiser stern. There were three holds, two forward of the engine and boiler room and one aft. As originally designed the length of the ships would have been 230 ft, but because of berthing limitations at the time in Jersey the stern sections of the ships were reduced before building commenced, thus eliminating a second cargo hatch aft. The hatch tops were located at shelter deck level, the space from there up to main deck being used for the carriage of railway containers and cribs of various types. Pre-1949 the shelter deck space each side and forward of the engine room and boiler casing was also used to carry cargo. Being covered by the main deck above it was ideal for fruit and other easily damaged products. In all, well over 500 tons of cargo could be carried in 67,000 cubic feet of space. Steam windlasses on deck provided power for rope handling and anchor work, and they were also equipped to drive the cargo derricks fitted to each mast. This latter feature

Above: A high level view, taken from the bedroom of a house in Pulteney Buildings and showing the fore deck arrangements of *Roebuck* during 1938 as she lay at the cargo stage. Note the elderly steam cranes that for many years handled the traffic, compared with the three electric cranes in the scene, *below*, photographed 19 years later, showing the aft deck arrangements of *Roebuck* alongside the new cargo jetty. *(Both) The late E. Latcham Collection*

was soon removed from both vessels, as there were quayside cranes at all ports. With a service speed of 12 knots they were not the fastest cargo vessels afloat, although they were faster than many coasters of the day, and they were not the most beautiful of ships. The missing section from their sterns spoilt their trim and gave them a 'bow up' look. However they were excellent sea boats, and throughout their lives were thoroughly reliable.

Roebuck arrived in Weymouth on Wednesday 29th April, from where she made her maiden voyage on the 18th May. *Sambur* arrived on the 14th May, her first sailing to Guernsey being on the 23rd. Although classified as cargo boats, 12 passengers could be carried in the small officers' saloon next to the officers' quarters on the main deck. This was not a very satisfactory arrangement for night crossings, and during the 1928 refit the saloon was converted into a cabin with 10 bunks for the passengers and a new officers' saloon was constructed aft of the engine room on the shelter deck.

Roebuck was at Weymouth unloading on Wednesday 29th May, 1940 when she was requisitioned, and she sailed to Dover at 4 pm as soon as her cargo was discharged. At 7 am the following morning she anchored off the latter port to await orders, and in the early hours of Friday 31st she sailed to La Panne, a small Belgian resort nine miles east of Dunkirk. Today, even with all the modern aids to navigation and control of shipping, when operating in the Straits of Dover the greatest care still has to be taken in these, the world's busiest shipping lanes, but looking back on the events leading up to the evacuation of Dunkirk it is almost impossible to imagine the task set *Roebuck's* master, Captain W.Y. Larbalestier. He had no maps or charts of the area, there was a total blackout, and no ships had radar. Added to this was enemy action, mines, wreckage, the general confusion of the situation, and the fact that even under normal conditions the route is not an easy one with the Goodwin Sands on the English side and various sandbanks along the French coast.

Roebuck set sail at 2 am, sailing south-east until, just off the French coast, she turned her course east towards Belgium. As she rounded No. 6 buoy a destroyer, HMS *Wolsey*, ran into her stern, but fortunately neither vessel received serious damage and they were able to proceed on their way. *Roebuck* also had to run the gauntlet of shore fire whilst proceeding along the coast to La Panne. Upon arrival it was found that little assistance could be given. A fresh north-east breeze had blown up, and small boats were unable to bring any of the thousands of waiting troops out to the *Roebuck* lying at anchor.

Later *Roebuck* was ordered to Dunkirk. She moored alongside a damaged jetty with an almost total lack of facilities, her crew improvising ramps to allow 47 stretcher cases, 72 walking wounded, and 570 troops to board, the jetty coming under shell fire all the while. She sailed at 3.35 pm and at 7.30 pm she arrived off Dover, but was unable to enter harbour and unload until 3 am the following morning. As *Roebuck* had not been fitted with degaussing equipment as protection against magnetic mines and vessels so equipped were by then available, she was returned to Weymouth.

On Thursday 6th June she resumed her Channel Islands cargo service, returning to Weymouth from Guernsey on the 8th with 380 tons of tomatoes. The next day *Sambur* also arrived loaded with tomatoes. At once both vessels

Roebuck lying in Weymouth Harbour during the early years of her life. Apart from the white lifeboats, the black hull, brown upperworks and red funnel gave the vessel a dull look which belied her excellent sea-going capabilities. *The late E. Latcham Collection*

Roebuck lying at Penarth awaiting repairs after the damage received at St Valery-En-Caux, which cost the lives of three of her crew and seriously injured two others. The meagre armaments on board (one gun is shown near the stern) and a quick coat of grey paint were little protection against the overwhelming odds that the Royal Navy had abandoned as hopeless.
The late E. Latcham Collection

were requisitioned by the Admiralty, *Roebuck* proceeding to Portland Dockyard where she was fitted with degaussing equipment and then returned to Weymouth, where both ships awaited orders. These came on Wednesday 12th June when they were both instructed to proceed to a point five miles off St Valery-En-Caux, west of Dieppe, to assist in the evacuation of 600 troops of the 51st Highland Division. Upon arrival at 2 am on the morning of Thursday 13th June the captains of both ships were to place themselves under the orders of a senior naval officer of any British warship in the area. The only vessels to be seen were the LNER steamer *Archangel* and a few French fishing boats. The captain of the *Roebuck* hailed one of the latter to enquire about the situation in St Valery, to which came the reply, 'Go in, they are waiting for you'. Both *Roebuck* and *Sambur* proceeded towards the shore but when about a mile out they came under concentrated fire from German batteries. It was all too obvious that they were sailing into a well-defended occupied area, so both ships turned around and zigzagged their way out to sea. The suspicions of Captain Pitman aboard *St Helier* two nights previously were borne out by the events unfolding, both ships making their escape and heading to Newhaven. The incident had not been without price as both vessels were damaged and there was death and injury to the crews. On board *Roebuck* W.M. Williams the second officer, able seaman R.J. Wills, and greaser H.H. Caddy were killed and V.W. Newton the chief officer and signalman R. Pitts were injured. Aboard *Sambur* signalman L.A. Scarlett and cook J. Jones were killed, chief officer J.P. Goodchild and able seaman T. Donovan were seriously injured and able seaman A. Pitman and gunner L. Laws injured to a lesser degree.

Ashley Brown, writing in *Dunkirk and the Great Western*, stated of the St Valery affair:

> There was no-one who at any particular moment could say precisely how things stood. Further, wireless equipment with the troops had been destroyed in the course of the retreat, so that the Admiralty must have experienced the greatest difficulty in ascertaining the facts. But however that may be, when all this has been admitted it is still difficult to understand how it happened that Great Western requisitioned steamers were kept at short notice for three days before they were dispatched to St Valery, and eventually, without assistance of any sort or kind were permitted to attempt a feat which the British Navy had already abandoned as hopeless.

Following temporary repairs both vessels departed on 24th June for Penarth. After a refit in which both vessels were fitted out as barrage balloon escort ships, they were commissioned into the Royal Navy as *HMS Roebuck* and *HMS Sambur* on 22nd November, 1940. Both ships departed from Penarth in early December 1940 and proceeded to Sheerness to operate from the Thames Estuary escorting convoys in the English Channel as far as the Solent.

With France occupied the English Channel was no easy place to operate as there was constant threat from air and sea attack and the U boat menace. *Roebuck* was machine-gunned on 27th December, 1940, and in March 1941 she was involved in a collision with the Danish vessel *Skjold* in Southampton Water. She then suffered underwater damage during an air attack off Folkestone on 7th June. *HMS Roebuck* was renamed *HMS Roebuck II* on 21st August, 1942 to release the name for a new destroyer, and *HMS Sambur* was renamed *HMS Toreador* on 20th October, 1942. In May 1943 the barrage balloon unit was disbanded and both ships were laid up at Southampton, reverting to their original names until required for the build-up to D-Day. They were sent for refit on 6th May, 1944, *Roebuck* to Penarth and *Sambur* to Cardiff. They were to be used by the Royal Engineers for work in connection with the 'Mulberry Harbour' sections built to form the temporary harbour off Arromanches. Fitted with special pumps, their task was to pump out sections that had been submerged around the South Coast to protect them from enemy detection. After refloating, the sections were handed over to tugs and towed to France.

Roebuck departed Cardiff on 27th May destined for the South Coast, but she collided with the monitor HMS *Roberts*, and was forced to put into Falmouth for repairs, and therefore did not arrive at Selsey until 13th June. As she was late she was no longer required and was engaged in carrying stores from Southampton and Plymouth to the beach heads. The plan had been for both sisters to cross the Channel to help manoeuvre the huge concrete sections into place. Loaded with cranes, bridgework, and other vital equipment they then serviced the harbours, later going on to assist with the restoration of recaptured French and Dutch ports.

Roebuck was alongside the Mulberry Harbour at Arromanches on 5th November, and is recorded as sailing from Caen to Southampton on 9th November, proceeding to Cherbourg (arriving there on 3rd December) then steaming to Le Havre on the 11th. She made a crossing between Ostend and Southampton during the period 13th-15th January, 1945, and then made a crossing from Southampton to Calais on 25th January. On 11th February she departed Southampton for Antwerp on the first of four trips to the Scheldt, completing her final voyage at Southampton on 5th May. The final sailing on war service was when she crossed from Rouen to Southampton on 4th-5th June, 1945 after which she laid up at Southampton.

Sambur departed from the Bristol Channel on 26th May and sailed to Dungeness where she was an accommodation ship for the assembled Mulberry Harbour and Phoenix breakwater sections. After assisting in their pumping out, transportation to the beach heads and assembly, *Sambur* was engaged in the supply of stores to the advancing forces. Captain Pitman joined *Sambur* at Barry on 19th August, 1944, joining a convoy in Barry Roads two days later. His records describe the next eight months' service. She left the convoy in Weymouth Bay and anchored in Portland Harbour during the evening of the 22nd, proceeding at midnight on 23rd to the Solent.

On 27th November she sailed from Marchwood to Cherbourg, thence to Ostend from where she returned to Southampton. She stayed there until the 5th December, then sailed again for Ostend. By the 11th she had sailed up the Westerschelde to Antwerp where the vessel suffered concussion caused by bombs, rockets and explosion of mines in the area. Departing thence on the 15th she was delayed by fog at Terneuzen, not arriving at Dover until the 23rd. On Christmas Eve she departed for Calais, where she stayed until 2nd January, 1945 before returning to Southampton.

Another return trip to Terneuzen was made during January, then following boiler cleaning at Southampton she sailed on 12th March for Antwerp. As she was steaming between Dungeness and Folkestone at 6.30 the following morning a 'V2' rocket passed overhead, and minutes later an explosion was heard ashore. Whilst unloading at Antwerp on 14th March, 1945 it was noted that enemy action was much reduced! She returned via Calais two days later, sailing to Southampton and anchoring at Netley to await orders. Captain Pitman left *Sambur* on 30th March to join the *St Andrew* at Birkenhead. *Sambur* continued her sailings to the Scheldt, from where she made her final departure for Southampton on 28th May her war service over.

Both *Roebuck* and *Sambur* went to Cardiff on 14th June for refits before recommencing the Channel Islands service, *Sambur* returned to Weymouth at 3.30 pm on Friday 14th September, 1945. As she entered the harbour under the command of Captain Larbalestier other ships sounded their sirens in salute. Her first post-war voyage took place on the night of Wednesday 18th September, when she carried a general cargo to Jersey to become the first Great Western ship to enter the Islands since the occupation. On Tuesday 25th September the first post-war cargo of tomatoes arrived at Weymouth. *Roebuck* returned to Weymouth at 9.30 am on Saturday 13th October. On her first four trips time was lost through bad weather and loading difficulties in the Channel Islands. However, both ships managed to maintain a service of cargo and mails plus their limited accommodation for 12 passengers.

During the 1947 refit on both vessels the space occupied by bunks for 10 passengers was used to improve the officers' quarters. *Sambur* ran aground whilst entering Weymouth Harbour in September 1947. She sustained damage, and had to be towed to Penarth for repairs by the tug *Empire Sanoy*, and did not return to Weymouth until 18th December. During her absence *Roebuck* served both Islands. In September 1948 *Roebuck*, under the command of Captain Goodchild, broke the record for the fastest crossing made by the sisters between Weymouth and Jersey by completing the trip in 7 hours 14 minutes, very narrowly beating the record then held by *Sambur* of 7 hours 20 minutes.

Although they were still very good, reliable, vessels, the crew accommodation up in the bows was by now considered somewhat sub-standard. In 1949 some improvements were made, the cargo space at shelter deck level alongside the engine room and boiler room and the space just ahead of it being converted into crew's quarters. Over the years very few other alterations were carried out, although radar and more up to date wireless equipment was added.

Throughout the 1950s the sisters continued with the cargo service from Weymouth. In July 1952 *Roebuck* carried the record cargo (to date) ever to have been loaded onto a Southern Region ship, when she brought 86,000 chips of tomatoes, equivalent to 538 tons, into Weymouth in one load. On Monday 29th February, 1960 *Sambur* ran into the quay wall whilst proceeding stern first up Weymouth Harbour as a result of a misunderstanding between the bridge and the engine room. The point where she struck was at the seaward end of the cargo berth where the pier is angled, that section of the structure consisting of a concrete top about five feet thick supported on concrete legs. The force of the

The *Roebuck* swinging in Weymouth Harbour. The mail steamers rarely swung, but the cargo boats - if they had entered harbour bows first, usually because of high winds - would do so if the wind dropped before their next outward voyage. *Author*

Sambur viewed from the GWR slipway on 1st October, 1961. In the foreground is one of the lifeboats from the *St Julien,* the vessel having departed to the breakers the previous April. To the left is one of the work boats and outward again the principal work boat which was the surviving lifeboat from the *St Patrick* following her loss in the Irish Sea in June 1941. *C.L. Caddy*

Roebuck lying alongside the pier at Weymouth during the Summer of 1964. The 'up front' effect of the planned longer stern section being omitted is clearly shown. Within a year she will have steamed out of the harbour for the final time to the breaker's yard, having served a record 40 years on the Channel Islands service.
A.E. Bennett/R.C. Clammer Collection

impact stove in the stern on the port side from just above the water line to main deck level. When the ship was unloaded, workmen from Cosens & Company cut away the damaged plates, and with the help of a quayside crane fitted several concave rolled plates. They worked all night and she was able to sail two days later, but continued until the 1961 refit with a very large dimple in her stern!

The Guernsey tomato traffic was revolutionised in 1961, by the introduction of pallets for transportation, a three-year contract being signed to convey the crop via Weymouth. This resulted in the *Elk* and *Moose* being used for the traffic with *Roebuck* and *Sambur* filling the gaps and running into Southampton with general cargo. The loss of the main tomato contract in 1964 resulted in a decrease in the number of ships required to operate the service. *Elk* and *Moose* together with the *Winchester* took a more active part in the Weymouth service.

Lifebouy from *Sambur* on display in the old Great Western Railway Museum at Swindon. *Author*

Sambur made her last sailing from the Islands on 29th March, 1964, and two days later she sailed to Southampton and was laid up. She was purchased by Frank Rijsdijk-Holland of Hendrick-Ibo-Ambacht for scrap and left Southampton in tow of the tug *Pool Zee* on 10th June, 1964. *Roebuck* continued in service throughout the summer of 1964, and that November was chartered by a film company and steamed to Poole where, with her funnel painted white, she appeared as the Norwegian coaster *Galtesund* in the World War II film 'Heroes of Telemark'. *Roebuck* made her final crossing from Guernsey on Saturday 27th February, 1965 with a cargo of flowers, after which she lay at Weymouth until the July, when, under her own steam, she proceeded to Sheerness. On board was able seaman Bert Williams, who 40 years previously had sailed with her on her maiden voyage. *Roebuck* had been purchased by Lacmot's of Queenborough, and on 17th September she was moved to Washer Wharf. In November she was resold to Scrappinco of Brussels and broken up early 1966. It is now over 38 years since the passing of these two fine vessels. However, some 8½ minutes of superb shots of *Roebuck* internally, externally, and steaming at sea can be seen at the start of the video release of the film 'Heroes of Telemark'.

Roebuck alongside the cargo stage at Weymouth on 25th November, 1964. Her funnel had been painted silver and the ship renamed *Galtesund* ready for the filming of 'The Heroes of Telemark' in which she featured in scenes filmed in Weymouth Bay and Poole harbour. In all 8½ minutes of film of *Roebuck* are preserved for posterity. *C.L. Caddy*

St Patrick (1930)

The loss by fire of the *St Patrick* (1906) in April 1929 gave the opportunity to build a dual-purpose vessel for both the Irish Sea and Channel Islands trade, thus an order was placed with Alexander Stephen & Sons of Linthouse, Glasgow. Mrs Milne, the wife of the Chairman of the GWR, launched 'yard No. 525' on 15th January, 1930. At a cost of £130,000, she became the second *St Patrick* to enter the GWR fleet.

With a length of 281 ft 3 in., a beam of 41 ft 1 in., draft of 16 ft 3 in. and gross tonnage of 1,922 she was an updated version of the 1925 sisters. Externally the differences were in the raised forecastle which was extended to the superstructure and the funnel, symmetrically positioned and of better proportions than on the previous vessels. The propelling machinery consisted of two sets of Parsons compound turbines driving their respective shafts through single reduction gearing giving 250 revolutions per minute to the propellers. Four single-ended Scotch type boilers, oil fired on the Clyde system with Howden's forced-draught, supplied steam at a working pressure of 230 psi. Two sets of Belliss & Morcom direct-coupled engines and dynamos supplied electricity, with a cold start direct injection Petters diesel engine available in emergencies or when steam was not raised. The anchor windless, amidships winch, and aft capstan were all steam operated, as was the steering gear situated in the aft compartment and controlled from the bridge by hydraulic telemotor.

The passenger accommodation, an improvement on the two 1925 vessels, consisted of first and third class (there was no second class) dining saloons fitted with large windows allowing diners to view the coastal scenery.The first class saloon was decorated in polished and quartered mahogany with seating for 68 passengers at small tables. The third class saloon on the aft promenade deck was decorated in polished oak and accommodated 62 passengers. Conveniently situated near both saloons the main galley was equipped with electric ranges and grills and there were also refrigerated chambers.

Teas and other light refreshments were served in alcoves on each side of the vessel between the entrance and the first class saloon. The first class smoking room was panelled in laurel wood with walnut furniture and the ladies' lounge in grey sycamore. Third class passengers had two large lounges with ample seating which could be converted into sleeping accommodation when working night services. Sleeping berths could be provided for 216 first class and 116 third class passengers. A number of single and two-berth cabins were provided and several were specially furnished and decorated state rooms, all cabins being provided with hot and cold running water whilst heating and ventilating was provided by the Thermo Reg Louvre system. She had a cargo capacity of about 23,000 cubic feet, the fore and aft cargo hatches being equipped to meet the requirements of fruit and vegetable traffic whilst the hatch wells could accommodate motorcars.

She was equipped with the latest safety and navigational aids of the period, the hull being divided into 13 watertight compartments with watertight doors that could be closed from the bridge. Six lifeboats were carried in Columbus davits and a Marconi wireless installation with direction finding apparatus and auto alarm was fitted.

St Patrick (1930) with flags flying enters Weymouth Harbour for the first time on 24th March, 1930 on her delivery voyage from Clydebank. A finely proportioned vessel, at last the GWR had managed to resolve the funnel problems of the past! A dual-purpose vessel for both the Channel Islands and the Fishguard-Rosslare services, she was sunk by enemy action off Strumble Head, Fishguard in June 1941. *Kestin/Caddy Collection*

A feature described in the press as 'Portable cabins on the promenade deck which can be removed during the summer to provide a tea lounge on the port and starboard side' created the impression of a set of hut-like structures, but in fact the internal fittings and divisions of existing cabins could be removed to allow a quick conversion!

Sailing from Glasgow under the command of Captain Richardson, with the Mayor of Weymouth, Percy Boyle (who was also the GWR traffic and marine agent at Weymouth), other representives of the GWR Marine Department and the builders, *St Patrick* arrived in Weymouth Bay early in the morning of Monday 24th March, 1930. Later that morning, dressed overall, she entered harbour, where she was welcomed by the deputy mayor and other representatives of the town's business community, after which various parties made tours of inspection of the vessel. Unfortunately during berthing she damaged her rudder and had to proceed to Southampton for the fitting of a replacement before the delayed maiden voyage could take place on 18th April.

Sailing from Weymouth at approximately 1.40 pm on Friday 5th August, 1932 under the command of Captain Charles Sanderson *St Patrick*, with 314 passengers aboard, was making a direct sailing to Jersey. About an hour out from Weymouth fog was encountered but her course and speed was maintained for 65 miles. At 5.13 pm a wireless bearing was taken on the Casquets, and as the fog was only patchy bearings were also taken off other landmarks. On reaching the northern tip of Jersey off Grosnez the fog thickened, but the speed and course were maintained. An indistinct explosive fog signal was heard from Corbière shortly after 6 pm, but being faint it was repeated twice at the request of the master and seemed muffled. Speed had by then been reduced. Before long officers on the bridge noticed a tide eddy on the port bow, and the order was given to alter course. As the vessel swung to starboard an underwater rock gave her a glancing blow, damaging the port bilge plates, flooding the boiler room and propeller shaft tunnel, rupturing a bilge fuel tank and damaging her propellers. Distress messages were immediately sent and the ship anchored. The Jersey States tug *Duke of Normandy* arrived at 8.30 pm and the Southern Railway steamer *Isle of Sark* under the command of Captain R.J. Large set out from St Helier Harbour, whilst *St Julien* - anchored fog-bound off the Platte Fougere awaiting entry to Guernsey - cautiously proceeded towards the stricken vessel.

The *Duke of Normandy* went alongside St Patrick and by means of a rope ladder 65 male passengers were taken aboard, the tug standing by whilst the remaining passengers and mails were transferred by boats to the *Isle of Sark*, the tug then returning to St Helier. Owing to the fog *Isle of Sark* remained at anchor off the Corbière overnight, entering St Helier Harbour at 8.15 am. *St Julien* under the command of Captain Richardson, stood by overnight, commencing to tow the *St Patrick* at 7.30 am towards St Aubin's Bay where she was anchored at 11 am, *St Julien* then proceeded to St Helier to disembark her Jersey passengers (those for Guernsey and Weymouth still being on board) and also picking up 200 delayed passengers as the busy weekend timetable was in disarray.

The Southern Railway vessel *Princess Ena* arrived at 9 am and was placed at the disposal of the GWR, and that evening, assisted by the *Duke of Normandy*,

The second class dining saloon of the *St Patrick* (1930). High standards of service prevailed on the GWR ships giving passengers the feeling they were aboard a liner - a far cry from the indifferent attitude and help-yourself arrangements on modern ferries. *Author's Collection*

A view from the port wing of the bridge of *St Patrick* (1930) looking aft on 20th May, 1937 whilst attending the Coronation Fleet Review at Spithead. Astern one of the Southern Railway 'Isle' class steamers can be seen. *Author's Collection*

towed the *St Patrick* to St Helier where temporary repairs were carried out before she was towed to Plymouth by the tug *Seaman* for dry-docking. She then went to Birkenhead for permanent repairs, the damage and expenses incurred amounting to £6,783.

The Board of Trade inquiry into the stranding was held in November, where it was stated, that:

> . . . if *St Patrick* had been a few feet more to the eastward going at the speed she appeared to be going there was very little doubt that she would have suffered very serious damage, possibly ripping the bottom right out. She would have listed heavily and sunk within a few minutes with 295 passengers and with comparatively little chance of getting the boats out. Though the damage was small the question was a very important one, because it concerned the proper navigation of passenger steamers which travelled at high speed and which had a very large number of passengers on board.

The inquiry found that the master had set too fine a course and although the bearings taken were accurate the estimated distances were unreliable and inadequate with the position of the vessel not being accurately fixed. Captain Sanderson was censured and ordered to pay £100 towards the expenses of the inquiry.

The unsatisfactory fog signal from La Corbière lighthouse and the need for an efficient lighthouse and fog signal at Grosnez Point were also raised by the inquiry.

The incident proved that despite all the advances in navigational aids and radio in the past 30 years since the *Stella* disaster, familiarity and over-confidence could breed contempt; it had been a close call!

St Patrick represented the GWR at the Spithead Fleet Review on 20th May 1937, departing Weymouth at 9 am with many passengers who had arrived in Weymouth by special rail services. She took her place in the row of assembled vessels before returning to Weymouth at 10 pm. For those who took part in that historic event the fare had been 12*s*. 6*d*.

Departing from the Channel Islands for the last time on 2nd September, 1939, she returned to Fishguard until requisitioned on 20th September, 1939. She was engaged as a troop transport between Avonmouth and France until 11th October when she returned to the Fishguard-Rosslare route, painted grey with a concrete shield over her wheelhouse and only 12 lb. guns for defence. In this condition she maintained the Irish Sea service, making three overnight crossings per week.

During 1940 she was attacked twice by enemy aircraft, on 17th August and 20th. On the first occasion a plane flew in low just above the masts from the direction of the sun, releasing two bombs that missed the vessel, but the decks were raked with machine gun fire resulting in the death of seaman Moses Brennan and injury to a passenger. On the second occasion aircraft attacking a tanker sighted the *St Patrick* and broke off the attack to drop five or six bombs. These again fortunately missed *St Patrick* which had quickly taken evasive action by steering a zigzag course at full speed. On 15th November she struck an unidentified submerged object, and on 28th November detonated an acoustic mine at Fishguard. On 13th May, 1941 she was again attacked from the air but made good her escape, suffering only minor damage.

Fate finally caught up with *St Patrick* on Friday 13th June, 1941. Having left Rosslare just before 1 am, she was 14 miles from Fishguard (10 miles off Strumble Head) when a plane suddenly appeared and dropped a stick of four bombs which struck the vessel between the bridge and funnel penetrating the cross bunker fuel tanks causing a fire and breaking the ship's back. There was great loss of life. Of the 45 crew and 44 passengers aboard 28 were lost, 18 of them crew members including Captain James Faraday and his son Jack who died in a vain attempt to save his father's life, first officer Frank Rowe, second officer S. De Candia, and seaman John Brennan of Wexford, whose father Moses had been killed in the incident the previous August.

Despite the short time in which the vessel sunk the heroism of the crew was of the highest standards of the Merchant Navy. Stewardess Miss Elizabeth May Owen made her way to berths on the lower deck, forced the doors open, led the passengers to the deck, helped them into their lifejackets and over the side, then, hearing the cries of a young woman trapped below, went back into the sinking vessel and dragged the girl to safety before they both jumped into the water without lifejackets. The stewardess kept the girl afloat for two hours until rescued. For her bravery Miss Owen was awarded the Lloyds Medal and the George Medal. She is thought to be the only woman to have received both honours. Chief Engineer Cyril Griffiths received the OBE for his part in rescuing the only first class passenger to survive. Second engineer Frank Purcell who rescued three men trapped in the engine room and saved a wounded man in the water was also awarded the OBE, whilst radio operator Norman Campbell who managed to send out a distress call as the vessel sunk was awarded the MBE.

Within six minutes the *St Patrick* had disappeared, the survivors being picked up by a warship and merchantman which came to her aid. Only one lifeboat managed to get away from the vessel. In post-war years it was fitted with an engine and served at Weymouth as a workboat - the only tangible reminder of a brave vessel.

For many years ex-servicemen from the area gathered on the Fishguard-Rosslare ferry to remember the *St Patrick* by holding a memorial service. In 1982 Miss Owen's medals were presented to Sealink and went on display at the Fishguard offices. On the 50th anniversary of the loss of *St Patrick* a short service was conducted aboard *Stena Felicity* 15 miles off Strumble Head, a wreath being laid in the sea by Will Perry, one of the survivors, and there was a fly-past by two aircraft from RAF Brawdy.

On the 50th anniversary of the loss of the *St David* (a Fishguard-based vessel) during the Italian landings in January 1944, a memorial in the form of a large piece of Welsh slate with a picture of a fouled anchor and the words 'In Memory of the Fallen' was unveiled at the Customs Hall at Fishguard Harbour to commemorate the loss of both vessels.

St David

To replace vessels lost during the war the keels of two new passenger ships were laid at the Birkenhead yard of Messrs Cammell Laird & Co. Ltd in April 1946. The first (yard No. 1182) was launched by the Countess of Dudley, wife of the Earl of Dudley, Deputy Chairman of the GWR, during a snowstorm on 6th February, 1947. She was named *St David* after her predecessor which was bombed off Anzio in January 1944.

Larger than the pre-war vessels, having a length of 306 ft 5 in., a beam of 48 ft 2 in., a draft of 17 ft 2 in. and a gross tonnage of 3,352, the *St David* differed from *St Patrick* in internal layout and having the space to carry 52 motor cars on the main deck and 350 tons of cargo in the fore and aft holds. In all 1,300 passengers were housed in accommodation on four decks concentrated amidships, first class public rooms being on the promenade deck and third class on the shelter deck. The first class dining room seated 52 persons, whilst the third class saloon on the shelter deck accommodated 24 passengers at each sitting. There were sleeping quarters for 355 passengers in single, double, or open berths and luxury cabins. Her machinery and general details were the same as for *St Patrick* (1947) and are therefore fully described under that vessel.

Making her maiden voyage from Fishguard to Rosslare in August 1947, she was the last ship to enter service with the Great Western Railway before Nationalisation on 1st January, 1948. To provide experience in handling larger vessels at Weymouth and the Channel Islands, *St David* arrived at Weymouth on 3rd September, 1947 under the command of Captain R. Pitman DSC. She lay

The *St David* (1947) departs from Weymouth during her short stay at the port in the autumn of 1947. *St David* was at the time the largest GWR ship to sail from Weymouth and the first to be fitted with radar. *The late E. Latcham Collection*

The last ship to be built and launched for the Great Western Railway, *St Patrick* slides into the Mersey from the yard of Messrs. Cammell Laird on St Patrick's Day, 20th May, 1947. Flying from her masthead are the tattered remains of the name pennant of her predecessor lost during the war.
National Museums & Galleries on Merseyside

in the bay dressed overall until entering the harbour in the evening when a party was held on board for invited guests. The largest cross-channel vessel up to that time to enter the port, on Thursday 4th September she made her first crossing to the Islands where thousands at both St Peter Port and St Helier awaited her arrival. At the end of the summer service at the beginning of October *St David* returned to Fishguard. Having been constructed purely for the Irish Sea route, she never returned to Weymouth.

She remained on the Fishguard-Rosslare sailings until 10th February, 1964, when she was sent to Cammell Laird where alterations took place to allow her to load cars over her side as a drive-on ferry. At the same time her passenger accommodation was improved. Returning to Fishguard she commenced the drive-on operation in May 1964, but as facilities had not been constructed at Rosslare cars still had to be craned on and off in the traditional manner until June 1965. In 1969 she was transferred to the Holyhead-Dun Laoghaire route - usually acting as a relief steamer. Sold in 1971 to Allies Finance SA of Greece, she was renamed *Holyhead* for the sailing to Piraeus where there had been plans to convert her into a small cruise liner operating for a subsidiary of Chandris Cruises. This project was abandoned, the vessel laying at Perama until broken up during the early 1980s.

St Patrick (1947)

Yard No. 1183 was launched by Vicountess Portal, wife of the Chairman of the Great Western Railway, from the Birkenhead yard of Messrs Cammell Laird on St Patrick's Day, 20th May, 1947. Appropriately named *St Patrick,* she was the last vessel to be built and launched for the Great Western Railway. As the new vessel slid down the ways she flew at her masthead the war-scarred pennant of her predecessor which had been washed ashore on the Welsh coast following her sinking. With a length of 306 ft 5 in., a beam of 48 ft 2in., draft of 17 ft 2 in., a gross tonnage of 3,482 and speed of 20 knots she was the largest vessel built for the GWR and as with the *St David* she was one deck higher than previous vessels, and the largest to date to enter Weymouth Harbour.

Being designed for both the Channel Islands and Fishguard-Rosslare runs the internal accommodation differed from *St David.* The main deck car space was reduced to 27, the space being taken up with lounges, smoking and dining saloons for both first and third class passengers and less space devoted to cabins, thus making her ideal for a daylight service with a capacity of 1,300 passengers, with 295 berths.

Amidships was the first class lounge, of an open design with aircraft type seats and adjustable tables with an open buffet beyond, and below it was the third class lounge and dining saloon. A feature of the vessel in the main vestibule was a wooden inlaid map of rail and sea routes of the GWR. Sycamore was used for the base, other woods being ash, birch, walnut, oak and ebony, with mahogany being used for the inlaying of the company coat of arms. The crew quarters gave a hitherto unknown level of comfort, all officers being accommodated in single berth cabins, the remainder of the crew having single,

St Patrick, the crest of the Great Western Railway mounted on her bows. Photographed on 28th June, 1948. *Author's Collection*

two-berth, or four-berth cabins, all air-conditioned and each having an electric heater.

Power was provided by two sets of Parsons single reduction geared compound turbines, the high-pressure turbines being of the impulse reaction type and the low-pressure all-reaction. The astern turbines provided 70 per cent of the ahead power and were incorporated in both the high-pressure and low-pressure casings. Transmission to the propeller shafts was via single reduction gearing giving a combined shaft horsepower of 8,500 to the two three-bladed propellers. Steam was supplied from three oil-fired Babcock & Willcox water tube boilers at 250 psi, working under forced draught on the enclosed stokehold system, whilst a turbo-generating set supplied electric power whilst at sea, and two diesel generating sets supplied power on other occasions.

St David, and *St Patrick* were the first Great Western vessels to be fitted with radar in addition to radio and direction finding equipment, and seigraph echo sounding equipment. They also had bow rudders allowing the vessels to manoeuvre more easily when going astern.

Following trials in Liverpool Bay on 23rd January, 1948 the vessel was handed over to her owners on the same day and proceeded to Cardiff where a celebratory luncheon was held on board on the 27th. She left Cardiff on 31st January, arriving in Weymouth Bay at 6 am on Sunday lst February. Dressed overall, she entered harbour two hours later. Also dressed overall was the cargo steamer *Sambur*, the only other GWR vessel in harbour to greet her. Later in the day visitors inspected the ship. Under the command of Captain R.R. Pitman she sailed on her maiden voyage on Wednesday 4th February, carrying 115 passengers on her outward sailing and returning with 267.

After the Nationalisation of the railways, the transfer of the management of Weymouth to the Southern Region and the resultant new British Railways livery, *St Patrick* became the odd vessel out by retaining her original Great Western livery. Being registered in the name of the Fishguard & Rosslare Company she was not affected by Nationalisation, although her management remained with the Western Region until 1950, when the management of the Fishguard steamers was transferred to the London Midland Region, and she flew the Fishguard & Rosslare Company's flag up to 1959 and retained the GWR coat of arms on her bow.

The *St Patrick* continued to serve the Channel Islands during the summer, providing the extra weekend sailings and operating excursions from both Weymouth and Torquay to the Islands during the week. She returned to Fishguard each winter to relieve vessels for refit and lay-up, later also covering the Holyhead-Dun Laoghaire service. On 17th December, 1959 *St Patrick* was transferred to the British Transport Commission and became a member of the Southern Region fleet at Weymouth. She then operated the winter service, the *St Julien* and *St Helier* being laid up for the winter of 1959/60. Painted in BTC livery early in 1960, *St Patrick* continued as the third vessel during the summer season, but with the pending arrival of two new ships *St Patrick* sailed to the Mount Stuart dry dock, Cardiff, during the winter of 1960/61 for an extensive refit costing £91,400. This converted her into a one-class ship to run alongside the new vessels. Alterations included additional catering facilities and the

Dressed overall shortly after her arrival at Weymouth for the first time on 1st February, 1948, *St Patrick* awaits to make her maiden voyage to the Channel Islands. With a gross tonnage of 3,482 she was the largest steamer built for the GWR. *The late E. Latcham Collection*

St Patrick (1947) alongside the landing stage on 2nd December, 1960, showing the crest of the Great Western Railway on her bows. On the right is the original 1889 passenger terminal, with the 1933 extension in the foreground. The width restriction on this section of the pier required the small swan neck crane shown in the centre to work the forward hold of vessels at this berth. *Author*

cabins at the forward end of the shelter deck being replaced by an open saloon with reclining aircraft seats, whilst cabins on the main deck were converted into crew accommodation. This reduced her gross tonnage to 3,459, and she became well known at Weymouth for rolling in poor sea conditions; the lack of space had precluded the proposed fitting of stabilisers. Whereas before passengers had often specified the *St Patrick* when booking their passage, she now became the poor relation. As with many conversions it was a compromise, making her of inferior standards to the new vessels whilst destroying her original character.

On 10th October, 1963 *St Patrick* made her last run from the Channel Islands to Weymouth and was then transferred to Southampton, where she took over the Le Havre service on 5th December until it closed on 10th May, 1964. *St Patrick* then took over the St Malo service, which included a fortnightly sailing from St Malo to Weymouth until this service also ceased in September 1964, making her final sailing on the 23rd. Following a refit at Smith's Dock, Hartlepool - which included the fitting of gangway doors amidships (and she was the first Southern Region vessel to have the new British Rail livery which included a red funnel) - she was transferred to Dover in December 1964 to operate the Calais service. Moving next to Folkestone on 25th May, 1965 to cover the Boulogne route, she remained there until September 1971, by which time she had reverted to a two-class vessel.

St Patrick photographed whilst moving berths on 13th January, 1962. By that time she had been converted into a one-class ship, her red funnel replaced by buff, and during the refit the black paintwork of the hull had been extended higher up to avoid some of the problems of rust stains on the previous white finish. At that time the GWR crest remained on the bow despite the other alterations. *C.L. Caddy*

However, her visits to Weymouth and the Channel Islands were not yet over. Owing to the *Caesarea* being out of service with collision damage in August 1968 *St Patrick* returned to Weymouth, arriving on Friday 23rd to take over the midday sailing, her short stay being the last-ever visit of a former Great Western Railway steamer to Weymouth. It was not, however, her final visit to the Channel Islands, as she returned to Jersey in April 1969 with a charter from St Malo, and in May 1970 she operated two excursions from Guernsey to Jersey and one from Jersey to St Malo. Her final visit to the islands came the following year when she spent a week conveying parties of school children from St Malo to Jersey, making her final departure from the Island on 8th May, 1971. Returning again to Folkestone, she made her final sailing from Boulogne on 25th September, 1971, then sailing to Newhaven to lay-up.

She was sold on 9th March, 1972 and departed Newhaven the same day for Piraeus, having been purchased by Greek ship owners Gerasimos S. Fetouris to operate a service between Greece and Italy under the name *Thermopylae*. The venture was unsuccessful and the vessel was sold the following year to Agapitos Brothers. Renamed *Agapitos I*, she sailed between Piraeus and the Cyclades Islands until replaced by another former Sealink vessel *Lisieux*. Laid up at Perama for four years, the rusting *St Patrick* was broken up in 1980, bringing to an end the long line of Weymouth-based vessels formerly owned by the Great Western Railway.

The end of the line. *St Patrick* (1947) lays at Perama in the Greek islands before breaking up in 1980. Her passing marked the end of GWR shipping from Weymouth. Fortunately the GWR crest from her bows, having been removed during her stay at Dover, is today housed in the National Railway Museum at York. *A. Scrimali*

Appendix One

Ancillary Vessels

Armine

The *Armine* was a steam launch/workboat, built by J. White of Cowes in 1886. Constructed of timber, her hull was 37 ft 8 in. long with a 9 ft beam and draft of 4 ft 3 in. Nothing is known of her means of propulsion (if any) before 1893, but in that year she was fitted with a twin-cylinder vertical-launch engine with 6 in. x 6 in. cylinders developing 2.4 nhp and fitted with a surface condenser supplied by Plenty & Son of Newbury, the unit giving a speed of nine knots. Steam was supplied by a coal-fired vertical-launch type boiler at 100 psi, constructed by Abbot & Son of Newark-on-Trent. This was replaced by a boiler from the same makers in 1910 at a cost of £121 10*s*.

Little is known of the *Armine* until 1894 when she was purchased by Charles Rushden to operate a Falmouth-Flushing ferry service across the River Fal. In January 1897 she was purchased by William Langrish Bussell, a sail maker of Weymouth. In October 1898 the GWR Steam Boat Committee gave authority for the purchase of a small tug or steam launch at a cost not exceeding £250, and in January 1899 *Armine* was acquired. The main need for such a vessel sprang from the pending extension to the west end of the cargo stage, which would eliminate the coal siding from which coal was transferred from railway wagons into barges for coaling the fleet. A new coal siding was constructed half a mile up harbour in the Backwater (at what is now the site of the Weymouth Angling Club), and a tug would be required to tow the barges up and down the harbour.

Painted with a black hull and red funnel with a black top like the steamers, she was a familiar sight at Weymouth, performing her task of towing coal barges between the Backwater siding and the lower harbour and the other odd jobs that befell a harbour launch. These duties continued until 1932 when the last coal burning steamer, the *Great Western*, departed. But *Armine* remained, her certificate to carry 12 passengers having always been renewed. Often referred to as 'Percy Boyle's yacht', she always played an active part in the annual Regatta, when Boyle would entertain leading townspeople to a close up of the event!

Following Boyle's retirement at the end of 1935 *Armine* was immediately put up for sale, and on 9th September, 1936 she was purchased by Pollock Brown & Company of Northam Ironworks, Southampton. Later she was resold, her certificate being cancelled and registry closed in January 1938. The vessel was then converted into a privately owned motor boat.

With the guests aboard the *Armine* and a junior officer from one of the steamers in command, a day out for the privileged few is about to commence. *Author's Collection*

Above: The steam launch *Armine* tows a coal barge up harbour. To the left the is *Reindeer,* with *Ibex* ahead with coal barges alongside.
Author's Collection

Right: A close up views of the interior arrangements of *Armine*. The fact that two picnic tables are aboard and cushions are placed on the seats in the passenger compartment indicates that she is to be used for entertainment purposes.
Author's Collection

Sir Francis Drake

She could well be described as 'The Little Lady That Followed The Fleet'. Although not directly connected with the Weymouth service, this vessel became involved with the Weymouth fleet on several occasions, and in her later years was often within sight and sound of her former fleet mates.

The emergence of Plymouth as a port of call for ocean liners involved the creation of railway-owned docks alongside the existing Naval establishments and the small commercial harbours within Plymouth Sound. The situation at Plymouth was complex, the railway docks being originally owned by the 'Plymouth Great Western Docks' until the passing of the 1874 South Devon Railway Act, after which ownership was vested in the South Devon Railway, the Bristol & Exeter Railway, and the Great Western Railway. The Great Western Railway and South Devon Railway Companies Amalgamation Act of 1878 brought the docks under the control of the Great Western Railway.

In 1872 the docks company decided to acquire its own tender rather than rely on locally hired vessels, an order being placed with William Allsup of Caledonian Works, Preston, Lancs. for the construction of an iron paddle steamer. Delivered to Plymouth in June 1873, she was named *Sir Francis Drake.* Her principal dimensions were 173 tons gross, 59 tons net, 131 ft 3in. long, 20 ft 1 in. beam, and a draft of 10 ft 1 in. She was powered by a simple diagonal engine with a cylinder diameter of 30 in., and a stroke of 48 in. developing 80 nhp. Within Plymouth Sound she held certificates for 352 passengers in summer and 251 in winter. The vessel was registered in the name of the West Cornwall Railway Committee until 1878 when the Great Western Railway became her legal owners.

Within three years a second steamer was ordered from the same builders, and subsequently other vessels were added as traffic increased. There were occasions when the vessel's capacity as a tug came to the fore. *Sir Francis Drake* had made her first recorded appearance at Weymouth on 5th June, 1884 when, with the other Plymouth tender *Sir Walter Raleigh,* they towed the liner *Frisia* into Portland Harbour after she became disabled in the English Channel with a broken propeller shaft. *Sir Francis Drake* went to the assistance of the *Ibex* in 1897 and 1900 *(as described on pages 113-115)*. The nature of tender work involved periods of inactivity, so to keep the vessels gainfully employed short excursions were operated along the South Hams and East Cornwall coastline. It was whilst on one of these excursions to the Eddystone Lighthouse during the summer of 1883 that *Sir Francis Drake* ran into and damaged a fishing boat. The Steamboat Committee were told that the accident had been caused by the captain taking charge of the wheel and allowing his attention to be drawn to the lighthouse.

The future of the *Sir Francis Drake* had been discussed in a report on the Plymouth tenders in February 1890, it being suggested that a new boat be ordered as a replacement, as in about 12 months' time the boiler would require replacement at a cost of £2,500. However, the ship was not disposed of and the boiler was replaced in 1896 when, with four tenders available, *Sir Francis Drake* was certified only during the summer months for passenger work, and mainly employed on excursions, a fore deck saloon being added for this purpose.

The increase in liner traffic and competition from the London & South Western Railway during the early 1900s had required the replacement of the older vessels. A new *Sir Francis Drake* arrived in April 1908, the former being renamed *Helper* and laid up in reserve. Thirty-five years of age and re-boilered in both 1880 and 1896 her future prospects were not good. However, in 1909 the GWR become involved in tendering at Fishguard from Liverpool-based Cunard liners, two Plymouth tenders being transferred to the Welsh port giving the *Helper* a reprieve.

The withdrawal of the LSWR from the liner trade in May 1910 and the return of the two tenders from Fishguard sealed the fate of *Helper,* the General Manager reporting the vessel as being sold to Joseph Constant the shipbroker in August for £575. She was resold to Cosens & Company of Weymouth who operated a substantial fleet of paddle steamers on the excursion trade at both Weymouth and Bournemouth, and also held the contract to provide liberty boats to warships laid at anchor in Portland Harbour and Weymouth Bay; *Helper* was ideal for this work and for short passenger excursions. Within days she again came into contact with the *Ibex* following the latter's engine failure off Portland, and she was also in contact with other vessels of the Weymouth fleet that had made regular appearances at Plymouth.

With the outbreak of World War I *Helper* was at first involved with ferry duties to warships at Portland, but by September 1916 she had moved to Newhaven where she was employed as an examination vessel and by January 1918 had become a minesweeper in the Irish Sea. Returning from Belfast at the end of hostilities, she put into Swansea in January 1919 for repairs, lying there for three months before agreement was reached for the reconditioning, this work taking place at Cardiff. Upon return to Weymouth she commenced a limited excursion programme during the summer of 1919.

However, the loss of the Naval liberty contract made her surplus to requirements. Towards the end of October 1919 she was sold to the Alderney Steam Packet Company to operate a service between Guernsey, Sark, and Alderney, arriving in Guernsey on 8th November. Again she came into contact with the GWR's cross-channel steamers, forwarding goods that they had brought over from the mainland. She again appeared with a red funnel and a derrick was fitted on the fore deck to handle light cargo. On 13th June, 1922 her port of registery was transferred from Weymouth to Guernsey. In 1926 *Helper* was damaged in Creux Harbour, Sark, during a severe gale, and after limping back to Guernsey she was laid up until she was taken to Appledore, North Devon, and broken up. Her register was closed on 8th July, 1929; *Helper* had been the last paddle steamer employed on the inter-island service.

Ironically, a later Plymouth tender, the *Sir Richard Granville* of 1931, was for a few years during the 1960s employed on excursions from Guernsey to Sark and Jersey, sailing under the name of *La Duchesse de Normandie.*

The *Helper* anchored off Sark Harbour whilst in the ownership of the Alderney Steam Packet Company. Note the derrick fitted to her fore mast to handle light cargo. Formerly the Great Western Railway Plymouth tender *Sir Francis Drake* (1873), her entire life had been spent within sight of and giving assistance to the GWR cross-channel steamers.

Author's Collection

Appendix Two

Chartered Vessels

From the start various vessels were chartered as required during the season to assist with extra traffic, to cover a shortage of available ships, or to relieve in the event of failure or misfortunes. As early as 1857 the Packet Company chartered a schooner for at least one crossing! This procedure continued, particularly after the potato trade developed; the absence of *Brighton* caused the chartering of four vessels during the 1877 season. One of these (the *Denia*) was the first vessel to unload at the new cargo stage on 12th June. Again the following year four vessels were chartered. The terms of the charter varied according to the tonnage of the vessel concerned. For instance, in 1877 the prices per calendar month were *Rosebud* £310; *Denia* £230; *Sixty Six* £240; *Undine* £245. The following year *Rosebud* still cost £310; but *Denia* was £290; *Otter* £300; and *Earl of Carrick* £290. These were inclusive charges for vessels and crew, but excluded coal which was supplied by the charterer.

The shortage of vessels caused by the accident to the *Lynx* in 1890 resulted in the charter of the Isle of Man Steam Packet Company *Snaefell* for two weeks; it was also the last occasion that paddle propulsion was used by the GWR for a cross-channel service.

The Guernsey fruit traffic required the chartering of the *Gipsy* in 1890 and *Lady of the Isles* the following year. Vessels from the fleet of James Fisher of Barrow were regularly employed for many years. Indeed between about 1887 and 1904 the seasonal potato traffic was almost dependent upon them, and they continued to visit the port regularly up to 1915 and made occasional appearances during the 1930s. The cost of hired vessels was also important. In the summer of 1900 the monthly hire fee was £370 for each of four vessels hired from James Fisher. By comparison the *Stream Fisher* cost £1,500 a month during 1919, whilst *Clare Monks* was chartered for a period of three weeks during September 1932 at a cost of £101 10*s*. per week, the cost reflecting supply and demand. The conversion of the *Lynx* and *Gazelle* to cargo boats reduced the hiring of outside vessels, during 1912, only two being hired.

The outbreak of World War I, and the requisitioning of the GWR steamers with the exception of *Ibex*, increased the need for chartering at a time when vessels were in short supply. During those difficult years a succession of both coasters and steamers from other railway companies were often employed just to relieve *Ibex* and keep a basic service operating. GWR records reveal that the LSWR passenger steamer *Vera* operated the service in November 1914 and February 1915, whilst the cargo steamer *Bertha* was on charter from 26th October, 1914 to 20th February, 1915. The passenger vessel *Galtee More* from the LNWR operated seven trips during June 1915, whilst *Mellifont* from the Lancashire & Yorkshire Railway made nine trips in that June and July. The latter company supplied the cargo vessel *Mersey* from 21st February, 1915 until 19th August, relieved then by *River Crake* until 30th March, 1916. The coaster *Aletta* was chartered during 1915, 1916 and 1917. Ironically in the final year she was sunk after a collision with the *Ibex*. At a Board meeting in May 1918 it was reported that the coaster *Earnham*, which had been used as a cargo boat at Weymouth, had been withdrawn by the Ministry of Shipping and the *Croham* substituted.

The unfortunate double accident with both *St Helier* and *Reindeer* hitting the pier head at St Helier caused the chartering of the Southern Railway steamer *Vera* to cover sailings on 13th-14th March, 1926.

At the outbreak of World War II the motor vessel *Guernsey Queen* was on charter for the seasonal traffic and continued until requisitioned on 19th September, 1939. With the requisition of *Robuck* and *Sambur* in June 1940 the LNER cargo steamer *Sheringham* took over the cargo service until 29th June. When she departed from Guernsey with the company agent and staff aboard she was the last vessel on the service to leave before the invasion. The *Felixstowe*, which had brought troops and refugees into Weymouth, never

The London & North Western Railway vessel *Galtee Moor* (1898) was on charter to the GWR to cover the Channel Islands sailings between 2nd and 17th June, 1915. She was also chartered by the LSWR to sail from Southampton due to a shortage of vessels in 1921. *Author's Collection*

The LSWR steamer *Vera* (1898) enters Weymouth Harbour in March 1926 whilst on charter to the GWR following the double incident whereby *St Helier* and *Reindeer* were both out of service after colliding with the pier head at St Helier. *Author's Collection*

The former LNER cargo steamer *Felixstowe* (1918) alongside the old cargo stage during the summer of 1948. The first vessel chartered for the Channel Islands trade by British Railways. *Felixstowe* had previously brought troops and refugees to Weymouth in June 1940 and was about to make a voyage to the Channel Islands with cargo she was loading on 1st July when the Islands fell to the Germans, thus concluding the service. In the foreground is the relief lifeboat *Hearts of Oak*, sold out of service in 1955 but still in use as a pleasure boat on the East Coast during 1994. *Author's Collection*

sailed with cargo, for as she was loading on 1st July the occupation of the Channel Islands concluded the service.

The last vessel chartered by the GWR was *Fredor* for the 1947 season, and she returned each year until 1956. She was a slow vessel with a tendency to take a list at the slightest opportunity, but she was not without interest. Built in 1943 at Lidingo, under the name of *Glucksburg*, but soon becoming *Stadt Glucksburg*, she was seized as a prize of war and became the *Empire Condart* before being renamed *Fredor* under the ownership of the Plym Shipping Company.

Felixstowe returned on charter for the 1948 season. By then all railway steamers were under the jurisdiction of the British Transport Commission, so the term 'charter' could well be substituted by 'temporary transfer'. Working alongside the former GWR ships during the season during in the early Nationalisation years were the former Southern Railway vessels *Hythe* from 1951 to 1956, *Whitstable* in 1956-1957, and the French Railway vessel *Brest* 1960-1965.

Fredor, the last ship to be chartered by the GWR, served at Weymouth during the summer season between 1947 and 1956. Chartered from the Plym Shipping Company, her 139 ft-long hull was lengthened by 30 ft during 1952. *Author's Collection*

Appendix Three

The Milford Connection

In the period between 1872 and 1906 references are made to Milford, and it is hoped that the following brief account will clarify the situation. Although referred to as 'Milford' the actual place was Neyland, also known as New Milford, situated on the Milford Haven in West Wales, from where the original ferry service to the South of Ireland operated. The promoter of this scheme was the South Wales Railway, which in 1846 commenced construction of a line westwards from Chepstow with plans for a ferry route to Ireland, where both the South Wales and Great Western railways had interests.

The first choice for a departure point was Fishguard, but the exposed coastline and the large expense of making a sheltered anchorage caused the scheme to be shelved. In March 1851 it was agreed that the terminus would be on the shore of Milford Haven, Neyland being chosen because a railway terminus and other quayside facilities could be constructed there at a tenth of the cost of Fishguard. Work commenced in November 1855, the station opening on 15th August, 1856. The shipping service started the same month, the 118 mile crossing to Waterford taking between 8½ and 9½ hours whilst the 285¼ miles from Paddington took 7½ hours. As the South Wales Railway had no Parliamentary powers to operate shipping services, a separate company, the Milford Haven and Waterford Steam Shipping Company owned by Captain Robert Ford and Captain Thomas Jackson, operated the service, and in 1860 marine workshops were added and a gridiron constructed to maintain the vessels.

Brunel had dreamed of greater plans for Neyland with an eye on the trans-Atlantic trade, but the Admiralty objected lest they impede naval movements at Pembroke Dockyard on the south side of the haven. A service to Brazil commenced in September 1859 but was abandoned after several voyages, and Brunel's *Great Eastern* visited in August 1860 on her return from New York and made a second visit in 1862, the ship undergoing repairs at Neyland on both occasions. Little other outside traffic developed, although a service to Cork was added in May 1857. The Irish trade was heavy, consisting mainly of cattle, sheep, pigs, and fish. There was also the mackerel trade during the season which was landed at a separate jetty. In August 1863 the South Wales Railway was absorbed into the GWR, and in the same year a railway opened to the town of Milford (renamed Milford Haven in 1894) the new station being named 'Old Milford'.

Like the Weymouth & Channel Island Steam Packet Company, Ford & Jackson had to be financially assisted by both the South Wales and Great Western railways on several occasions, and there had been some deterioration in services owing to lack of investment. The passing of the GWR Steam Ship Act in 1871 allowed the takeover of the Ford & Jackson operation on 1st February, 1872. Jackson remained as manager until July 1873 when Captain W.H. Haswell became the first marine superintendent of the GWR, New Milford becoming the headquarters of the Marine Department and a majority of GWR vessels were registered there. In July 1883 Captain T.S. Lecky took over as marine superintendent until resigning in 1898, when John Dunster became marine and dock superintendent based at Paddington, resulting in the New Milford department being reduced and Milford no longer being the registration port for new vessels.

In 1895 there had been plans for improvements to the facilities at New Milford, but these were not proceeded with because of a threat by the LNWR to build a railway to Fishguard and offer a shorter sea crossing. This spurred the GWR into action, and by 1899 the new line from Clarbeston Road had reached Goodwick, where a 27 acre terrace was cut from vertical cliffs to form a station, cattle lairage, a deep water quay, and a 2,000 ft breakwater to protect the new works. On 30th August, 1906 the new line opened - complete with a steamer service

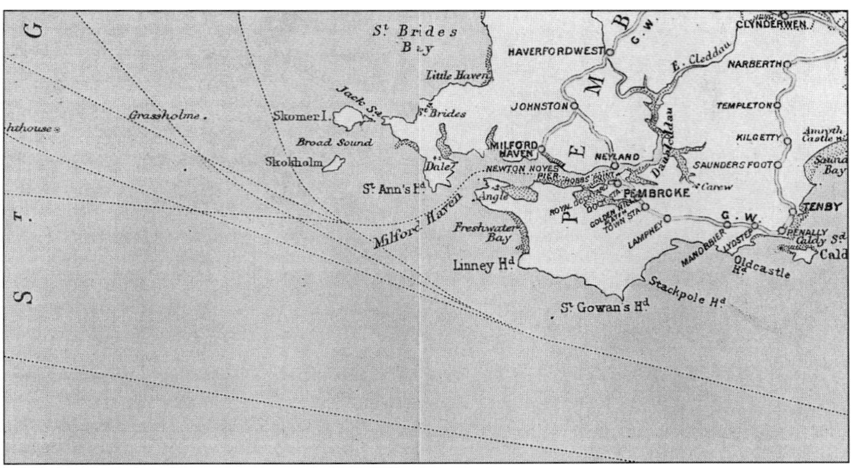

Railway Clearing House map showing Milford Haven.

which made the 54 mile crossing to Rosslare in 3 hours. New Milford then closed, the marine workshops, 200 workmen and port staff being transferred to Fishguard. Milford's association with railway steamships thus ended; only during times of war did they return when several railway steamers sought sanctuary in the Haven on various occasions. New Milford reverted to its original name of Neyland and in 1908 a fish dock was set up with the assistance of the GWR, although this closed in 1914.

GWR Marine Department Officer's cap badge. Above the laurel leaves is the GWR coat of arms. *Author's Collection*

Appendix Four

Table of Weymouth Vessels

London & South Western Railway (New South Western Steam Navigation Company)

Name	*Official No.*	*Built* *Acquired* *Sold* *Scrapped*	*Builder* *Ship* *Engines*	*Length (ft)*	*Beam (ft)*	*Depth (ft)*	*Tons*	*Engine type* *Cylinder dia. (in.)* *Stroke (in.)* *No. of cyl.*	*NHP*	*Speed (knots)*	*Notes*
South Western		1843 1843 1863 1868	Ditchburn & Mare John Seaward	143.0	18.0	10.8	203	side lever 36½ 36 2	80		Paddle Wrecked 15.11.1858
Wonder		1844 1844 1874 1874	Ditchburn & Mare Seaward & Chapel	158.0	20.6	10.0	250	atmospheric 53 42 3	130		Paddle
Express		1847 1847 1859 1859	Ditchburn & Mare Maudslay & Field	159.0	21.4	10.4	255	atmospheric 55 42 2	160		Paddle Wrecked 20.9.1859

Weymouth & Channel Islands Steam Packet Company

Name	*Official No.*	*Built* *Acquired* *Sold* *Scrapped*	*Builder* *Ship* *Engines*	*Length (ft)*	*Beam (ft)*	*Depth (ft)*	*Tons*	*Engine type* *Cylinder dia. (in.)* *Stroke (in.)* *No. of cyl.*	*NHP*	*Speed (knots)*	*Notes*
Aquila	18602	1854 1857 1889 1896	Henderson, Renfrew McNabb & Clarke	180.4	21.0	10.9	264	oscillating 42 42 2	110		Paddle Wrecked 17.12.1896
Cygnus	17807	1854 1857 1889 1899	Henderson, Renfrew McNabb & Clarke	182.0	21.4	9.7	245	oscillating 42⅜ 42 2	120		Paddle

Brighton	11918	1857 1858 1887 1887	Palmer, Jarrow	193.5	20.9	10.0	286	oscillating 43¾ 48 2	140		Paddle Wrecked 29.1.1887
Great Western Railway											
Great Western	53553	1867 1872 1890 1904	Simons, Renfrew	220.4	25.2	12.4	447	oscillating 48 45 2	190		Paddle
South of Ireland	56817	1867 1872 1883 1883	Simons, Renfrew	220.2	25.8	12.4	474	oscillating 50 48 2	200		Paddle Wrecked 25.12.1883
Vulture	50102	1864 1872 1886 1886	Aitken, Whiteinch	243.2	25.7	17.3	793	oscillating 54 60 2	200		Paddle
Gael	44394	1867 1884 1891 1924	Robertson, Greenock Rankin & Blackmore	211.0	23.2	10.6	403	oscillating 45 63 2	150		Paddle
Lynx	93434	1889 1889 1925 1925	Laird Bros	235.5	27.6	13.1	596	vertical triple expansion 16½ x 26 x 41 30 3	168	16½	Twin screw
Antelope	93435	1889 1889 1913 1933	Laird Bros	235.5	27.6	13.1	596	vertical triple expansion 16½ x 26 x 41 30 3	168	16½	Twin screw
Gazelle	93436	1889 1889 1925 1925	Laird Bros	235.5	27.6	13.1	596	vertical triple expansion 16½ x 26 x 41 30 3	168	16½	Twin screw

Great Western Railway (continued)

Name	*Official No.*	*Built Acquired Sold Scrapped*	*Builder Ship Engines*	*Length (ft)*	*Beam (ft)*	*Depth (ft)*	*Tons*	*Engine type Cylinder dia. (in.) Stroke (in.) No. of cyl.*	*NHP*	*Speed (knots)*	*Notes*
Ibex	98375	1891 1891 1925 1925	Laird Bros	265.0	32.6	14.2	1,160	vertical triple expansion 22 x 34 x 51 33 3	282	19	Twin screw
Roebuck	108422	1897 1897 1915 1915	Naval Arm. & Con.	280.0	34.5	16.8	1,281	vertical triple expansion 23 x 36 x 56 33	330	20¼	Twin screw Sunk 13.1.1915
Reindeer	108424	1897 1897 1928 1928	Naval Arm & Con.	280.0	34.5	16.8	1,281	vertical triple expansion 23 x 36 x 56 33 3	330	20¼	Twin screw
Pembroke	82973	1880 1880 1925 1925	Laird Bros	254.0	30.9	15.0	976	vertical triple expansion 19 x 30 x 46 30 3	650	16	Twin screw. The vertical triple expansion engine replaced a compound oscillating engine 51 x 91 84 stroke (2cylinders). 400 hp pre-1896.
Melmore	99833	1892 1905 1912 ?	Dunlop, Glasgow	156.2	25.8	11.3	412	vertical triple expansion 15 x 23 x 28 27 3	n/a	10	Single screw
Great Western	115805	1902 1902 1934 1934	Laird Bros	275.8	36.3	15.2	1,339	vertical triple expansion 19 x 29½ x 33 (2) 30 4	228	16	Twin screw
Great Southern	115823	1902 1902 1934 1934	Laird Bros	275.8	36.3	15.2	1,339	vertical triple expansion 19 x 29½ x 33 (2) 30 4	228	16	Twin screw

Roebuck	148583	1925 1925 1965 1966	Swan Hunter	201.2	33.7	15.3	776	vertical triple expansion 14½ x 23 x 38 27 3	226	12¼	Twin screw Oil fired
Sambur	148590	1925 1925 1964 1964	Swan Hunter	201.2	33.7	15.3	776	vertical triple expansion 14½ x 23 x 38 27 3	226	12¼	Twin screw Oil fired
St Julien	148585	1925 1925 1961 1961	John Brown	282.2	40.0	16.3	1,885	single reduction geared turbine	819	18	Twin screw Oil fired
St Helier	148612	1925 1925 1961 1961	John Brown	282.2	40.0	16.3	1,885	single reduction geared turbine	819	18	Twin screw Oil fired
St Patrick	161385	1930 1930 1941 1941	Stephen, Linthouse	281.3	41.1	16.3	1,922	single reduction geared turbine	887	19	Twin screw Oil fired Sunk 13.6.1941
St David	181676	1947 1947 1971 1981	Cammell Laird	306.5	48.2	17.2	3,352	single reduction geared turbine	1,559	20¾	Twin screw Oil fired
St Patrick	181830	1947 1947 1972 1980	Cammell Laird	306.5	48.2	17.2	3,482	single reduction geared turbine	1,559	20	Twin screw Oil fired

Note: Tonnages are those recorded when the ships were constructed; over the years there were alterations to the vessels and changes in the tonnage rules which have been omitted.

Acknowledgements

Many people have assisted with the composition of this work, ranging from the answering of a single question to allowing me access to their records. In particular the late Eric Latcham and the late John Lucking, the latter's *Great Western At Weymouth* having inspired this work. Fellow author Richard Clammer opened up connections in shipping circles, putting his photographic collection at my disposal, and checking the draft copy, and Maureen Attwooll, whose knowledge of local history is unsurpassed, put me right on local matters. Acknowledgement is also given to George Pryer for proof checking and his vast knowledge of railway matters; Bill Macy for his knowledge of Weymouth Harbour and associated interests; G. Millsott for details of the life of Captain Pitman, Captain John Attwood, formerly of Sealink; B. Moody, G. Prichard, R.C. Riley, Brian Seale, the late W. Symons, and the late D. Hoppins.

Various organisations have given invaluable assistance, especially the Dorset County Library and the staff of Weymouth Library; the Dorset County Record Office; Pembroke County Record Office; Haverfordwest Public Library; Priaulx Library, St Peter Port; Societe Jersaiase, St Helier; Glasgow University; The Museum of the Royal Scots Regiment; The Public Record Office, Kew; The British Library, Newspaper Library, Colindale.

The following publications are amongst those consulted

Boyle, P., *The Channel Islands Service* (GWR Debating Society)
Couling, D., *Wrecked on the Channel Islands* (Stanford Marine)
Cowsill & Hendy, *The Sealink Years* (Ferry Publications)
Davies, D.N., *End of the Line, History of Neyland*
Duckworth & Langmuir, *West Highland Steamers* (Stephenson)
Farr, Graham, *West Country Steamers* (Stephenson)
Kitteridge, A., *Plymouth Ocean Liner Port of Call* (Twelveheads Press)
Le Scelleur, K., *Channel Islands' Railway Steamers* (Patrick Stephens 1985)
Lucking, J.H., *Great Western at Weymouth* (David & Charles 1971)
Lucking, J.H., *The Weymouth Harbour Tramway* (OPC)
Masterton, S., *A Century of Shipping in the Channel Islands* (Guernsey Press)
Robins, Nick, *Turbine Steamers of the British Isles* (Colour Point)
Thornton, E.C.B., *South Coast Pleasure Steamers* (Stephenson)
Winser, John de S., *Short Sea Long War* (World Ship Society)

Periodicals & Newspapers

The Comet (Guernsey)
Dorset County Chronicle
Dorset Evening Echo
Engineering
The Engineer
Great Western Railway Magazine
Guernsey Evening Press
Illustrated London News
Liverpool Journal of Commerce
Sea Breezes
Ships Monthly
Southern Times
The Star (Guernsey)
Weymouth Telegram